CW00747222

Kant on Judgment

"This is a superb treatment of Kant's third *Critique* in its entirety – in depth, in careful analysis, and in understanding in a way not articulated by others of the integration of Kant's aesthetic theory with the rest of his philosophy."

Donald W. Crawford, *Emeritus Professor of Philosophy, University of California, Santa Barbara*

Kant's *Critique of Judgment* is one of the most important texts in the history of modern aesthetics. This GuideBook discusses the third *Critique* section by section, and introduces and assesses:

- Kant's life and the background of the *Critique of Judgment*
- The ideas and text of the *Critique of Judgment*, including a critical explanation of Kant's theories of natural beauty
- The continuing relevance of Kant's work to contemporary philosophy and aesthetics.

This GuideBook is an accessible introduction to a notoriously difficult work and will be essential reading for students of Kant and aesthetics.

Robert Wicks is Associate Professor of Philosophy at the University of Auckland, New Zealand.

ROUTLEDGE PHILOSOPHY GUIDEBOOKS

Edited by Tim Crane and Jonathan Wolff,
University College London

Routledge Philosophy GuideBook to

Kant on Judgment

Robert
Wicks

Routledge
Taylor & Francis Group

LONDON AND NEW YORK

First published 2007
by Routledge
2 Park Square, Milton Park, Abingdon, Oxon OX14 4RN

Simultaneously published in the USA and Canada
by Routledge
270 Madison Ave, New York, NY 10016

Routledge is an imprint of the Taylor & Francis Group, an informa business

© 2007 Robert Wicks

Typeset in Aldus and Scala by Taylor & Francis Books
Printed and bound in Great Britain by
TJ International Ltd, Padstow, Cornwall

British Library Cataloguing in Publication Data
A catalogue record for this book is available from the British Library

Library of Congress Cataloging in Publication Data
Wicks, Robert, 1954–
  Routledge philosophy guidebook to Kant on judgement / Robert
Wicks.
      p. cm. -- (Routledge philosophy guidebooks)
  Includes bibliographical references and index.
  1. Kant, Immanuel, 1724–1804. Kritik der Urteilskraft. 2. Judgment
(Logic) 3. Judgment (Aesthetics) 4. Aesthetics. 5. Teleology. I. Title.
  B2784.W53 2006
  121--dc22

                          2006020182

ISBN10: 0-415-28110-5 (hbk)   ISBN13: 978-0-415-28110-2 (hbk)
ISBN10: 0-415-28111-3 (pbk)   ISBN13: 978-0-415-28111-9 (pbk)
ISBN10: 0-203-64297-X (ebk)   ISBN13: 978-0-203-64297-9 (ebk)

" . . . to take an immediate interest in natural beauty is always the sign of a good soul . . . " (§42)

" . . . no human reason can ever hope to understand the generation of even a tiny blade of grass from merely mechanical causes." (§77)

"There is a God in the human soul. The question is whether he is also in nature."

(Opus Postumum, 22: 120)

CONTENTS

PREFACE AND ACKNOWLEDGMENTS

The dates 1790 and 1970 are easy to memorize. Prior to the 1970s, the bulk of English-language scholarship devoted to Kant's philosophy was focussed mainly on his theory of knowledge, ethics, and historical relationships between Kant and other philosophers. Works addressing Kant's aesthetic theory were relatively few, constituting only a small neighborhood within the wider array of books and articles about Kant and his influence. Up until the 1970s among English-language publications, for instance, there was only one typically consulted, full-length study of Kant's third *Critique* – *A Commentary on Kant's Critique of Judgment*. This was written in 1938 by H. W. Cassirer, the son of Ernst Cassirer (1874 – 1945).

Cassirer's book was reprinted in 1970, and after the reappearance of his study, scholarly attention to Kant's aesthetics developed dramatically with the publication of Donald W. Crawford's *Kant's Aesthetic Theory* (1974), Francis X. Coleman's *The Harmony of Reason: A Study of Kant's Aesthetics* (1974), Paul Guyer's *Kant and the Claims of Taste* (1979), and Eva Shaper's *Studies in Kant's Aesthetics* (1979). These landmark publications stimulated three decades of serious attention to Kant's aesthetics – decades within which some of the most refined Kant scholars contributed, and continue to contribute, to our understanding of Kant's theories of beauty and fine art.[1]

From the standpoint of the general reader, introductory philosophy students interested in Kant's aesthetics, aestheticians who specialize in areas other than Kant, not to mention philosophy professionals and academics who focus upon other thematic specialties, the number of introductory studies on Kant's aesthetics that include an exposition of the book's second half – a segment that does not obviously concern art and beauty – presently compares with the condition of scholarship in Kant's aesthetics as a whole prior to 1970. To many of those who are not Kant scholars, Kant's *Critique of the Power of Judgment* (1790) largely remains a work whose name might now be well known, but whose detailed contents from beginning to end, still need to be clarified and explained in an accessible exposition. This is the purpose of the present work.

This guide to Kant's third *Critique* aims to stay close to the text while remaining intellectually approachable. The third *Critique*'s own sequence of exposition is respected fairly rigidly, and the commentary and explanation follows the internal logic of the *Critique* itself from beginning to end. At the same time, Kant's broader purposes are set forth during the exposition to help establish an integrated vision of the book as a whole. The leading idea is to show, while remaining focussed on Kant's third *Critique*, how it fits into his primary philosophical project of coordinating his theory of scientific knowledge with this theory of moral behavior, for it is clear that Kant's primary philosophical interest is in philosophically coordinating what scientifically happens to be, with what morally ought to be. He aims to align to the best extent possible, facts with values, and actualities with ideals. His key works aim to define those ideals as steadfastly as possible.

As hinted at above, one of the limits of contemporary attention to Kant's aesthetics is that the *Critique of the Power of Judgment* is not typically viewed as a whole and within the context of Kant's other two *Critiques*.[2] Even those texts that intend to introduce Kant's aesthetics, despite their usefulness in relation to specific topics, tend to focus only on the first half of the third *Critique* – the segment that explicitly concerns aesthetic judgment – and give accordingly only an abbreviated characterization of the contents of the concluding half of the *Critique* that concerns teleological (i.e., purpose-specifying) judgments about living organisms and the natural purposes of things. The thematic affinities between the two parts of the book are only infrequently brought forth in introductions to Kant's aesthetics, although this trend is slowly changing to include wider perspectives.

Without viewing aesthetic judgment in conjunction with teleological judgment, however, one lands in the truncated situation of acknowledging, with Kant, that moral awareness can be attained through pure introspection and that the contemplation of beautiful objects helps foster this awareness, while dropping out of sight Kant's complementary claim that reflection on the mystery of life helps foster this moral awareness as well. As we will see, both sorts of reflection serve as moral supports, both are similarly structured, and both lead ultimately to the same postulation of God's existence. If one is to appreciate the function of Kant's aesthetics within his overall philosophy, it is short-sighted to ignore the Critique of Teleological Judgment and its relation to Kant's moral theory. Consequently, this GuideBook encompasses the entire third *Critique* with the hope that the exposition will help situate Kant's aesthetics within its philosophically systematic context more clearly and explicitly.

With respect to my own studies of Kant's aesthetics, my greatest thanks is due to Donald W. Crawford, who introduced me so positively to Kant's aesthetic theory at a time when it was hardly a mainstream discipline in Kant studies. The effect of this fortunate situation – one whose power of philosophical *Bildung* I was able to appreciate retrospectively only many years later – was to establish an unexpectedly fertile intellectual foundation for appreciating the history of philosophy during the sevententh, eighteenth, and nineteenth centuries. Kant is known as a Janus-head figure that summarizes eighteenth-century philosophical tendencies and anticipates the nineteenth-century ones, and there is much to be discerned in nineteenth-century German philosophy by using the *Critique of the Power of Judgment* as one's intellectual center, as opposed to the *Critique of Pure Reason*, as is standardly, and certainly effectively, done. This book is dedicated to Don.

I would also like to express my thanks to the Department of Philosophy and the Faculty of Arts at the University of Auckland, who provided a substantial research leave during 2005 when most of this book was written. Special thanks is due to Professor John Morrow, Dean of Arts, for his intellectual interest and moral support of this project. I am also grateful to an anonymous reviewer for the invaluable observations I have been able to incorporate into the final manuscript.

There are two people, who, as sagacious teachers, played a formative and constitutive role in my appreciation of art, philosophy, personal character and scholarship. To John F. A. Taylor (1915–96) and William H. Hay (1917–97) – whose inspirational magnitude of urbanity and learning have always been a guiding light for me – I also owe a timeless thanks.

Auckland, New Zealand
March 2006

A note on the English translations of the *Critique of the Power of Judgment*

There are four complete English translations of Kant's *Critique of the Power of Judgment* (which is also referred to as the *Critique of Judgment*). These are by J. H. Bernard (1892), James Creed Meredith (1911/1928), Werner S. Pluhar (1987), and Paul Guyer and Eric Matthews (2000). The Guyer–Matthews translation is the best representative of Kant's original wording, and in this respect it stands as a distinguished improvement over the previous translations. For the purposes of reading, in English, a text that reflects what Kant actually wrote, this is surely the translation to have in hand. The long sentences are not clipped into shorter segments, the syntax is largely preserved, and the words chosen usually come as close to the original German as one can reasonably expect. Many segments of the translation simply cannot be improved upon.

The following set of examples gives a sense of the variability to be encountered in the English translations. Here is a crucial passage from §57:[3]

> *Denn nähme man eine solche Rücksicht nicht, so wäre der Anspruch des Geschmacksurteils auf allgemeine Gültigkeit nicht zu retten;* . . .
>
> (Ak 340 (236), G 216, P 212, M 207, B 185)

[2000] For if one did not assume such a point of view, then the claim of the judgment of taste to universal validity could not be saved . . . [G]

[1987] For unless we assumed that a judgment of taste relies on some concept or other, we could not save its claim to universal validity. [P]

[1911] For unless such a point of view were adopted there would be no means of saving the claim of the judgment of taste to universal validity. [M]

[1892] For if we do not admit such a reference, the claim of the judgment of taste to universal validity would not hold good. [B]

It nonetheless remains that what is best from a scholarly point of view is not always preferable from a student's point of view. The Guyer–Matthews [2000] translation impeccably provides the most accurate reflection in the English language of Kant's original text, but Bernard's translation [1892] is still the most user-friendly for the student who has time constraints and who is trying to comprehend Kant's thought in the most direct and efficient manner for the first time. Bernard is more clearly understandable than Kant himself is in the original, and his English formulations have a linguistic economy and stronger semantic impact than what Guyer and Matthews were obliged to convey in their effort to be as faithful as possible to the original text. Bernard, though, often does not replace the German words in the closest one-to-one correspondences that are available.

Meredith's sensible translation [1911/1928] is reliable and its rhetorical tone is comfortably light, but it does not accurately reflect the original text's syntactic structure. It also periodically conveys an archaic quality in the choice of words and linguistic formats, and introduces a few odd terminological coinages in places. Overall, it offers an approachable rendition, while sacrificing some philosophical clarity in the process.

Pluhar's translation [1987] advances philosophically over Meredith's, and in terms of its ease of use, it stands halfway between Bernard's clarity of expression and Guyer and Matthews' accuracy of rendition. Pluhar frequently does not use Kant's exact words, but he impressively conveys the sense of the original text, and his translation is generally the most useful and insightful for deciphering difficult passages that the Guyer–Matthews translation has no choice to present as vague. This weighty interpretive benefit is achieved, however, by artistically rephrasing, segmenting, and augmenting the wording beyond Kant's original formulations. Nonetheless, with respect to its usefulness in deciphering obscure passages, Pluhar's translation can be a blessing for the student at critical junctures, when used in conjunction with Bernard's.

Bernard's translation, all factors considered, is probably the best for someone who is approaching Kant's aesthetics for the first time, desires to consult only one translation, and who immediately needs a clear, efficient, and reliable rendition of the original's meaning. The more advanced, English-speaking student of the third *Critique* would obviously do well to work with Kant's original and/or all four complete translations side-by-side to appreciate with some illumination how the key passages have been alternatively rendered, or as a second option, with the Guyer–Matthews translation in conjunction with Bernard's, if the German version is linguistically inaccessible. It is memorable to experience how many of the meanings in the Guyer–Matthews literalistic translation that become present upon extended reflection and that are indeed right before one's eye, but that inevitably fall into the background and are easily overlooked, are there on the surface in Bernard's semantically sparkling formulations. Comparing and contrasting the four existing English translations itself provides an education in different attitudes towards what a translation of a philosophical text is supposed to achieve.

None of the existing translations were optimal to use unmodified for the purposes of the present GuideBook, which aims to respect the accuracy of rendition that we find in the Guyer–Matthews translation, but also to enhance it with some of the clarity and accessibility of Bernard's translation. Consequently, the quoted passages have been newly translated with both aims in mind. For example, for the sake of clarity, the more literalistic "purpose" is used for "*Zweck*" instead of "end," although "end" fits better within the context of some of Kant's other books, especially his moral writings; "purposiveness" is correspondingly used for

"*Zweckmäßigkeit*" instead of "finality" to preserve the parallelism between *Zweck* and *Zweckmäßigkeit*; "teleological causality" is used instead of "final causality" to match the book's theme and subtitling more accurately, since Kant uses "*teleologische Causalität*" interchangeably with the less perspicuous "*Causalität der Endursachen.*" The effort at every point has been to render Kant's meanings as straightforwardly comprehensible as possible without disproportionately modifying the original wording.

Readers familiar with the third *Critique* will notice that in most instances, the more focussed and theoretically descriptive phrase, "judgments of pure beauty" – a phrase that contrasts easily and usefully with "judgments of adherent beauty" – is used to translate the generic and multi-purpose term "*Geschmacksurteil.*" It is used in place of the more literal, but less informative and confusion-generating phrase, "judgments of taste." The implicit position expressed is that Kant's canonical analyses are almost always directed towards illuminating *ideal* judgments of taste rather than actual ones, since his project is to define an idealized standard of pure beauty against which all actual judgments of taste should be measured and understood. The rationale for this phrasing is explained further in §1 below.

INTRODUCTION

A GUIDE TO THE ENTIRE THIRD *CRITIQUE*

Kant's *Critique of the Power of Judgment* (1790) is also known as his third *Critique*, since it followed upon the *Critique of Pure Reason* (1781 and 1787) and the *Critique of Practical Reason* (1788). It is one of the most influential systematic aesthetic theories in the history of philosophical aesthetics. It is also among the penultimate components of Kant's thought as a whole, as it builds a small contingent of ferry boats (owing to the lack of bridges) between two distinct modes of interpreting the world, namely, in reference to science, with its attendant mechanical causality and determinism, and in reference to morality, with its attendant teleological causality and freedom.

The tension and ultimate resolution between scientific determinism and moral freedom is a leading theme in Kant's philosophy. Accordingly, the third *Critique* introduces reflections on the nature of beauty and on living organisms – and more generally, reflections on the nature, extent, and presuppositions that accompany our power of judgment – to reconcile philosophically our physical circumstances with our moral freedom. Kant's ultimate hope is to strengthen the ideal of acting morally as best as we can, given a natural world that on the arbitrary and violent face of things does not display much of an inner moral fabric supportive of our efforts to do actually what our voice of reason within us obliges us to do.

The *Critique of the Power of Judgment* divides into two parts, namely, the Critique of the Power of Aesthetic Judgment (§§1–60) and the Critique of the Power of Teleological Judgment (§§61–91). The German title of the book, *Kritik der Urteilskraft*, refers to "*Urteilskraft*," which is often translated as "judgment," but is better translated as "power of judgment." "*Urteil*" by itself signifies "judgment" and "*Kraft*" signifies "power" or "force."

The word "*Urteilskraft*" refers consequently to a power, capacity, faculty or facility that we have to make judgments, and within his philosophical theory, Kant descriptively coalesces this power into a particular kind of mental "faculty" that operates in conjunction with other mental faculties or capacities. The two main parts of the third *Critique* thus refer respectively to the power of aesthetic judgment and the power of teleological, purpose-specifying, goal-oriented, judgment. These two parts work side-by-side, for each defines an avenue that helps us conceive of a compatibility between nature, considered with respect to its thoroughly mechanical operations, and free, moral activity.

At the same time, the two main parts of the third *Critique* have distinct subject matters, equally daunting technical terminology, and a common theme that becomes obvious only after having had some familiarity with Kant's philosophy as a whole. Such obstacles partially explain why, if one is interested primarily in philosophical aesthetics and is approaching the third *Critique* with the exclusive aim of understanding Kant's views on art, it is difficult to develop a solid standpoint from which one can incorporate the significance of book's second half into aesthetics-related issues. These latter involve, for instance, reflections on the nature of beauty, artistic creativity, the division of the arts, and the relationship between beauty and morality. The subject matter of the second part of the book appears foreign to such themes, since it essentially concerns whether living organisms are comprehensible in mechanical terms, and unexpectedly introduces arguments for God's existence. The immediate relevance of these issues to philosophical aesthetics is obscure, and the historical result has been that studies of Kant's aesthetics have gravitated towards only the first half of the book.

Kant's account of the logic that governs our judgments of biological organisms – notwithstanding its direct relevance to contemporary debates surrounding the issue of intelligent design – is itself a less predominant field of study within Kant scholarship in general. The resulting selective approach to Kant's aesthetics has thus had the unfortunate result of suggesting that the second half of the book that concerns teleological judgment, is not central to understanding his aesthetic theory. To be sure, there is some independence between the two halves of the book, and there is some noticeable expository overlap between Kant's *Critique of Practical Reason* and the second half of the third *Critique*. The following exposition, though, will show that without conceiving of the *Critique of the Power of Judgment* as a whole, the motivations and systematic functions of several of Kant's key ideas in his philosophical aesthetics (e.g., aesthetic ideas) remain close to invisible, owing in part to a close connection between Kant's theory of artistic genius and his theory of living organisms. For such reasons, the present GuideBook covers the entire third *Critique*, with the primary aim of illuminating Kant's aesthetic theory.

KANT'S PHILOSOPHICAL STYLE

Kant spent his life (1724–1804) in the European harbor-city of Königsberg (now Kaliningrad, Russia) and it is natural to ask how a person who ventured from home no farther than a day's journey by horse-drawn cart and who, during the 1700s, lived in a small and relatively remote, although not insignificant, city in the Prussian empire, could have become one of the most intellectually awesome philosophers in the history of Western civilization. Part of the answer is explained by Kant's philosophical style, which was introspective. Kant looked inside of himself, tried his best to adopt the universalistic standpoint of a human being in general, and discerned an intellectual core to his presence as a human being, independently of the historical circumstances, physical limitations, and cultural soil within which his daily life took place. He tried out-standingly to articulate what makes us all human, whether one happens to be an ancient Egyptian, an eighteenth-century German, or person of the distant future.

In this effort, Kant shares a place with Plato. In a likewise man-ner, Plato sought for universal constancies both within and without us, and noted that if truth requires something permanent for us to grasp – that if sandcastles, clouds, and passing smoke cannot repre-sent the foundation of the world, and if even the strongest blocks of granite are dissolved eventually by the passing of time – then ultimately, the truth can reside only in what is absolutely, and not merely relatively, steadfast. Plato located such an unshakeable truth in a timeless realm that we can apprehend through pure con-templation, using our mind's power alone. He believed that we can conceive of this timeless, colorless, textureless, odorless, tasteless, and silent realm simply by using our minds, just as we use our five senses to perceive the physical world. For Plato, this conceivable world is more than an imaginary ideal; he regarded the act of con-ceiving of it as itself a metaphysical act through which we appre-hend the absolute truth – a truth that resides beyond the ordinary world of sensory experience. This is a realm of perfect circles, num-bers, goodness, beauty, courage, and the like, that are instantiated in the material objects that continually come and go.

Kant never went so far as to claim that we can exactly know of such a timeless world, and he did not sympathize with Plato's metaphysical optimism. He nonetheless acknowledged that if any-thing is to be characterized as unconditional and true, then it must be unchanging, stable, and self-sufficient. The noteworthy and rev-olutionary aspect of his philosophizing is that he claimed to have discovered within the human being – although not necessarily within the constitution of the universe as it is independently of us – formal structures of thought whose character can be known independently of experience, can be referred to as unconditional *for us*, and that can be shown to constitute the steadfast structural foundations of our experience, both scientific and moral.

Kant discovered these structures by a philosophical thought process that resembles analytic chemistry, where we take some mixture, alloy or compound and separate it into its various elements. We will see this analytic process operating once more in his aesthetic theory. Most famously, Kant performed this philosophically analytic process not within the context of beauty, but more ordinarily and foundationally on our perception of ordinary objects. Here, he distilled out conceptual contents from variable sensory contents, and then both of these from formal, spatio-temporal structures. We can see this in an excerpt from his *Critique of Pure Reason* (1781 and 1787):

> In the transcendental aesthetic we will therefore first isolate sensibility, such as to remove everything that the understanding thinks through its concepts, so as to leave nothing more than empirical intuition. Second, we will also separate from this everything that belongs to sensation, so as to leave remaining nothing more than pure intuition and the mere form of appearances, which is exclusively what sensibility can provide *a priori*. From this investigation it will be found that there are two pure forms of sensible intuition as principles of *a priori* cognition, namely space and time . . .
>
> (*Critique of Pure Reason*, Transcendental Aesthetic, A21 / B36)

With some further argumentation, the above distillation process identified space and time as structures within us that we bring to our experience. These structures, Kant maintained, are knowable independently of experience, and most importantly, are *invariant* from person to person. Kant concluded that for every human being and for every human experience, it certainly will take place at some time, and for every experience of a sensory object that is perceived to be mind-independent, it certainly will be in some place or other. For human beings, the forms of space and time are subjective constants. Their infinity is fundamentally within us, and not without us. To discover this, he did not need to leave Königsberg, let alone his own sitting-room.

Kant's doctrine of the subjectivity of space and time is arguably his most famous and influential contribution to the history of philosophy. However, his allegiance to Aristotelian logic – a discipline that in Kant's own time, had not changed substantially in 2000 years – is a more permeating and characteristic factor in his thought in general. Without referring to Aristotelian logic and to the associated type of rationality that stems from it, Kant's philosophy cannot be well understood.

Aside from using standard logical deduction to style his philosophical arguments, as do virtually all philosophers, Kant also employed what he referred to as a "transcendental" style of argumentation, and both of these styles lend a characteristic form to his philosophy. To display the difference between these two modes of logical argumentation, let us consider the arithmetical statement "2 + 2 = 4."

There are at least two ways to consider the statement "2 + 2 = 4" in reference to alternative styles of argumentation. The first articulates what the statement implies; the second articulates what the statement presupposes. Each exemplifies a different style of logical argumentation. Most straightforwardly, the statement "2 + 2 = 4" implies "(1 + 1) + 2 = 4" or "(.5 + .5) + 1 + 2 = 4" along with an inexhaustible number of similar instances of this analytic and extractive sort. In such cases of straightforward logical deduction we simply analyze, or draw out implications from, what is already given in the initial statement.

More interestingly and less mechanically, we can also ask what must be presupposed for "2 + 2 = 4" to be true. We can ask even more fundamentally what must be presupposed for "2 + 2 = 4" to be possible at all. For instance, we would need to presuppose the existence of a mathematical language, and more basically, that each term has a precise meaning that remains constant over time. Kant would add specifically that we also need to presuppose the presence of time, since he believes that the number line and arithmetic in general derive from the sequence of points that constitutes the linear format of time itself.

By revealing such presuppositions, we reveal the underlying, and ideally, most basic preconditions for the statement or object at hand, i.e., the bottom-line conditions for the very possibility of the thing. This is to engage in transcendental argumentation, and Kant uses this sort of argumentation to establish most of his core philosophical tenets. The illuminating aspect of transcendental argumentation is its power to penetrate beyond given axioms and given presuppositions to discern what the presuppositions – often accepted unquestionably and dogmatically as self-evident – *themselves* presuppose.

Transcendental argumentation is a characteristic feature of Kant's thought, but it stands side-by-side with the elementary Aristotelian structures of logical form and deductive argumentation. The most basic is the dyadic form of logical judgment "*S is P*" that refers to some subject or individual "*S*" (what Kant calls an "intuition") to which some general property "*P*" (what Kant calls a "concept") is ascribed. In addition, there are the triadic forms of logical syllogism, where we have an initial pair of judgments such as "All As are Bs" and "All Bs are Cs" which are brought together logically to imply that "All As are Cs."

Having been influenced by Aristotle, some of the most famous logic treatises prior to Kant's time began with the analysis of *single* concepts, proceeded to investigate *dyadic* combinations of concepts in the form of judgments, and continued to explore *triadic* combinations of judgments in the form of syllogisms. A prime historical example is the *Logique, ou l'art de penser* (1662), by Antoine Arnauld (1612–94) and Pierre Nicole (1625–95), also known as the *Port-Royal Logic*. This type of logical structuring and sequencing also informs the conceptual framework upon which Kant built his *Critique of Pure Reason*.[1]

We will see how these logical forms – especially the dyadic form of judgment – influence and structure Kant's aesthetic theory in what follows below. For the present, it is important to keep in mind only how Kant believes that the forms of Aristotelian logic constitute a virtually unshakeable discipline, how these logical forms are abstract and have no sensory content, and how they presumably are the same in every human being, if we assume the classical definition of a human being as a "rational animal." In Kant's view, this classical definition amounts to saying that the Aristotelian logical forms constitute the essence of human beings and that, for us, they are absolutely reliable.

Kant's philosophical achievement involves investigating the foundations of scientific judgments, moral judgments, and judgments of pure beauty, and discerning that underlying each of these forms of judgment there is an abstract logical form whose unconditional nature, if respected, recognized, and properly acted upon, will guarantee agreement between people, no matter when or where they might live. Of greatest importance to Kant was his discovery that the foundations of morality can be defined exclusively in reference to our common human rationality, and that the ultimate ground of doing the right thing consequently has nothing essentially to do with the pursuit of pleasure, sense-gratification, personal inclination, and the contingencies that vary from person to person.

In Kant's aesthetic theory, we will witness much the same as what can be found in his moral theory in terms of its formality and degree of high abstraction, except that the basic topic will be judgments of pure beauty rather than moral judgments. Kant will similarly argue, however, that sensory charm, sense-gratification, historical contingencies, and empirical variabilities in general cannot be the basis of judgments of pure beauty. His view is that when judging an object's beauty, our attention should be directed only towards the object's rational form – a form whose capacity to resonate with our common human way to know things produces a disinterested, non-sensory, and knowledge-centered satisfaction of its own.

Indeed, as we shall see, Kant's theory of knowledge, his analysis of the disinterested pleasure in beauty, along with his association of beauty with both morality and science, are all based on his Aristotelian conception of logic, his assumption that this logic is inherent and invariant in the human being, and his assumption that our powers of knowing are themselves modeled upon these elementary structures of logic. The power and attractiveness of Kant's philosophy is based on having identified this common rational constitution that everyone shares, and on having subsequently developed accounts of science, morality, and beauty that issue from this universal and unconditional basis. At the same time, he conceived of this common rational constitution as being relative only to human beings as far as we can know, and left it as a tantalizingly open question and eternal mystery, whether or not the world in itself has such rational qualities. His own rational faith was that it does.

THE HISTORICAL COMPOSITION OF THE *CRITIQUE OF THE POWER OF JUDGMENT*

For most of his career, Kant assumed that judgments of beauty and sublimity are empirical, experience-based judgments that vary from person to person and from circumstance to circumstance. He held this belief as late as 1781, as can be inferred from a footnote in the *Critique of Pure Reason* (A21) where he states, in effect, that aesthetics is largely an empirically variable discipline.

The turning-point in Kant's mind – those months when he discovered a way to formulate a solidly non-empiricist theory of beauty, and when the idea for a third *Critique* was born – can be traced to several letters Kant wrote from mid-1787 to the end of that year, immediately after completing his *Critique of Practical Reason*. In a December 1787 letter to Karl Leonhard Reinhold (1757–1823), Kant mentioned that his new discoveries about the possibility of writing a "critique of taste" stemmed from attending closely to the elements of knowledge (viz., concepts and intuitions) and the mental powers associated with them (viz., understanding and imagination). This suggests that in his reflections on the relationship between the cognitive faculties of understanding and imagination in their aim to acquire scientific knowledge, Kant was able to discern a non-sensory, universalistic, *a priori* foundation for judgments of pure beauty.

In the *Critique of Practical Reason*, Kant had just succeeded in identifying a different type of feeling which, however, was similarly universalistic and independent of sensory pleasure. This was a feeling related to morality. With his subsequent recognition of a universal feeling related to the cognitive operations of the understanding and imagination in their aim to acquire scientific knowledge, Kant not only discerned a way to establish a non-empirical theory of beauty. He also saw a way to close the gap between science and morality in reference to beauty, since the feeling of beauty bears relationships to both. Insofar as a theory of beauty could thereby serve as a logical connecting link between science and morality, the possibility emerged for a third *Critique* that would complement the first two *Critiques*, which had addressed science and morality respectively.

There is some uncertainty regarding the thematic and historical sequence in which Kant composed the various sections of the third *Critique*. What seems to be clear, is that he first analyzed judgments of pure beauty in reference to the above-mentioned, universalistic, non-sensory feeling, to explain how they can have a universal validity (§§1–22; §§30–40). Then, he built the rest of the book up from this foundational insight. Attending to this question of universal validity is how Kant presumably started his work in later 1787 as the "Critique of Taste," and why it bore that initial name.

The segment on the sublime (§§23–29) is a curiosity for textual archaeologists, since it stands peculiarly between the thematically-connected §§1–22 and §§30–40 and begins with a noticeably new terminology – one that introduces a systematically useful distinction between "reflecting" and "determining" judgment that some historians of the text trace to mid-1789. If accurate, this dating suggests either that Kant composed the section on the sublime after mid-1789, or that he revised it to incorporate the phraseology concerning reflecting judgment. Kant had long been thinking about the sublime, having published *Observations on the Feeling of the Beautiful and Sublime* in 1764, and it is an open question whether he wrote the third *Critique*'s section on the sublime after mid-1789, or whether he revised earlier material to include references to reflecting judgment, even though its structure suggests it was written hastily.[2] This uncertain situation holds for most of the work. It is consequently fair to say that much of what can be said about the composition of the third *Critique* remains speculative, since Kant was previously interested in all of its main topics in one way or another. This makes it difficult to tell whether the segments were newly conceived or were ideas that he already had in mind semi-composed.

Such archaeological considerations have little bearing on the actual and resulting philosophical exposition (which is our main concern here) and strength of Kant's arguments, but they do help to resolve some puzzles about why certain topics appear in the text when they do, and why different terminologies are used in different parts of the work, sometimes seeming to appear out of nowhere. For such purposes, the basic point to keep in mind is that Kant's original 1787 title for the third *Critique* was the *Foundations of the Critique of Taste*, centering exclusively on judgments of pure beauty. By 1789, the title had evolved into the *Critique of the Power of Judgment*, centering (in part retrospectively, since Kant had continued to work on the project in 1788) not only on judgments of pure beauty, but also on judgments of natural beauty, artistic beauty, and natural teleology. This expansion of themes was in view of a more theoretically encompassing emphasis upon the faculty of judgment in general that could systematically integrate Kant's overall philosophical project of coordinating nature and morality, not only in reference to judgments of pure beauty, but also in reference to teleological, purpose-specifying, judgments.

EIGHTEENTH-CENTURY AESTHETIC THEORY PRIOR TO KANT

In conjunction with its status as an exceptional philosophical treatise, Kant's third *Critique* is also a historical document whose contents, despite the manuscript's ahistorical tone, display the influence of earlier writers. With respect to the *Critique of the Power of Judgment*, these influences are located mainly within German and British philosophies of the earlier 1700s. In Britain, most of the thinkers involved were writing under the influence of John Locke (1632–1704); in Germany, most were writing in light of the philosophy of Gottfried Wilhelm Leibniz (1646–1716). There are variations in approach and emphasis within each group, but speaking generally, the British philosophies tended to ground themselves on empirical observation and the results of experimental science, whereas the German philosophies were more directly inspired by the logical certainty of mathematical reasoning. Kant's aesthetic theory acknowledges both approaches: he accepts that beauty is based on a kind of satisfactory feeling that is paradigmatically stimulated by an encounter with some given empirical object, but he accounts for this feeling, not through an external reference to a resulting physical sensation, but through a more reflective and internal reference to a formal, non-sensory interplay between mental capacities that everyone shares.

In conjunction with the possibility of undertaking an archaeology of the text as briefly described above, investigating when each segment was composed, and so on, it is also possible to undertake a genealogical study of Kant's third *Critique*, whereby one traces each key theme back to earlier writers in a threadlike manner, with the aim of subsequently weaving all of the threads together in the end – acknowledging the essential contribution of Kant's own genius in the final stylistic combination – to reconstitute the third *Critique*. This is not the aim of the present GuideBook, but I will indicate some of these threads in a generalized manner to provide some historical perspective on the main themes that Kant introduces and sometimes discusses at some length. These themes can be grouped under the three headings of "disinterestedness," "perfection," and "beauty and morality."

Many authors were writing in Britain and Germany on the above topics, far in excess of what Kant had directly available in Königsberg, and it is important to identify which among them Kant had read or had heard about reliably. The question is straightforward within the field of German philosophers – at least in reference to the key topics that appear in his aesthetic theory. Although the following list is not exhaustive, we can indicate that Kant was immediately conversant with the works of G. W. Leibniz, Christian Wolff (1679–1754), Alexander Gottlieb Baumgarten (1714–62), Georg Friedrich Meier (1718–77), and Moses Mendelssohn (1729–86). Among British writers, we know that with respect to topics discussed in his aesthetic theory, Kant read in German translation, the works of Francis Hutcheson (1694–1746), Henry Home, Lord Kames (1696–1782), David Hume (1711–76), Alexander Gerard (1728–95), and Edmund Burke (1729–97).[3]

From the tradition of Leibniz and Wolff – who had themselves absorbed an assortment of conceptual distinctions from the philosophy of René Descartes (1596–1650) – Kant inherited a threefold manner of classifying ways of apprehending an object. Specifically, an object can be apprehended distinctly, clearly or obscurely.[4] A distinct apprehension involves identifying the object clearly against some background and then specifying its essential properties; a clear apprehension involves identifying the object sharply against some background, but without necessarily being able to specify its essential properties, since they remain confused; an obscure apprehension is where one cannot clearly identify the object against some background. The greater the clarity, the greater the basic articulation and separation of perceptual ingredients; the greater the distinctness, the greater the conceptual understanding.

According to Leibniz and Wolff, distinct apprehensions are only possible within the realm of thought. Clarity can be a property of either purely conceptual or sensory apprehension (since both perceptions and conceptions can be well articulated and can have sharp contours) and it therefore represents an intermediary stage between obscure perception and distinct conception. Within this hierarchical arrangement, one would, for instance, first apprehend an object in an obscure manner, then sharply isolate it from its background in an effort to clarify its perceptual presence, and then apply a process of reflection and abstraction to remove the confusion within the object for the purpose of apprehending it at the non-sensory level of thought and definitions.

This tripartite distinction between obscure, clear, and distinct apprehensions anticipates and inspires (although it does not exactly match) a tripartite Kantian distinction that we will discuss below. The latter is a distinction among three types of satisfactions, namely, those of sensory gratification (the agreeable), the satisfaction in beauty (the beautiful), and the satisfaction in moral consciousness (the good). In accord with this, we will find in some parts of the third *Critique* a gradual ascension from sensory gratification to moral awareness via the intermediary experience of beauty. For instance, given an object that is clearly apprehended, but where its sensory charm is initially confused with its form, we can then abstract from its sensory charm and attend only to its spatio-temporal form, reflect accordingly upon the object's form, and experience a satisfactory feeling in the object's beauty. From this, we can then additionally draw an analogy between the experience of beauty and moral awareness, owing to their mutual abstraction from sensory gratification in conjunction with their both having a kind of universality.

To accomplish this ascension to moral awareness, Kant called upon accounts of disinterested attention and the nature of the satisfactory feeling associated with beauty, the most salient of which was from his contemporary, Moses Mendelssohn (1729–86), whose views lead one to appreciate that the satisfactory feeling associated with beauty need not have a sensory ground. From the British theorists such as Hutcheson, who referred to an internal sense of beauty (among several internal senses) that differed from our external five senses, there is some impetus to formulate an account of the satisfactory feeling associated with beauty in reference to a non-physical, or non-external, sense that – with some further argument – can be assumed to be the same in everyone. In addition, Alexander Baumgarten referred to the power of genius as involving the harmony of the mental faculties, and this allows not only for the satisfactory feeling associated with beauty to be explained in reference to the harmony of the cognitive faculties, but also allows for the theory of genius to play a central role in bringing together beauty and morality. Baumgarten's conception of the perfection of sensory apprehension also has affinities to Kant's notion of aesthetic ideas and common sense.

The central relationship between beauty and morality that we encounter in Kant's aesthetics can also be traced back to British aesthetic theory in the works of Anthony Ashley Cooper, the 3rd Earl of Shaftesbury (1671–1713). Enhancing this with a theistic element, are some reflections from Hutcheson, who speculated on the role of God as a being who coordinates nature with our moral aspirations. In further development of the relationship between aesthetic experience and morality, we also have Kant's discussion of the sublime, which was influenced significantly by Mendelssohn, Edmund Burke, and Kames, whose writings on the sublime he had read.

These authors represent the bulk of the sources from which Kant adopts his terminology, distinctions, formulation of problems, and philosophical emphases that constitute his aesthetic theory. His aesthetic theory nonetheless carries his own stamp and expresses his own particular formulation of a philosophical project that aims to coordinate the mechanical, empirical, and factual natural laws with the ideal, subjectively-discovered and purely rational moral law that he adamantly believes prescribes how we ought to behave. This interest in coordinating nature and morality is the driving force of Kant's aesthetics, as we shall see presently in the pages that now follow.

1

THE PLEASURE IN PURE BEAUTY
(§§1–22; §§30–40)

[First Part, Critique of Aesthetic Judgment. Section I. Analytic of Aesthetic Judgment. Book I. Analytic of the Beautiful.] In the first 22 sections of the *Critique of the Power of Judgment*, Kant analyzes the structure, grounds, and objects associated with "judgments of taste" (*Geschmacksurteile*). To do this systematically, he organizes his exposition according to a fourfold division inherited from the logic books of his time. This fourfold division also guided his earlier analyses in the *Critique of Pure Reason* and *Critique of Practical Reason*. In the first *Critique*, for example, Kant structured his expositions of the logical preconditions for any human experience into the four logical aspects of "quantity," "quality," "relation," and "modality." These will be further described below, since they apply similarly to Kant's present analysis of judgments of taste. In the second *Critique*, he used the same fourfold structure to organize his treatment of moral issues.

Kant's topic in the third *Critique* as a whole is concerned specifically with judgments of a particular sort, namely, those that are *purpose-related* in a manner that is either determinate (i.e., when the purposes are specified) or indeterminate (i.e., when they are not). The fourfold logical format referred to above continues to apply, and Kant utilizes this division as a template – with varying degrees of success – to organize his expositions of aesthetic and teleological judgments, both of which are purpose-related types of judgment.

As outlined in the *Critique of Pure Reason*, logical *quantity* concerns whether a judgment's scope extends to only a single thing, to some things or to all things; logical *quality* concerns whether a given judgment is positive, negative or unlimited;[1] logical *relation* concerns whether the judgment is categorical, hypothetical or disjunctive; logical *modality* concerns whether the judgment is presented as only a possibility, as an actuality, or as a necessity. A judgment such as "This rose is red," for instance, is a singular, positive, and categorical judgment that asserts a matter of fact. Kant will argue that a judgment such as "This rose is beautiful" is a singular, positive, categorical judgment that, rather intriguingly, asserts a matter of necessity. His analytic exposition of judgments of pure beauty is accordingly partitioned into four main logical aspects or "moments" (*Momente*), following the above divisions, and any instance of a judgment of pure beauty will embody the four aspects simultaneously.

A judgment such as "this is beautiful" also, however, has a peculiar subjective component in that it amounts to a person's report about how, upon disinterestedly contemplating an object's form, the object makes him or her feel. This entails that judgments of beauty will require furthermore a specialized analysis within the basic parameters of the standard fourfold division of logical judgments, since this crucial subjective factor needs to be additionally elucidated.

To highlight the different moments of judgments of pure beauty and to introduce an assortment of aesthetics-related themes, Kant organizes his analysis of judgments of pure beauty – an analysis that grounds the remaining discussions in the Critique of Aesthetic Judgment – according to the four following logical headings, which we will discuss in the sequence, following Kant's text. He presents:

§§1–5: [Quality][2] The first moment of the judgment of pure beauty, with respect to its quality. This concerns the judgment's **disinterestedness**.

§§ 6–9: [Quantity] The second moment of the judgment of pure beauty, with respect to its quantity. Although the judgment of pure beauty is always singular in logical form, this second moment concerns the judgment's **universality** in reference to its grounds.

§§ 10–17: [Relation] The third moment of judgments of pure beauty, with respect to the relation of the purposes that such judgments bring into consideration. This concerns the judgment's **purposiveness**.

§§ 18–22: [Modality] The fourth moment of pure judgments of beauty, with respect to the modality of the satisfaction in the object. This concerns the judgment's **necessity**.[3]

As noted above, in the initial sections of the Critique of Aesthetic Judgment, Kant is concerned with analyzing the features of a particular kind of judgment that he calls a "judgment of taste" (*Geschmacksurteil*). It is easy to assume that this type of judgment is made every time someone intends to judge a thing's beauty and makes the pronouncement, "X is beautiful." In fact, however, the majority of such "actual" judgments of taste might not be attending to the object's beauty at all, but to other features of the object, such as its sensory charm or its attractive meaning. We must therefore distinguish between actual judgments that are intended to be judgments of taste and ideal judgments of taste. Ideal judgments of taste attend to the object's beauty exclusively.

The bulk of Kant's initial analyses in §§1–15 concern ideal judgments of taste. His concern is to describe the essential features of such judgments, and he aims to characterize the perfect attitude that would stand as the ideal for anyone who would like exclusively to judge an object's beauty. In such an ideal situation, as we shall see, the judgment of taste would be disinterested, would demand universal agreement, would attend to the object's purposiveness, and would involve a kind of necessity. To underscore such idealizing intents on Kant's part, I will refer to a "*Geschmacksurteil*" (which would literally be translated as a "judgment of taste") as a "judgment of pure beauty."

THE FIRST LOGICAL MOMENT: JUDGMENTS OF PURE BEAUTY ARE AESTHETIC AND DISINTERESTED (§§1–5)

Aesthetic Judgments vs. Cognitive Judgments

[§1: "The Judgment of Taste is Aesthetic"] The most fundamental assertion in the *Critique of the Power of Judgment* is that judgments of pure beauty are *aesthetic* judgments. They are based on feelings of pleasure or displeasure, i.e., how something makes us feel:

> To decide whether something is beautiful or not, we relate the representation, not through the understanding to the object for cognition, but through the imagination (perhaps joined with the understanding) to the subject and its feeling of pleasure or displeasure.
>
> (§1, Ak 203 (4), G 89, P 44, M 41, B 37)

Kant formulates this characterization with several background assumptions about how the human mind operates. To start, he distinguishes a representation(s) of an object from the object itself, as when several people all perceive the same object and where it is possible to distinguish the object itself from the way each person perceives it. For instance, if each person drew a picture of the object that he or she was seeing, the pictures would each look different, given the different angles from which each was drawn. The object itself, however, would remain constant and independent of the various perspectives or representations taken upon it. When judging an object's beauty, Kant maintains that we refer immediately to how the object presents itself to us, and we attend thereby to our own representation of the object. An object's beauty concerns first and foremost how the object appears to you or to me, and we each reflect upon how that appearance makes us feel.

The above excerpt also reveals how Kant identifies and isolates various mental capacities and how he describes our psychological processes in terms of the interaction of those capacities. In the present case, we have the representation of an object, and two ways to relate ourselves to this representation, either for the purposes of cognition (i.e., to obtain knowledge of the natural world), or in reference to how the representation makes us feel. To comprehend, cognize or empirically know the object in some determinate way, we call upon the understanding. To judge how the representation makes us feel, we presumably call mainly upon the imagination. As we read the very first sentence of the *Critique of the Power of Judgment*, we thus have before us (1) the representation of an object, (2) two stated ways to interpret that representation, and (3) two mental capacities – understanding and imagination – through which we can focus the interpretation in one direction or another.

Distinctive in this philosophical arrangement is the claim that when we judge the pure beauty of an object, we are not deciding whether the representation of the object tells us anything true about the object or provides empirical or scientific knowledge of it. The relevant factor in beauty is not objectively directed to securing factual information about the object. Rather, what is relevant is subjectively centered, for it initially concerns only how the object's appearance makes us feel. We disengage our interest from the cognitive, knowledge-related contents of our representation of the object, and in judging the object's beauty we attend only to the pleasurable or displeasurable feelings that the object's presentation generates through our judging of it.

Judgments of pure beauty thereby concern themselves in the first instance with subjective feelings of pleasure and displeasure, although they are directed towards objects that have properties with the power to generate these feelings. Judgments of pure beauty are not cognitive judgments where we attend to an object's qualities to determine what sort of thing it is. From the outset, then, there is a distinction between cognition (i.e., objectively knowing about or comprehending an object) and merely experiencing how the object makes us feel (i.e., aesthetic awareness).

Kant consequently refers to judgments of pure beauty as aesthetic judgments, in contrast to cognitive judgments. The term "aesthetic" does not refer exclusively to beauty, however, and – this is a crucial point – not all aesthetic judgments are judgments of pure beauty. Some aesthetic judgments do not involve beauty at all. Kant refers to judgments of beauty as aesthetic judgments, as one might refer to diamonds as minerals, as opposed to plants.

The term "aesthetic" derives from the Greek "*aistheta*" (αισθητα), which means "sensible particulars." Within the present context, "aesthetic" refers simply to that which is related to feeling. An aesthetic judgment is about how something makes us feel, and there are different kinds of feelings that have respectively different sources or grounds. Some of these feelings and grounds are peculiar to judgments of pure beauty and some are not.

It is consequently important to note at the outset that in the absence of added qualifications such as "pure" or "reflective," it is terminologically confusing if the term "aesthetic judgment" is used flatly as a synonym for either "judgment of pure beauty" or "judgment of taste" within Kant's aesthetics. "Aesthetic judgment" is a comprehensive generic category under which judgments of pure beauty (e.g., "this object (which happens to be a snowflake) is beautiful") along with judgments of sensory gratification (e.g., "this wine has a spicy, citrus aroma"), not to mention judgments of the sublime (e.g., "the starry skies are mathematically sublime"), are included as distinct species, just as primates, rodents, and marsupials are included under the class "mammal."

Kant concludes §1 with some examples that foreshadow his upcoming analysis of judgments of pure beauty. The first example is of some given regular, purposive construction (*ein regelmäßiges, zweckmäßiges Gebäude*). Such a construction, as "purposive," is one whose organization very strongly suggests, although it does not necessitate, that it was intelligently designed. Kant states that in view of such a purposive presentation, we can either begin to wonder what sort of thing it specifically is, or we can more generally and less determinately "hold the presentation up to the entire faculty of representation" and derive a feeling from the overall intelligibility of the presentation's design, quite independently of being concerned with what sort of thing we have before us. Kant associates this latter activity of judging a presentation's abstract and formal intelligibility with judging the presentation's pure, or free, beauty.

In later sections, Kant expands upon what this sort of aesthetic judgment more specifically involves, and indeed, the above example of the purposive construction encapsulates the rudiments of his theory of beauty. At present, though, he only states that when we judge a presentation with respect to its degree of overall intelligibility with respect to its design, we derive a pleasure or displeasure that can be present independently of trying to comprehend what sort of thing we are perceiving. Kant adds that even if we had a presentation that had no sensory content (e.g., some abstract mathematical or geometrical structure), our judgment would still be an aesthetic judgment, if we were to consider solely how the presentation's configuration makes us feel. Whether the presentation has a sensory content or whether it is purely conceptual or formal makes no difference. We can aesthetically judge the formal configuration of either sort of presentation in a judgment of pure beauty.

Judgments of Pure Beauty are Not Grounded upon Interests

[§2: "The feeling of approval that determines the judgment of pure beauty is devoid of all interest"] After having established that the basic quality of judgments of pure beauty is "aesthetic," Kant continues with a definition of the term "interest" (*Interesse*) and asserts that when we have an *interest* in something, the representation of that thing's existence produces a liking, satisfaction, or feeling of approval (*Wohlgefallen*).[4] He maintains further that *desire* is necessarily related to the feeling of approval in the existence of things, and that interests therefore accompany desires. Interests and desires go together, for if one has an interest in something, then one has the desire that the object will be a reality. It follows that if there is some pleasure that arises *independently* of whether the object that causes it is physically real or merely imaginary, then interests and desires would not be involved in explaining the basis of the pleasure. Kant maintains that the latter is exactly the case in the satisfaction that is associated with pure beauty, and he concludes that judgments of pure beauty are *disinterested* judgments and are independent of the faculty of desire. Judgments of pure beauty accordingly require an attitude of disinterestedness on the part of the person making the judgment.

To support this contention that the pleasure in pure beauty is distinct from the pleasures associated with interests and desires, Kant offers a thought experiment to show that judgments of pure beauty are independent of practical affairs. Suppose that we have an image of a palace before us. To deny that the palace is beautiful because it took an excessive amount of money and human labor to build it would be to confuse the cause of the building with how the building looks. Similarly, supposing alternatively that the palace were only a vision in the air, to deny consequently that the building is beautiful because it is only an imaginative vision would be to confuse the building's possible physical existence with how it happens to appear as a mere image. If the building looks exactly the same as a vision and as a physically real palace, then the distinction between imagination and reality makes no aesthetic difference. The palace's merely imaginary existence would not detract from how it looks. Neither would the palace's actual existence need add anything to how it looks. The situation is similar to how, if one had ten imaginary dollars in one's pocket, or if one had ten actual dollars in one's pocket, the "ten" remains the same in both cases.

Kant concludes from such examples that reflection upon the actual causes of the presentation – an activity which introduces the issue of whether or not the presentation refers to an existing object, either natural or artificial – is beside the point when judgments of pure beauty are concerned. What is exclusively relevant, once again, is simply how the intelligibility of the presentation's design makes us feel. Judgments of pure beauty should not, in other words, depend upon the existence of the object of the judgment, as would be the case, for instance, if we were praising the quality of a satisfying restaurant.

In §§1–2, then, Kant argues that judgments of pure beauty are independent of both cognitive (i.e., theoretical) determinations and desire-and-interest-related (i.e., practical) determinations. The former are essentially scientific concerns, the latter are moral concerns in the broad sense, and Kant claims that judgments of pure beauty are reducible to the contents of neither. Judgments of pure beauty stand as a third sort of judgment within an independent philosophical sphere of their own.

In sum, judgments of pure beauty are a species of aesthetic judgment and, owing to their non-knowledge-producing and disinterested quality, are distinguished from cognitive judgments, moral judgments, any type of aesthetic judgment that involves interests (e.g., judgments of sensory gratification), along with concerns about whether or not the object actually exists as either a natural or artifactual object. Kant detaches the judgment of beauty from all of these considerations and it is consequently a rather purified form of judgment.

To elaborate on these distinctions, Kant contrasts such judgments of pure beauty with two different types of judgments that carry an interest with them. The first is a contrasting type of aesthetic judgment, namely, judgments of sensory gratification. These he discusses in §3. The second is moral judgments, which are the topic of §4.

Varieties of Interest-grounded Judgments (I): Judgments of Sensory Gratification

[§3: "The feeling of approval in the agreeable is bound up with interest"] Having established that judgments of pure beauty are disinterested aesthetic judgments, Kant sets the stage for distinguishing more explicitly between the two main species of aesthetic judgment, one of which includes judgments of pure beauty. To establish this distinction, he begins by disentangling a confusion associated with the word "sensation" (*Empfindung*). In the broadest scope of the word, it is possible to say that any satisfying experience is a sensation of some sort. If one adopts this extended meaning, then it is tempting to infer that since only input from the five senses stimulates and establishes our cognitive and practical connections to the physical world, then all satisfaction is ultimately a form of sensory gratification. This would transform beauty into a kind of sensory gratification.

Kant rejects this line of reasoning and distinguishes between satisfactions that are grounded in the five senses, and satisfactions that are otherwise grounded (e.g., they can be grounded in exclusive reference to non-sensory concepts and mental processes). As a rule, he reserves the word "sensation" specifically for pleasures and displeasures related to the five senses, and uses the term "feeling" (*Gefühl*) more generally to refer to aspects of experience that include non-sensory satisfactions, lest one beg the question about whether there are, in fact, any non-sensory satisfactions. This opens the door to recognizing non-sensory satisfactions, and allows for further discussions that explain how such non-sensory satisfactions are possible.

Kant now recalls the earlier distinction drawn between disinterested pleasures as opposed to interest-grounded pleasures (i.e., related to the existence of objects) and he associates sensory pleasures with the latter. He refers to these as satisfactions related to what is agreeable (*angenehm*) in sensation, or what can also be referred to as satisfactions related to sensory gratification.

Having now differentiated feeling from sensation, Kant further distinguishes within the sphere of sensation itself, one meaning of the term "sensation" where we refer simply to the way some raw sensory experience, say, of "greenness," subjectively feels, as opposed to how we can apprehend the same patch of green as being a quality of some external object. This yields two ways to interpret any given sensation, either subjectively or objectively, and it structurally matches the initial sentence in §1 where a representation is considered either in reference to feeling or to cognition. With respect to sensations, he states presently:

> The green color of the meadows belongs to *objective* sensation, as a perception of an object of sense; its agreeableness belongs, however, to *subjective* sensation, through which no object is represented, i.e., to feeling . . .
>
> (§3, Ak 206 (9), G 92, P 48, M 45, B 40)

An implication-filled aspect of Kant's analysis of subjective sensory satisfactions – what he refers to as the agreeableness of the sensation – is his claim that when there is a subjective sensory satisfaction, we necessarily *desire* that the satisfaction continue, and therefore have an *interest* in the item that is objectively related to the sensation. No subjective *sensory* satisfaction can consequently be a disinterested satisfaction. To express this fact about sensations, Kant states that what is agreeable in sensation produces a feeling of gratification (*Vergnügen*). All sensory gratification is consequently bound up with interests.

This brings us to an important conclusion about judgments of pure beauty: the feeling of approval peculiar to them cannot rest on sensory stimuli, interests, sensory satisfaction or, what is the same thing, sensory gratification. To judge that a gratifying spoonful of sugar, or a glassful of wine, is beautiful, is to misuse the word "beautiful" within Kant's aesthetics. In view of examples of this gustatory kind, his claim about the non-sensory foundation of judgments of pure beauty is compelling.

It should be mentioned, though, that we should wonder whether it is equally mixed up to refer to a rose's delicate perfume, or a sunset's charming colors, as beautiful, since setting aside sensory gratification cancels out the relevancy of these qualities as well. Some of the paradigm cases of beautiful things – roses, lotus blossoms, sunsets, diamonds, certain birdsongs, peacocks, and the like – derive much of their beauty from sparkling colors, soft textures, and pleasing sound qualities. All such sensory qualities, however, cannot enter centrally into judgments of pure beauty on Kant's view.

Kant has now set before us the generic sphere of aesthetic judgment, along with a specific, yet fundamental, distinction between judgments of pure beauty and aesthetic judgments of sensation. Judgments of pure beauty are disinterested, whereas aesthetic judgments of sensation are combined with a gratifying interest and, strictly speaking, do not directly relate to beauty.

Varieties of Interest-grounded Judgments (II): Judgments of Goodness

[§4: "The feeling of approval in the good is bound up with interest"]
Kant has distinguished judgments of pure beauty from judgments that yield empirical knowledge of objects (i.e., cognitive judgments) and also from judgments that involve an interest in an object's existence (i.e., practical judgments). This differentiates judgments of pure beauty from judgments characteristic of science and morality. He has also distinguished judgments of pure beauty from aesthetic judgments of sensation (*Sinnenurteile*). This corresponds to his distinction between pure aesthetic judgments and empirical aesthetic judgments, and it reinforces the independence of judgments of pure beauty from the activity of accumulating bits of empirical knowledge. In §4, he now attends to distinguishing clearly between judgments of pure beauty and judgments of goodness.

Kant introduces the conception of moral goodness that he developed in previous works and states that that which is good, "by means of reason, pleases through the mere concept." In feelings of approval related to moral goodness, we thus have before us a *second* type of non-sensory satisfaction that might easily be conflated with the disinterested satisfaction associated with judgments of pure beauty. The difference is that moral goodness and the feeling of approval associated with it, is practically oriented towards the world and carries with it an interest in the existence of objects, whereas judgments of pure beauty do not. Unlike judgments of pure beauty, moral goodness is directed practically towards doing the right thing, and in this way Kant underscores, despite their affinities, how judgments of moral goodness and judgments of pure beauty, along with the respective, non-sensory feelings associated with them, are distinct.

In Kant's moral theory, the morally good is behaviorally realized by formulating a maxim of one's action – a definite rule relative to the type of situation at hand, e.g., "when under duress, I will act dishonestly to escape the problem" – and determining whether that rule can succeed in being generalized into a universal law, applicable equally to everyone. Essential in this process of generalization is knowing initially what sort of situation one is in, defining it accurately, and employing a set of specific concepts that allow one to judge the rationality of one's action. To decide whether any action is morally possible or not, one holds the action up to rational scrutiny, in other words.

In the above case, the universal generalization would fail, since it is contradictory to assert as a universal law for people's behavior, "for any person under duress, he or should act dishonestly to escape the problem." This is because the institutionalization of lying, in principle, would undermine the very meaning and possibility of lying. To express the general situation philosophically, Kant employs the categorical imperative (i.e., unconditional command), "act so that the maxim of your will could always count at the same time as a principle of universal legislation."[5] The effect is to assert that for moral purposes, one should always act from the perspective of a human being in general, in the interests of humanity, and independently of one's personal interests.

With respect to judgments of pure beauty, not only does Kant distinguish them from judgments of goodness on the ground that the former include no interests, whereas judgments of goodness carry with them an interest in realizing certain effects in the world, he also distinguishes between the two sorts of judgments in reference to the need to employ concepts that specify the sort of thing we are judging. In moral judgments, it is essential to specify what sort of situation we are in. When making a judgment of pure beauty, it makes no difference whether or not we know what sort of thing we have before us. Judgments of pure beauty do not specify the sort of thing we are judging, and this distinguishes them further from judgments of goodness.

In the following excerpt, Kant draws a short summary of his reflections up until this point, and distinguishes on the one hand, judgments of pure beauty from judgments of goodness, and on the other, judgments of pure beauty from judgments of sensory gratification. His characterization of judgments of goodness, as we shall see, is stated in reference to judging "what kind of thing the object ought to be" – a style of reflection he will later associate generally with "judgments of perfection." He writes:

> To find something good, I must always know what kind of thing the object ought to be, i.e., I must have a concept of it. To find beauty in something, I do not need that. Flowers, free delineations, lines wanderingly intertwined in each other called "foliage" – signify nothing, depend on no definite concept, and please nonetheless. The feeling of approval in the beautiful must depend upon the reflection on an object that leads to some sort of concept or other (it is undetermined which). It thereby also separates and distinguishes itself from the agreeable, which rests entirely on sensation.
>
> (§4, Ak 207 (10–11), G 93, P 49, M 46, B 41)

Assuming that we require no prior concept of an object's purpose to judge whether or not it is beautiful, a mystery in the above quotation – soon to be resolved – concerns how, in the act of making the judgment of beauty, our reflection on an object nonetheless leads to some sort of concept or another, even though it makes no difference what the particular concept happens to be. This is a puzzling view on the face of things, since we now encounter judgments that involve no specification of what the purpose of the thing we are judging happens to be, but nonetheless lead to some concept or other, even though we are not concerned with acquiring empirical knowledge of the object.

We will describe what constitutes this peculiar activity of judging in §9. For the present, we can see that judgments of pure beauty are somehow involved with conceptual activity. They are, however, clearly not concerned with the existence of objects and are not grounded in sensory pleasures. Moreover, despite their similar emphasis upon conceptual activity and despite their holding a presentation up to rational reflection as we find in judgments of moral goodness, neither do judgments of pure beauty involve knowing what sort of thing we are judging, and by implication, do not involve knowing what the object is for.

Varieties of Satisfaction: Disinterested vs. Interested

[§5: "Comparison of the three specifically different kinds of feelings of approval"] Kant began the *Critique of the Power of Judgment* with a series of considerations that would soon allow him to distinguish the sphere of pure beauty from the spheres of cognition, morality, and raw sensation. In particular, judgments of pure beauty are subjectively-grounded and disinterested whereas the latter three involve interests and are related to objective conditions in the world. Judgments of pure beauty are also contemplative and they set us at a distance from practical affairs. Kant refers further to the satisfaction in pure beauty as a *free* satisfaction, insofar as our judgment of an object's pure beauty ought *not* to be determined by practical concerns or conceptual definitions. What remains to be articulated is a positive account of our mental operations, when we judge an object's pure beauty. Kant concludes the First Moment with the following summation:

> *Taste* is the capacity to judge an object or a kind of representation through a satisfaction or dissatisfaction *devoid of all interest*. The object of such a satisfaction is called *beautiful*.
>
> (§5, Ak 211 (16), G 96, P 53, M 50, B 45)

So far, we have identified a specific way of judging objects in reference to their pure beauty, called "taste," along with a reference to the sort of feeling of approval involved in this mode of judgment, namely disinterested. We also have the consequence that although we are judging the object's presentation and reflecting upon how that presentation's design subjectively makes us *feel*, our judgment of pure beauty in its upshot leads us to assert more objectively that the presentation *itself* is beautiful.

There is here an obvious analogy to the act of attributing objectively determinate properties to an object, e.g., as when we say that an object weighs three pounds, as opposed to saying merely that the object's presentation gives me, personally, individually, and subjectively, a feeling of approval. Kant addresses this objectivistic aspect of judgments of pure beauty in the Second Moment of his exposition, to which we will now turn. He also reviews and elaborates upon these themes in §§30–40 in the context of justifying the claim to universal validity that accompanies judgments of pure beauty. We will discuss the contents of the remarks from those sections in this chapter's conclusion.

§§1–5 can now be summarized as follows: Kant begins with the claim in §1 that the judgment of taste is *aesthetic*. This means that it is based on a feeling of pleasure or satisfaction. In §2 he argues that this feeling of pleasure or satisfaction is *not* based on any interests, which implies that it is distinct from both the satisfaction in what is pleasant in sensation (§3), and the satisfaction in what is good (§4), whether good for something (the useful) or good in itself (the morally good). In §5, Kant then compares and contrasts these three different kinds of satisfaction.

THE SECOND LOGICAL MOMENT: JUDGMENTS OF PURE BEAUTY ARE GROUNDED UPON A UNIVERSAL FEELING OF APPROVAL (§§6–9)

Pure Beauty is Based on a Non-Personal, Public Feeling of Approval

[§6: "The beautiful is that which is represented, without concepts, as the object of a universal feeling of approval"] Kant maintains that the disinterestedness of judgments of pure beauty entails that the feeling of approval associated with such judgments must be independent of one's own personal conditions, desires, and interests. Since all modes of sensory gratification, along with utilitarian and moral interests, have been disconnected from judgments of pure beauty, nothing related to the specific structures of one's taste buds, eyes, ears, nose, and nerve endings in general can enter constitutively into the satisfaction that grounds such judgments. Neither will anything enter that is related to conceptual definitions and determinate rules of behavior. Kant believes that this *leaves nothing personal* upon which the satisfaction associated with judgments of beauty can be grounded, and for this reason he maintains that we can expect – or certainly can begin to expect – every person to experience this feeling identically in relation to any beautiful object, if everyone were to judge the object in an equally disinterested fashion.[6]

An important implication of the universal feeling of approval that grounds judgments of pure beauty is the quality of *objectivity* that the judgment carries along with it. To account for this, we must recall Kant's theories of space, time, and the categories of the understanding, insofar as they account for the objective validity of more specific empirical judgments, such as those whereby we ascribe mathematical, geometrical, and causal properties to physical objects. Kant maintains that everyone identically projects space, time, and *a priori* concepts such as causality, and that this shared projection defines a necessary ground for our communal awareness of objects that have publicly apprehensible properties. The public and empirically real qualities of objects arise fundamentally from how we all similarly project space, time, and the categories of the understanding upon an unknowable mind-independent reality. This projection commonly structures our human experience and lends objectivity to our empirical judgments.

The general idea is that if there is a mode of awareness that everyone necessarily and universally shares – if there is a mode of awareness that is founded in *a priori* conditions – then this mode of awareness generates a sense of publicity and objectivity, and contributes to our apprehension of being together in a shared and common world. Kant explained in the *Critique of Pure Reason* how this sense of publicity is generated by the experiential application of the determinate *a priori* forms of space, time, and the categories of the understanding, and he now brings these results into his account of the universality of judgments of pure beauty.[7]

Here, in the *Critique of the Power of Judgment*, Kant analyzes judgments of pure beauty in reference to our universally-shared mode of awareness that lends objective validity to specific judgments about the qualities of natural objects, and he extends to pure judgments of beauty, the sense of publicity and validity that he more basically associates with the former. Specifically, Kant claims that the disinterestedness of the feeling of approval associated with judgments of pure beauty embodies the very sense of publicity that stems from the *a priori* grounds through which we, for instance, ascribe mathematical and geometrical properties to objects. Indeed, as we shall see, it will be such mathematical and geometrical properties (which are formal properties related to time and space, respectively) that will in fact stimulate the beauty-related, universal feeling of approval to begin with.

The peculiarity of judgments of pure beauty, however, is that they do not entail that we specify what sort of thing we are contemplating, and indeed require that we disregard such knowledge. (The situation is similar to how, as a medical doctor, we would disregard a person's name when measuring a person's height, although we might well know who the person is.) The ascription of beauty to the object refers to the same shared cognitive structures that Kant discusses in the *Critique of Pure Reason*, except that in the case of beauty, he refers to these shared structures at a higher, generic level that is independent of giving conceptual definitions of the object's purpose. This type of validity, as I will describe later in more detail, is therefore closely akin to the validity of mathematical, geometric, and causal attributions. The difference is that in the absence of any determinate conceptual specification of the apprehended object, the sense of objectivity involved can only be generically characterized in reference to a specific feeling that is related to the optimal operation of cognitive functioning in general.

The universal validity of judgments of pure beauty does not require us to refer to the application of determinate concepts in the acquisition of empirical knowledge, but as noted, this universal validity is based nonetheless – at a higher level of abstraction – on the same *a priori* cognitive processes that make empirical judgments possible. We will see this in further detail below. Judgments of pure beauty have a universal ground, and they are, for instance, akin to mathematical, geometric, and causal judgments, but since their ground is apprehended only by means of feeling in the absence of determinate concepts, their universality will not be a logically provable matter.

What we can gain so far is a sense of the abstractness of judgments of pure beauty with respect to both the type of properties in the object they reflect upon, and the type of universality and public quality they embody and convey. No defining concepts are involved, but their ground can nonetheless be subjectively defined in reference to a universal feeling of approval. In one respect, their objectivity is akin to that of mathematical and geometric judgments insofar as the objectivity is directly related to cognitive functioning. On the other hand, the objectivity of judgments of pure beauty is subjectively and also more abstractly defined, and like moral judgments, the feeling of approval associated with them is non-sensory. Nonetheless, judgments of pure beauty involve a rationality-related judgment of an object insofar as the object is held up for scrutiny "to the entire faculty of representation" although, unlike moral judgments, the rationality involved does not involve trying to define or comprehend the object, and is of a different order.

Although Judgments of Pure Beauty are Not Provable, they Nonetheless Oblige Everyone's Agreement

[§7: "Comparison of the beautiful with the agreeable and the good through the above characteristic"] Since the disinterested nature of the satisfaction associated with judgments of pure beauty leads us to ascribe beauty to the object itself, as if it were an objective, public quality of the object, and since this disinterestedness is independent of our private conditions and interests, it makes no sense to say of something, that it is merely beautiful "for me." When we believe that we are making a judgment of pure beauty and are assuming that we are judging disinterestedly, there is the expectation that everyone else who judges disinterestedly will arrive at a very similar, if not exactly the same, conclusion, for we are not judging as private individuals, but are judging solely in light of our capacities as human beings in general.

Hence, as in the related case of moral judgments, where the universality of everyone's capacity to reason is equally assumed in making such judgments, and where there is a comparable, if not stronger, demand for agreement, Kant maintains that when we believe that we are making judgments of pure beauty, we demand (*fordern*) that others agree. To the extent that we are confident that our judgment is disinterested, the demand follows. In both moral judgments and in judgments of pure beauty, then, a sense of "ought" consequently accompanies the judgment, for in both sorts of judgment, we judge as human beings in general, rather than as private individuals with personal interests. This is the key idea that later allows Kant to make deep-rooted linkages between beauty and morality.

It is also undeniable that people often disagree in their actual judgments of pure beauty. To eliminate some of the confusion involved in such situations, Kant notes that it is helpful to keep in mind the distinction between what is beautiful as opposed to what is gratifying or agreeable in sensation. Judgments about the quality of wine, food, or attractive musical instrumentation, for instance, refer to what is agreeable and it is therefore important to append the phrase "for me," when making aesthetic judgments in reference to these items. Rule-of-thumb empirical generalizations are possible in such cases, as when cooks use salt, sugar, and pepper, or when they add lemon to a curry mixture, or a bit of cardamom to coffee, but such rules admit of exceptions.

One can "have taste" in matters of cooking, but in Kant's aesthetics this sense of gourmet taste is independent of judgments of pure beauty. Such a gourmet taste involves a different species of aesthetic judgment altogether, viz., judgments of sensory gratification that are relative to the individual who makes the judgment. In contrast, judgments of pure beauty carry with them in principle an agreement-forcing universality that admits of no exceptions. They are not sensation-based and are grounded on a disinterested feeling of approval whose exact source in our common human nature still remains to be specified.

From this discussion we can see how judgments of pure beauty stand in a theoretical space between judgments that literally and appropriately ascribe mathematical and geometric properties to objects (i.e., the objects can in fact have the properties ascribed) and judgments that ascribe objective properties to objects in only a figurative and projective way. Among the latter would be a judgment that the untasted sugar crystals in a sugar bowl are themselves "sweet."

Strictly speaking, the ascription of sweetness to untasted sugar is inappropriate, since sweetness is a property that arises only when the sugar is tasted and experienced. Moreover, to some people the sugar might taste simply sweet, whereas for others with differently-structured taste buds, the sugar might, for instance, have a bitter taste as well. The feeling associated with pure beauty compares to the pleasant taste of sugar in that it refers to the quality of someone's experience. It differs, however, in that the quality of the feeling associated with pure beauty does not vary from person to person as can the taste of sugar. Owing to the universality of the feeling of pure beauty, it makes greater sense to say that the object itself is beautiful, even though strictly speaking, this is not true.

[§8: "The universality of the feeling of approval is represented in a judgment of taste only as subjective"] Kant now summarizes the results from the preceding discussions, highlighting how the phrase "aesthetic judgment" is not synonymous with "judgments of taste" (i.e., judgments of pure beauty), and how it is a generic categorization that encompasses both judgments of sensory gratification and judgments of pure beauty:

> I can call the first the taste of the senses [*Sinnen-Geschmack*], the second the taste of reflection [*Reflexions-Geschmack*], insofar as the first makes merely private judgments, while the second makes presumably generally-valid (public) judgments, although both make aesthetic (not practical) judgments about an object, regarding merely the connection with the relation of its representation to the feeling of pleasure and displeasure.
>
> (§8, Ak 214 (22), G 99, P 57–58, M 54, B 48)

Kant is careful to emphasize that the logical form of judgment embodied by judgments of pure beauty is always the singular judgment, e.g., of the form "this rose is beautiful." All judgments of pure beauty are also first-person judgments: in every instance of a judgment of pure beauty, it is necessary to perceive the object for oneself and experience the disinterested feeling of approval involved. At the same time, the attitude one adopts is the general standpoint of a human being in general. In this respect, one sets aside personal considerations, and the judgment of beauty is made with the intention of expressing a universal voice. One states, in effect, "when considered exclusively in reference to my capacity to judge simply as a human being in general, I find this object beautiful," and aims to judge as all people would disinterestedly judge.

Despite the universal voice one adopts in judging an object's pure beauty, this universality does not involve a process of generalization to other objects of the same kind. That is, it contradicts the aesthetic nature of judgments of pure beauty to reason from premises that refer to some objects judged to be beautiful, to other objects that have not yet been experienced. One could indeed see a few examples of beautiful objects (that happen to be roses), and then judge logically that the rest of the examples in the same setting are beautiful, but this generalization would not be a judgment of pure beauty.

Given these reflections, Kant reaffirms that judgments of pure beauty are not logical judgments that involve relationships of validity between conceptual premises and conclusions, and that judgments of pure beauty do not issue from drawing logical implications or constructing proofs. Accordingly, it is impossible to persuade someone that an object is beautiful, if he or she has not somehow perceived the object in question. These considerations show how logical judgments and judgments of pure beauty are distinct, even though both involve the assertion of a universal validity.

The Key to the Critique of Taste

[§9: "Investigation of the question: whether in the judgment of pure beauty the feeling of pleasure (*Lust*) comes before the judging

of the object, or whether the judging of the object comes before the feeling of pleasure"] The unusual title of §9 asks whether in a judgment of pure beauty, the satisfaction is prior to (*vor der*) one's judging of the object, or vice-versa. Kant announces importantly that determining an answer to this question is essential for understanding the nature of such judgments. It is, as he says, the key (*Schlüssel*) to the critique of taste.

Kant's question is difficult to comprehend at first sight, since nothing that he has explained up until this point in the *Critique of the Power of Judgment* has suggested that there can be alternative sequences between "having some sort of positive feeling" and "making a judgment," with respect to whether the former could be prior to the latter or vice-versa (or perhaps, even be simultaneous). We will consider each alternative in a moment.

The situation here in §9, however, is very similar to some of the discussions in Kant's other works, the most obvious of which is his account of the universality of moral judgment in the first chapter of the *Critique of Practical Reason* (see theorems 1–3). In that discussion, Kant argues that if the empirical objects whose reality we desire are prior to (*vor der*) our moral principles, then the moral principles themselves would depend on the qualities of the given objects, and would therefore only be empirical, contingent principles, rather than universal principles. They would also thereby concern mainly our sensory gratification and individually-variable happiness and would therefore have no universal force.

Kant argues that if the foundations of morality are to be universal and necessary, then the empirical objects desired cannot be prior to the moral principles themselves. It must be the other way around: the moral principles must be prior to the empirical objects whose reality would be their consequence. This entails that the foundational moral principles need to be considered in abstraction from their empirical content, and hence for Kant, considered only with respect to their form. The result is to identify the mere form of law itself, or the basic idea of lawlike, regular, rule-bound behavior at the foundation of moral awareness.

Kant's analysis of judgments of pure beauty follows the same reasoning pattern in an effort to explain how such judgments can have a universal validity. This aligns his theory of pure beauty with his moral theory in terms of its underlying structure and it hints at an idea to be developed at the end of the Critique of Aesthetic Judgment, namely, that beauty is a symbol of morality. We will explore this symbolic relationship in Chapter 4. At present, we can consider Kant's discussion of judgments of pure beauty and explore the alternatives he outlines in the title of §9.

Suppose that one apprehends an object, feels some immediate satisfaction and then judges – somehow based on the felt quality of the satisfaction – that the object is beautiful. In this case, the judgment depends upon an immediately pleasurable feeling. Kant believes that in such a situation it would be impossible, or at least mysterious, to discern the exact nature of the approval, such as to decide whether it is disinterested or interested. Moreover, in aesthetic judgments of sense – the sort of aesthetic judgment that immediately contrasts with judgments of pure beauty – the pleasure is in fact prior to the judgment, such as when we taste food, so the above scenario aptly describes what occurs in aesthetic judgments of sense. This suggests that in relation to judgments of pure beauty, if the satisfaction is prior to the judgment, then the satisfaction related to judgments of pure beauty will be on a par with aesthetic judgments grounded on sensory pleasure. Such a result is dangerously consistent with the reduction of the pleasure in beauty to sensory gratification, even though it does not imply such a reduction.

To distinguish sensory satisfaction from the satisfaction in beauty, the theoretical results are more promising if we reverse the sequence. In this alternative, the judgment of the object must be foundational, and a feeling of satisfaction must radiate from the very act of judgment. This alternative allows for a sharp distinction between aesthetic judgments of pure beauty and aesthetic judgments of sense, based on the priority of the elements in the judging process. Here, one would initially adopt a disinterested attitude towards an object, apprehend the object through this attitude, i.e., judge it accordingly, and feel, or not feel, some consequent approval. The approval would thereby depend upon an initially disinterested attitude that one adopts along with the associated judging activity, and it would reflect and embody the disinterested attitude.

Given that Kant has already characterized judgments of pure beauty as disinterested, as being grounded upon a universally-ascribable feeling of approval, and as independent of determining what sort of thing the object that we are judging happens to be, this second option, where the judging is a precondition for the feeling of approval, is obviously the position to adopt for consistency's sake, assuming one can articulate the details. This calls for identifying a kind of judgmental activity that captures all of the characteristics that Kant has so far ascribed to judgments of pure beauty.

The Harmony of the Cognitive Faculties of Understanding and Imagination

To identify this judgmental activity, Kant begins by recalling that the satisfaction which grounds judgments of pure beauty is universal, and carries with it the same style of general validity (but of an indeterminate kind) that we encounter when we refer to the public, intersubjective, spatio-temporal qualities of things. Within his philosophy as a whole, this validity is paradigmatic of empirical knowledge insofar as our experience is conditioned by space, time, and the categories of the understanding. This is the exclusive sphere in which we can ascribe an intersubjective validity to our judgments where the knowledge involved is a determinate empirical knowledge of objects. Hence Kant asserts that "nothing . . . can be universally communicated except cognition and representation so far as it belongs to cognition." The universal feeling of approval that grounds judgments of pure beauty must therefore be directly related to cognition in *some* manner.

Cognition, which ordinarily results in the determinate empirical knowledge of an object, involves a situation where we are either given an object and subsequently apply some concept to the object, or where we start with some concept and then apply it to an object. The former are "reflecting" cognitive judgments and the latter are "determining" cognitive judgments. In the former case, we reflect upon the object's presentation and then ascertain, for example, what sort of thing it is, such as when we see some person in the distance and recognize the person as our friend John. In the latter case, we look for some object that fits a prior concept, such as when we are going to meet our friend John, and are trying to pick him out from within a crowd of people. The cognitive results are the same in both cases: an object "S" and a definite concept "P" are linked together to form a judgment of the form, "S is P."

Although this is the standard model for cognitive judgment, it cannot be the model for judgments of pure beauty. Kant has already argued that the universal feeling of approval that grounds judgments of pure beauty is independent of knowing anything about what sort of object we are judging, so this feeling must be independent of any specific cognition that yields empirical knowledge. The only way to account for the feeling in relation to cognition, then, is to refer to cognition as it can be conceived of independently of asserting of an object, determinately and with closure, that the object is of this or that type, kind, or species. This point is of the essence in Kant's theory of judgments of pure beauty.

When judging a rose's pure beauty, we need not know, and should not take into account, that the flower is called a "rose," or that it has this or that biological function. Cognition must nonetheless be involved, since the universality of the feeling of approval that grounds judgments of pure beauty is explained in reference to the universality of cognition. The situation is a peculiar one, and these considerations shed some light on Kant's remark in §4 above that the satisfaction in pure beauty involves reflecting upon an object in a way that leads to some sort of concept or other, but to no specific concept.

Kant infers that the satisfaction that grounds judgments of pure beauty can therefore only be related to "cognition in general," rather than to cognition as it operates specifically in the definite assignment of concepts to objects. This importantly shifts his analysis to a higher level of generality, for attention is now being given to the interrelationships of the faculties involved in acquiring empirical knowledge in general, as they operate in all instances of empirical knowledge, and that, despite this level of generality, carry with them a sense of public validity. His exposition is as follows:

> Now if the determining ground of the judgment regarding this univer-
> sal communicability of the representation is to be conceived of merely

subjectively, namely without a concept of the object, it can be nothing other than the state of mind that is met with in the relationships of our representational powers to each other insofar as they relate a given representation to *cognition in general* (*Erkenntniß überhaupt*).

The cognitive powers that are set into play through this represen-tation are thereby in a free play, because no determinate concept lim-its them to a particular rule of cognition. Therefore the state of mind in this representation must be that of a feeling of the free play of the powers of representation in a given representation in reference to a cognition in general.

(§9, Ak 217 (28), G 102, P 61–62, M 57–58, B 52)

Kant's strategy in explaining the nature of the universal satisfac-tion that grounds judgments of pure beauty is ingenious. Knowing that he cannot refer to specific acts of cognition and their attendant satisfactions to account for this feeling, and knowing that it must nonetheless be related to cognition to account for its universality, he resolves the difficulty by considering the conditions and pur-poses of cognition in general – or, what amounts to the same thing, to "the power of judgment in general" – and states that when judging an object's beauty, we regard the object in view of the con-ditions and purposes of cognition in general.

This is roughly analogous to looking at some object, and approving of the object in light of its capacity to lead us to appreci-ate the sheer pleasure of being able to see at all, or of hearing some sound, and approving of the sound, not as an instance of this or that type of sound, but approving of the sound in light of its capac-ity to lead us to appreciate the satisfaction in simply being able to hear, or of walking down the street, and approving of that activity, not in view of where one is going, but in light of its capacity to lead us to appreciate the satisfaction in being able to move at all. Similarly, it is analogous to approving of one's daily activities, not in view of some job that one has, but in view of their capacity to lead one to appreciate the pleasure of simply being alive. Not all objects achieve such effects to the same degree. Some epitomize the experience of sight, hearing, movement or life itself.

In each of these analogies, we attend to the specific perception insofar as it supports an experience of the general pleasure of the sense modality or living condition in abstraction from the situation's specific aims and practical details. In the analogous case of pure beauty, we apprehend an object, and do not approve of the object for the sort of knowledge it provides. Instead, we approve of its formal structure in light of its capacity to lead us to appreciate our general capacity, or power, for knowing anything at all. Beauty is linked to a general satisfaction in being cognitively active and alive, and Kant suggests this at the outset when he states in §1 that the feeling of approval in beautiful things is related to the feeling of life. This is all consistent with saying that some sorts of objects and activities more easily lead us to approve of the general conditions of life.

To identify the nature of the satisfaction that pure beauty provides, we thus need an account of how the general processes of cognition are structured in general, and how Kant believes they operate when we judge a thing's beauty. Since we are referring to a feeling of approval associated with cognition in general, no specific cognitions can play a substantial role in producing this universal feeling. So when some object is appreciated in relation to cognition in general, the cognitive powers will be stimulated and will remain active, but will remain active in a disengaged condition, free from applying concepts to the object to determine what sort of thing it is.

As noted previously in the introductory chapter above and now worth reiterating, Kant's theory of knowledge extends from the nuclear idea that in an act of knowledge, an individual is specified by some concept, as symbolized in the judgment "S is P," where S is an individual and P is some concept. In the *Critique of the Power of Judgment*, Kant takes this account for granted, along with his primary assumption that, with respect to cognition, the elementary parts of the mind correspond to the elementary parts of the judgment. He maintains accordingly that the mind has a storehouse of mental images (the imagination), and associated with this, a storehouse of concepts (the understanding). In an act of cognition, these two parts of the mind – more exactly and technically, the imagination for the composition of the manifold of intuition and understanding for the unity of the concept that unifies the representation – are brought into relationship, just as the two elementary parts of the judgment are brought into relation in a specific act of judgment.

The imagination is the storehouse of "S's" (i.e., intuitions or representations of individuals) and the understanding is the storehouse of "P's" (i.e., concepts or universals) and when the imagination and understanding are stimulated into a free play – when they are harmoniously coordinated with each other, and set for making some specific judgment – the very structure of the mind expresses the general union of intuitions and concepts. This reflects the logical structure of the "S is P" judgment and it pleasurably instantiates "cognition in general."

We can see here how Kant's psychological and epistemological theories are inspired by the basic form of logical judgment, which itself expresses his assumption that human beings are essentially rational animals. With respect to the "S is P" logical structure of the harmony of the cognitive faculties, Kant writes later in §35:

> . . . as a subjective power of judgment, taste contains a principle of subsumption, not of intuitions under concepts, but of the faculty of intuitions or presentations (i.e., of the imagination) under the faculty of concepts (i.e., the understanding), insofar as the former in its freedom is attuned with the latter in its lawfulness.
>
> (§35, Ak 287 (146), G 167, P 151, M 143, B 129)

We can thus refer to the free play of the cognitive faculties as themselves embodying at a higher, generic level, the elementary form of judgment, "S is P." One could say that the harmony of the cognitive faculties directly expresses the power of judgment in general, and that the universal feeling of approval in beauty is the pleasurable expression of the power of judgment. Since we are involved here with cognition and hence, with public, communal agreement and validity, Kant maintains that this feeling of approval that grounds judgments of pure beauty is none other than the postulation and projection of the idea of public, social, intersubjective validity in general (i.e., the feeling and the sense of a social or communal agreement are not separate). For this reason, he maintains that judgments of pure beauty carry with them the demand that other people agree.

Kant concludes the Second Moment with the statement, "beautiful is that which is universally appreciated, without a concept." In this section, however, he has done more than develop the view that judgments of pure beauty do not involve applying concepts to objects for the sake of attaining empirical knowledge. He has specified the nature of the universal satisfaction that grounds judgments of pure beauty and he has identified its source in the attunement, or harmony, of the cognitive faculties of understanding and imagination – a harmony that makes the acquisition of empirical knowledge possible to begin with. In the course of this, Kant has shown how the very harmony of these faculties reflects the general form of logical judgment, "S is P," and by implication, has revealed how we have at the basis of judgments of pure beauty, a genuine form of judgment – in this instance, a kind of meta-judgment – as opposed to an immediate sensory pleasure, as is the case in aesthetic judgments of sensation.

In the key to the critique of taste, then, the "judging of the object" is prior to the pleasure in the following sense. Let us assume that we are apprehending an object that has a purposive form (i.e., it is highly organized and systematic). To judge the object in terms of its pure beauty, we try to apprehend the object disinterestedly, and if successful, the object's purposive form will then generate a harmony of the cognitive faculties to a degree that radiates a satisfaction associated with cognition in general. This satisfaction is the activity of the harmony of the cognitive faculties which, most importantly, can be seen itself to have the form of a judgment in general ("S is P"). The experience of the harmony of the cognitive faculties is thus a mode of judgment that issues in an experience of satisfaction, owing to the mind's operating effectively as it ought to operate as a precondition for the acquisition of knowledge.

The judging of the object thus turns out to be the very experience of the harmony of the cognitive faculties, albeit instantiated to a degree of intensity (i.e., these degrees can vary) that matches the intelligible quality of the object's purposive form. All of this takes place within the context of the object being subsumed under the two faculties considered in unison, in a condition where the two faculties are in free play with respect to each other, operating as if they were themselves a "concept" under which the object is being aesthetically determined. In this particular case, though, the faculties are in a free play with respect to each other, and the quality of the object stands in relation to the faculties in a way that determines this free play to some degree of intensity.

In sum, there are two judgmental forms operating, where (1) contains (2) as a component:

(1) "P" = The imagination and understanding in unison and free
            play with respect to each other, which jointly subsume
      "S" = The object

(2) "p" = The understanding, which subsumes under it
      "s" = The imagination

This yields: (S is [s is p]), i.e., "the object is beautiful" where "beautiful" designates the meta-judgment "s is p" that represents the harmony of the cognitive faculties. The pleasure is located in (2), but only (2) as considered within the larger context of (1) where the object in (1) is responsible for the pleasure in (2).

The harmony of the faculties, or meta-judgment exemplified by that harmony – a harmony that is universally communicable, since it is the expression of "cognition in general" – is analytically prior to the pleasure that that judgment produces, since first of all, without the harmony there could be no such pleasure, and secondly, when the degree of harmony is low, there would be no noticeable pleasure, or possibly even a displeasure if the object's configuration is disorganized.[8] In the case where the intensity of the harmony is high, however, we express our feeling of the harmony of the faculties as the judgment, "the object is beautiful."

The key to Kant's key to the critique of taste, in sum, resides in noting first, how the harmony of the cognitive faculties itself embodies the form of judgment in general, "S is P," and second, how this harmony constitutes thereby a kind of meta-judgment that functions in the judging of the object where we "hold the presentation up to the entire faculty of representation" (§2). From what Kant states in other sections (see preceding note), it appears that the object resonates initially with the imagination and produces a free play within the imagination itself, and then depending upon the quality of this free play, the imagination then resonates to either a high or low degree with the understanding, thus producing a pleasure or displeasure in the free play of the two cognitive faculties to some degree.

Since the harmony of the faculties embodies the very form of judgment, the satisfaction taken in beauty – a satisfaction that radiates from the harmony of the cognitive faculties – must therefore be construed as being grounded upon the judging of the object, where this "judging" is none other than the harmony of the cognitive faculties itself. At a point where the satisfaction radiating from the harmony of the cognitive faculties reaches a certain intensity, one would be disposed to refer to the object that occasions such a harmony as "beautiful." The judging of the object would thus be theoretically prior to the feeling of satisfaction, even though judging and the satisfaction might be experientially simultaneous in every case.

The situation is comparable to how an electrical current running through a wire must be prior to, and yet nonetheless under certain conditions can be simultaneous with, any visual glow that the wire emanates. If the current is too low, there will be no glow, but when the current is sufficiently strong, the movement of the electricity and the glow of the wire can happen simultaneously, if they are indeed not one and the same, as the glow varies directly with the electricity's current. To equate the two, one could say that the glow is the manifestation of the strong current, rather than the effect of it. Analogously, one could say that the satisfaction related to pure beauty is the manifestation of the harmony of the cognitive faculties at a certain level of intensity, rather than the effect of it.

THE THIRD LOGICAL MOMENT: JUDGMENTS OF PURE BEAUTY REFLECT UPON HOW AN OBJECT'S CONFIGURATION APPEARS TO HAVE BEEN THE RESULT OF AN INTELLIGENT DESIGN (§§10–17)

Purposiveness Without Purpose

[§10: "Concerning Purposiveness in General"] We now have before us a substantial portion of Kant's account of the universal and disinterested feeling of approval that grounds judgments of pure beauty. What immediately stands ahead is an account of an object's features that occasion the universal feeling that radiates from the harmony of the cognitive faculties. Even if every comprehensible object has a small measure of beauty, objects are beautiful to different degrees. The harmony of the cognitive faculties can consequently occur with different intensities, and an account of these differences is necessary to complete the core account of judgments of pure beauty. Central to this is Kant's discussion of purposiveness within the context of beauty, and the Third Moment attends to this concept's role. Since the harmony of the cognitive faculties is a logically-structured harmony, and since the purpose of cognition is the acquisition of knowledge, we will be attending to features of objects that are directly resonant with these conditions and purposes.

The terms "purpose" (*Zweck*) and "purposiveness" (*Zweckmäßigkeit*) are closely associated in Kant's account and he begins §10 with some definitions. He defines a "purpose" as the object of a concept whose meaning suggests a plan or intention. For example, the purpose of the concept "tonight's dinner" would be the actual dinner on the table later in the evening. Within this situation where a prior concept is given, the "purposiveness" of a concept is correspondingly "the causality of a concept with regard to its object," and in the above example, it would be the inner tendency of the concept to refer to its end or purpose and indeed even stand as a causal power of a teleological sort that produces the end, as when a cook has it in mind and is guided by the idea of "tonight's dinner," to make the dinner for tonight.

Having drawn this distinction between "purpose" and "purposiveness," Kant adds a further proviso and rigid constraint upon the concept of purpose. He maintains that we refer to an object itself as a purpose (although we would say ordinarily that the object "has" a purpose) only when the object can be thought of in no other reasonable way than as the result of some plan or concept. Nothing can count as a purpose, if it can be easily considered to have come about by accident or by merely mechanical, natural means. To speak of purposes involves postulating with no other reasonable recourse, an intelligence and intentional activity, or teleological causality, as the source of the object that is referred to as a purpose. This happens, for example, when we look at a large building and are compelled to think of the architects, engineers, and construction workers who made the building. No one can imagine how a building could materialize by sheer accident from natural causes alone, as flowers and plants materialize. Even if the building's presence were regarded as a miracle, the miracle would postulate God's intelligent activity as the divine cause of the building.

With respect to comprehending the origins of some object, it might appear to be too strong a requirement to postulate intelligence and rational activity with no other reasonable recourse, if we conceive of the object as a purpose or end, and indeed it is a strong requirement. But Kant is explicit in this regard:

> Thus where not merely the cognition of an object but the object itself (the form or existence of the object) as an effect is thought of as possible only through [*nur als durch*] a concept of the object, there one thinks of a purpose.
>
> (§35, Ak 287 (146), G 167, P 151, M 143, B 129)

In effect, if we call some object a purpose, it is tantamount to saying that if we did not postulate some intelligence as the teleological cause of the object, the object's presence would be absurd. Given such a strong relationship between a plan (i.e., a concept) and its realization (i.e., an object), the concept of purposiveness enters into the situation by referring to the causal relationship between a plan and its realization. It refers to the directedness of a concept towards some specific end and expresses the presence of a planning intelligence that specifies how things will happen.

Within this context, Kant introduces the adjective "purposive" (*zweckmäßig*) to refer, not to concepts that have a purposiveness or causal power, but to objects, states of mind, and actions, i.e., the sorts of things that could count as purposes. This introduces a subtle distinction between objects that are regarded as purposes and objects that are regarded as purposive.

The distinction is as follows: when we regard an object as a purpose, the object is regarded as possible only through the existence of some prior plan or concept; when we regard an object as purposive, we admit the possibility that the object might have come about by accident, but add that the object nonetheless compels us to consider it as having been brought about by a concept. In the case of referring to an object as a purpose, we face an absurdity in supposing that object could have happened by accident; in the case of referring to an object as purposive, we can appreciate in the abstract how the object might have arisen by accident, but trying to imagine how this accident might have actually come about leads to the postulation of unlikely and virtually absurd scenarios. The two conceptions are quite close. Kant writes:

> An object or state of mind or even an action is called purposive – even if its possibility does not necessarily presuppose the representation of a purpose – merely because its possibility for us can only be explained and conceived insofar as we assume as its ground a causality according to purposes, i.e., a will that has arranged them so in accordance with the representation of a certain rule.
>
> (§10, Ak 220 (33), G 105, P 65, M 61–62, B 55)

According to these definitions, to say that an object is purposive is not to say that it looks like it might have been designed and that it is easy to conceive of it as having arisen by accident, as we might say of a large rock formation that happens to look like a face, or of the sound of a strong wind blowing through an old cabin that resembles a howling voice. To the contrary, to refer to an object as purposive is to assert that our ordinary common sense does not allow us to think otherwise. We are compelled to ascribe an underlying intelligent cause to the object, as would be the case if we were to observe a set of seashells on the beach in an arrangement that spelled out the words, "we are seashells." Although the arrangement could have happened by accident and it remains conceivable to us that the seashells assumed that form through the accidental movements of the surf, such a hypothesis seems absurd, and it remains virtually impossible to dismiss the thought that some intelligence intentionally arranged them that way.

To refer to something as purposive is to assume that the ascription of a background intelligence is compelling, psychologically unavoidable, and impossible to remove from consideration. The word "designedness" partially captures the meaning of the term "purposive," but "designedness" must be understood in the strong sense of there being the undeniable suggestion of design. As we will see in the last chapter on teleological judgment, Kant believes that living organisms are purposive in this strong sense, owing to the mysterious nature of life.

In attributions of purposiveness, despite the compulsion to project an intelligence as the teleological cause of an object concerned, the logical possibility of there having been no intelligent design allows one to speak of a purposiveness without an actual purpose. This describes the seashell situation above, where we admit that the arrangement might have arisen by accident, but where we cannot reasonably conceive of it as having so arisen. The residual uncertainty, though, allows for a detachment of purposiveness from purposes, and this yields a use of the term "purposiveness" that is detached from any given concept, which refers merely to the strong appearance of a purpose, as opposed to implying that an object is actually an end or purpose. In this sense, "purposiveness" would refer more abstractly to general notion of a directedness between a plan and an object, independently of any given plan or concept.

This general notion of purposiveness in abstraction from the definite activity of any given concept can itself take two forms. The first is where we have an object, are compelled to ascribe a definite purpose to it, but remain unsure whether the object was in fact designed for that particular purpose. This fits the seashell example above. The second is where we have an object, cannot resist the thought that it has some purpose or other, but either cannot or do not ascribe any particular purpose to it. This fits the case of beauty. The first case is a purposiveness without purpose that depends upon, or adheres to, a projected concept of a purpose; the second case is a purposiveness without purpose that is free of such projections.

In the larger view, Kant's terminology of "purpose," "purposive," and "purposiveness" is dually-intended to help organize his aesthetic theory, and to provide a philosophical reference to natural items whose internal design is so amazing and intellectually impressive – Kant is writing in pre-Darwinian times, so he is thinking of the designs of living things as instances – that we cannot but suppose that they are the products of a superhuman intelligence. We will later consider this issue in more detail, but it is worth mentioning at present that between the lines of Kant's theory of beauty are reflections on the teleological argument for God's existence (i.e., the argument from design). As we will see in the Critique of Teleological Judgment (§§61–91), natural beauty and living organisms will become indicators, but not altogether determinate and conclusive ones, of God's existence. When we consider Kant's theory of the sublime, we will also notice the presence of the two other traditional arguments for God's existence, namely, the ontological and cosmological arguments that underscore the Critique's broader, divinity-related themes.

Kant maintains that judgments of pure beauty are grounded on the apprehension of the appearance of purposes – they are grounded upon the apprehension of an object's purposiveness – rather than upon the apprehension of actual purposes or ends. This is partially because judgments of pure beauty do not involve knowing what the purpose of the thing judged happens to be. Moreover, since judgments of pure beauty are not based on sensory gratification, only the object's spatio-temporal design – at least on the face of things – can be relevant to the apprehension of an object's purposiveness, and relevant to stimulating the harmony of the cognitive faculties. This helps to reveal what sort of purposiveness in the object we need to consider in making judgments about the object's pure beauty.

Unlike what John Locke called ideas of secondary qualities such as the taste of wine or colors, which Kant considers to be mere sensations, only ideas of primary qualities (i.e., spatio-temporal forms) belong to the objective, scientific determinations of the object. They are the only ones that yield empirical knowledge of the object, insofar as it is a public object (see Critique of Pure Reason, A28–29 / B44). Given the judgment of pure beauty's necessary relationship to cognition in general and to the universal validity of cognition, the restriction to spatio-temporal configurations follows straightforwardly.

This primary attention to spatio-temporal form seems to be Kant's standard view. In §14, for instance, he uses words such as "Form," in contrast to color (which suggests that the meaning of

"*Form*" here is "shape"), "*Gestalt*" (which can also mean "shape"),"*Zeichnung*" (i.e., drawing; delineation; configuration), "*Komposition*," and "*Abriß*" (i.e., outline or sketch).

It is nonetheless possible to expand the scope of the term "form" to include formal interrelationships between meanings, inter-relationships between colors (as in the case of simultaneous contrast of complementary colors) or between tastes (as in the case of relationships between sweet, bitter, etc., in culinary art), compositional considerations, and the like. This yields a broader type of aesthetic formalism that coheres more easily with other sections of Kant's text, such as his §49 account of aesthetic ideas within the context of art. As we shall see below, aesthetic ideas attend mainly to semantic configurations, rather than spatio-temporal configurations.

The Purposiveness of an Object's Form

There are a number of ways that an object could compellingly suggest that it was produced according to a design, i.e., how it could exhibit a purposiveness without purpose, and some of these ways do not concern its form, design or configuration, but rather the material of which it is composed (e.g., plastic). To isolate those aspects of the object's purposiveness that are relevant to the object's pure beauty, Kant consequently refers to the apprehension in an object of a species of purposiveness without purpose. This is, namely, a purposiveness without purpose concerning only the object's form. Our reflection upon an object's purposive form independently of the object's sense-gratification qualities and conceptual determinations, in effect, is what he believes occasions the harmony of the cognitive faculties and generates a universal feeling of approval in reference to the object's pure beauty, if the purposive form is significantly impressive.

[§11: "**The pure judgment of beauty has for its ground, nothing but an object's form of purposiveness (or mode of representing it)**"] When we reflect upon an object for the purpose of judging its pure beauty, we consider only its form, and consider this form only in relation to whether it compels us to ascribe an intelligent cause to that form. This is to reflect upon the purposiveness of the object's form, or its "purposiveness of form." In the title of §11 above, Kant introduces a different notion which he calls an object's "form of purposiveness." This expression simply reiterates the claim that when we reflect upon an object with respect to its beauty, we ascribe a purposiveness without purpose to the object.[9]

Kant refers synonymously to purposiveness without purpose as the "form of purposiveness," because he coordinates the content of purposiveness with those situations where the perceived purposiveness is not merely apparent, but actual, such that an actual purpose is linked with the perceived purposiveness. He states that every purpose, whether it is subjective or objective, involves an interest and a concept, and since judgments of pure beauty are disinterested and not based on conceptual determinations, the purposiveness involved in such judgments is a purposiveness considered in abstraction from its purposes or content, and hence is only the "form" of purposiveness.

Given these reflections on the concept of purposiveness without purpose (i.e., the form of purposiveness) and the instantiation of the form of purposiveness in the more specific purposiveness of an object's form, Kant augments his account of the feeling of approval that grounds judgments of pure beauty and states generally that the purposiveness without purpose in a representation through which an object is given, constitutes (or more precisely, occasions) the feeling of approval that we judge to be universally communicable, and hence is the determining ground of the judgment of pure beauty.

Implicit here is the assumed requirement that the sort of purposiveness without purpose under consideration can only be the purposiveness of the object's form, for as noted above, Kant believes that we paradigmatically reflect specifically upon to the object's spatio-temporal form in our judgment of pure beauty. This is because on the face of things, the spatio-temporal forms and their link to cognition in general establish the reason why we require others to agree with our judgments of pure beauty. To make full sense of Kant's claim that the disinterested feeling of approval that grounds judgments of pure beauty stems from the apprehension of an object's purposiveness without purpose (i.e., the form of purposiveness), it is important to underscore that the form of purposive-ness is instantiated exclusively in the object's purposiveness of form. That is, it is instantiated in the intelligence-indicating quality of the object's configuration, either narrowly or broadly construed.

These reflections coordinate the harmony of the cognitive facul-ties with the purposiveness of the object's form, and indicate that when we disinterestedly contemplate an object aesthetically, the intelligibility of the object's form resonates with our cognitive fac-ulties and generates a feeling of approval – a feeling that is inde-pendent of sensory gratification and which concerns merely the quality of the object's configuration. Owing to its effort to account for the universality that we ascribe to judgments of pure beauty, Kant's theory of beauty becomes unquestionably formalistic.

The Purposiveness of the Harmony of the Cognitive Faculties

[§12: "The judgment of pure beauty rests on *a priori* grounds"]
§12 is a conceptually dense and important section where Kant adds detail to his position that judgments of pure beauty rest on structures of cognition that are knowable *a priori*. He draws an analogy to the feeling of pure rational respect that arises in moral judgment to illuminate the nature of the disinterested feeling of approval related to beauty. This is an association we have already noted above in §9 concerning the key to the critique of taste. To recall, in the case of moral judgments, a non-empirical, rationally-grounded teleological cause determines us to act morally, and Kant claims that there is a feeling of approval in the very condition of being rationally-determined. It is a feeling of self-approval related to acting with respect towards who we essentially are as rational beings.

Kant introduces his account of moral satisfaction to put aside a potential problem that he sees implicit in his account of beauty. With respect to moral satisfaction, he notes that this feeling does not issue from the rational determination of the will as a side-effect or independent consequence, but is identical to the very experience of being rationally-determined. This construal avoids the problems inherent in saying that the rational determination of the will causes a satisfaction – an account that would introduce the need to explain the relationship between the two, which itself could turn out to be tenuous.

Kant claims that in the case of judgments of pure beauty, the structure of the situation is the same: the feeling of approval that grounds judgments of pure beauty emerges as a manifestation of the activity of the harmony of the cognitive faculties, and is not a detachable side-effect of the cognitively harmonious activity. With this reasoning, Kant more easily circumscribes the satisfaction that grounds judgments of pure beauty within the bounds of the *a priori* structures of cognition and accordingly maintains that judgments of pure beauty rest exclusively on *a priori* grounds.

In light of this explanation, Kant characterizes the harmony of the cognitive faculties in more exact terms, stating that when the cognitive faculties are in harmony, they are geared towards producing of knowledge natural objects. In the satisfaction related to pure beauty, the cognitive faculties are not, however, directed towards attaining any specific knowledge. There is instead an inter-relationship between them that is the power of judgment itself as it stands in a disengaged and abstracted form. By definition, the cognitive faculties are directed towards the goal of attaining empirical knowledge – this is their purpose or end – but in their disengagement from specific application, the purpose or end is suspended.

Given this characterization of the harmony of the cognitive faculties, the concept of purposiveness enters once again. This time, however, it is used in reference to the harmony of the cognitive faculties themselves, which can now be seen to embody a purposiveness without purpose, or form of purposiveness, of their own. The harmony of the cognitive faculties is purposive with respect to attaining knowledge of natural objects, but since these faculties remain in a free play, they remain at the level of cognition in general, and hence at a disengaged level where the purpose of the harmony of the faculties is not being realized. There nonetheless remains a feeling of approval in the experience of the very power of judgment, considered generally, and this is identical to the satisfaction in pure beauty. It is comparable to the feeling of approval in flexing, limbering, and loosening up one's muscles before lifting a heavy weight. In the case of beauty, the satisfaction amounts to a feeling of self-approval related to one's cognitive power – a cognitive power that all humans share.

To say that the purpose of the harmony of the faculties is not realized, however, is not to suggest negatively that in the experience of pure beauty there is any failure involved in their operation. We would not say, for instance, that a person fails to lift a weight when the person is busy limbering up his or her muscles and enjoying the feeling of physical power. Nor would we say that a car fails to move when the driver is only revving up the engine and appreciating the car's power. Nor would we say that since a car is meant for driving that the car's idling should be understood as some mode of the car's failure to drive. The case is the same for positively appreciating the power of judgment in general.

This leads us to distinguish between several senses of the term "purposiveness" that arise within Kant's discussions. First, there is the generic distinction between purposiveness with purpose (i.e., purposiveness with content) and purposiveness without purpose (i.e., the form of purposiveness, or purposiveness without, or in abstraction from, content). Second, there are three specific applications of the phrase, "purposiveness without purpose." The first of these does not depend upon a concept and refers objectively to the presentation of an object. This is the object considered with respect to its internal configuration and the configuration's associated purposiveness of form, relative to the systematic quality of that configuration, such that we cannot but postulate an intelligence as the object's cause. This fits the objective aspect of the experience of a thing's beauty.

The second application of "purposiveness without purpose" depends upon a concept of an actual purpose. It refers subjectively to the quality of the harmony of the cognitive faculties that is stimulated by the apprehension of an object's purposiveness of form. With respect to this quality of this harmony, this would be a purposiveness dependent upon a purpose in that we can specify what the harmony's purpose happens to be (viz., to serve as a precondition for empirical knowledge), and a purposiveness without purpose in that the harmony of the cognitive faculties remains in free play, indeterminate and suspended from the realization of their purpose. This fits the subjective aspect of the experience of a thing's beauty.

The third application of "purposiveness without purpose" depends upon a concept of a projected purpose. It refers to how a beautiful object can be said to be purposive in the sense that it seems (for whatever reason) to have been designed for the express purpose of stimulating the harmony of the cognitive faculties. This would be a purposiveness dependent upon a projected purpose in that we can specify what the object's aesthetic purpose appears to be (viz., to stimulate the harmony), and a purposiveness without purpose in that we cannot be certain that the beautiful object was indeed designed, let alone designed for us in particular.

Central to Kant's account of judgments of pure beauty, then, is a coordination between an object's perceived purposiveness without purpose with respect to its configuration (viz., its designedness) and the harmony of the cognitive faculties' purposiveness without purpose that the apprehension of that object occasions (viz., the positive feeling of the power of judgment in relation to cognition in general). The first is an object-related form of purposiveness and the second is a subject-related form of purposiveness. Both are coordinated in the experience of pure beauty via the third form of purposiveness mentioned above. We will see this same sort of coordination between subjective and objective aspects of the experience of pure beauty arising in the "deduction" or legitimation of judgments of pure beauty, when Kant explains how their universal validity has an objective basis.

Such distinctions are important to draw, because the formal structure of the beautiful object is not identical to the corresponding formal structure of the mind, and because neither of these is identical to the relationship that brings them together, even though all three are described with the phrase "purposiveness without purpose." Kant claims that the harmony of the cognitive faculties radiates the universal feeling of approval that grounds judgments of pure beauty, but this harmony and feeling of approval cannot be equated with anything in the object itself, which remains as it is, whether or not we attend to it disinterestedly and bring it into an aesthetic relationship with us.

Finally, to reiterate, it is important to distinguish an object's purposiveness without purpose (the form of purposiveness) from the object's purposive form, which is what we attend to specifically in the object when we judge its beauty. As noted, the two are not the same, since in general it is possible to discern an object's purposiveness without purpose in a way that involves qualities over and above the object's configurational qualities (i.e., as when we recognize an object's material as being non-natural, but as being of a substance we cannot easily classify). More important for Kant's systematic exposition, though, is the distinction between the objective and subjective sorts of purposiveness without purpose, as related respectively either to the object's configuration, or to the structure of the harmony of the cognitive faculties.

Judgments of Pure Beauty are Independent of Emotions and Sensory Charms

[§13: "The judgment of pure beauty is independent of charm and emotion"; §14: "Elucidation through examples"] Some might count it to be a significant point against Kant's theory of beauty that some ordinarily-recognized, paradigm cases of beautiful things conflict with his foundational claim that judgments of pure beauty are disinterested. As we have seen, sensory gratification, along with any considerations that carry an interest with them, cannot be included among the defining qualities of pure beauty. Kant maintains accordingly that sensory charms (e.g., a sunset's bright orange, or a rose's sweet perfume and soft texture) cannot enter constitutively into judgments of pure beauty. When they do, they render the judgment of beauty impure and in the worst cases, "barbaric" (*barbarisch*) or vulgar. Kant reiterates that only the object's purposiveness of form (i.e., its configurational qualities insofar as these compellingly suggest an intelligent designer) constitute the relevant properties of the object that can enter into a judgment of beauty and that render the judgment pure.

Kant is aware that the elimination of sensory charms could stimulate objections to his theory, and he carefully explains why sensory charms need to be set aside. The main reason is that they undermine the judgment of pure beauty's universality, and the universality of the judgment of pure beauty, in Kant's view, is of the judgment's very essence. He does admit, though, that although an object's delineation, drawing, shape or abstract configuration is paramount, the awareness of that configuration can be highlighted through the use of pleasing colors. In every case, though, such charms must remain in the service of illuminating the configuration and must be set aside when making a judgment of the object's pure beauty.

If it turns out that shapes are inseparable from colors in actual perceptual experience, then in actual circumstances, the optimal beauty-related awareness would be one where the presence of colors in the perception of shapes always helps to highlight the perception of shapes. This is analogous to saying that if rationality is inseparable from feelings in actual human experience, then in actual circumstances, the optimal moral awareness would be one where the presence of feelings in the activity of rationality always helps to highlight the rational awareness of duty. In both optimizations, colors and feelings would have an instrumental value with respect to focussing and supporting our attention upon the non-sensory dimensions of beauty and goodness.

Kant does add, parenthetically, that colors can be beautiful in themselves in relation to their "form," even though colors are merely charming for the most part and vary in their agreeableness from person to person. He has in mind the respective purity (e.g., pure blue, pure red, etc.) that colors can display. His inspiration is due to Leonhard Euler's (1707–83) wave theory of color, which characterized colors as vibrations upon analogy to sounds. Since all pure colors are identical with respect to their purity *per se*, however, Kant's admission of beauty in reference to color is fairly limited.

With respect to emotional factors involved in making judgments of pure beauty, Kant is quickly and perhaps disappointingly dismissive, stating that all emotions are related to gratification or agreeableness, and that emotion therefore has essentially nothing to do with pure beauty. In §14, he observes that the experience of the sublime is based on emotion, and that this indicates the need for an entirely different explanation for the sublime, in contrast with pure beauty. Unlike some authors (e.g., Arthur Schopenhauer) who interpret sublimity as an attenuated form of beauty, Kant keeps them distinct with respect to the particular mental faculties and qualities of experience that are involved in each, although he regards judgments of pure beauty and judgments of pure sublimity as species of pure (i.e., universalistic) aesthetic judgment. We will address Kant's theory of the sublime in the next chapter.

Despite the brevity of Kant's treatment of emotional factors in judgments of pure beauty, his position has a long and weighty history in its recall of Plato's classical characterization of art (as *mimēsis*) in Book X of the *Republic*. Plato did not leave much room for a positive assessment of art in general, since he associated artistic creation with sense-perception and emotion – and rejected it on account of this very association – but he shares with Kant a negative valuation of these qualities. In a Platonic spirit, by focussing upon the geometrical, linear features of objects and in reference to judgments of pure beauty, Kant aims to raise our attention to dimensions of objects that are independent of sensory charm and emotion.

Judgments of Pure Beauty are Independent of the Concept of Perfection

[**§15: "The judgment of pure beauty is completely independent of the concept of perfection"**] Returning to the format of the first several sections of the *Critique of the Power of Judgment*, Kant continues with his efforts to distinguish judgments of pure beauty from other sorts of judgments with which they might be easily confused. Until now, he has made much of the disinterestedness of judgments of pure beauty, using the quality of disinterestedness to distinguish judgments of pure beauty from judgments of sensory gratification (which he also refers to as "empirical aesthetic judgments," "aesthetic judgments of sense," and "material aesthetic judgments"). In this section, Kant once again turns in the opposite direction and develops the distinction between judgments of pure beauty – which are not grounded on any definite concepts – and judgments of perfection, which always have a concept of the object's ideal condition in view.

Kant spends some extra time refuting the classical position that judgments of pure beauty involve a judgment of an object's perfection. This intuitively-attractive position states that a thing is more beautiful, the closer it measures up to its ideal type or condition. He explores this view in §§16–17, but as a prelude, his argument here in §15 is brief: he simply reiterates his main position that the universal feeling of approval that grounds of judgments of pure beauty requires that the judgments depend on no specific concepts, and hence, cannot depend on conceptions of ideal types, whether they are *a priori* or empirically derived.

Adherent Beauty (I): The Amalgamation of Pure Beauty and Perfection

[§16: "The judgment of beauty is not pure, through which an object is declared to be beautiful under the condition of a determinate concept"] Kant nonetheless appreciates the intuitive appeal of the view that beauty involves apprehending the degree of perfection that an individual instantiates. We speak easily of "beautifying" a person's face in traditional portraiture, and refer self-evidently to a "beautiful specimen" when an animal exhibits an appealing, crisp, textbook-like presentation. In such cases, beauty is conceived of as being directly related to the degree to which an individual measures up to its ideal condition, often in the context of realizing its natural purpose. The same conception of beauty-as-perfection operates within an artistic context when an artist sculpts the form of a human body in proportions more perfect than appear in any particular human. With little hesitation, we refer to such forms as representing beautiful human bodies.

Kant goes a long way towards incorporating the beauty-as-perfection view into his own theory, and he begins §16 with an accommodating claim. Contrary to what one might expect in parallel to his negative attitude towards the role of sensory gratification in judgments of pure beauty, Kant does not assert that perfection is irrelevant to judgments of pure beauty and let the matter rest. Instead, he defines "two kinds" of beauty. The first is the type of pure beauty familiar from Kant's exposition so far, which his theory has been circumscribing in some detail. The second is a type of beauty that is not pure and that adheres to the presence of concepts.

The former, Kant calls "free" or "pure" beauty – *freie Schönheit* (*pulchritudo vaga*) – and the latter he calls "adherent" or "dependent" beauty – *abhängige Schönheit* (*pulchritudo adhaerens*). Kant refers to adherent beauty as a different type of beauty, but the structure of his theory suggests that it is more accurately understood as the hybrid result of affixing pure beauty to a purpose-related (i.e., conceptual) component to which the pure beauty adheres, structurally comparable to what we encounter when such beauty is mixed with sensory charm.

Kant refers to free beauty as *pulchritudo vaga*, and the Latin word "*vaga*" (from "*vagus*") has the sense of "wandering," "roaming," "diffuse," "strolling about," "unfixed," "unsettled," and "aimless." The term "aimless" is perhaps the most revealing, since it directly suggests the absence of a determinate purpose. This fits nicely with Kant's examples in §4 (viz., flowers, free delineations, lines wanderingly intertwined in each other called "foliage"). The words "doodles" and "doodling" used in reference to aimlessly drawn lines, also capture this idea to some extent. Rendering "free beauty" as "doodling beauty" would be linguistically unattractive, but it does capture much of the sense of "*vaga*."

On the other hand, Kant's account of adherent beauty aims to do justice to the view that beauty involves the idealization and the perfection of individuals, while preserving his account of pure beauty as the baseline account. He writes:

> There are two kinds of beauty: free beauty (*pulchritudo vaga*) or merely dependent beauty (*pulchritudo adhaerens*). The first presupposes no concept of what the object ought to be; the second presupposes such a concept and the perfection of the object in accordance with it. The free kinds are called (self-subsisting) beauties of this or that thing; the other, as dependent upon a concept (conditioned beauty) is attached to objects that stand under the concept of a particular purpose.
>
> (§16, Ak 229 (48), G 114, P 76, M 72, B 65)

Kant explains this distinction by noting how certain objects invite judgments of free beauty, whereas others invite judgments of adherent beauty. Flowers, some birds, some sea creatures, wandering spiral figures, and abstract wallpaper designs all invite judgments of pure beauty, since their respective purposes are either not obvious or not immediately pressing. In contrast, people, horses (given their social function during Kant's time), along with buildings such as churches, palaces, arsenals, and greenhouses, all strongly manifest their purposes and accordingly invite judgments of adherent beauty.

A motivation behind the distinction between free and adherent beauty stems from the form-content distinction considered in conjunction with Kant's conception of purposiveness. In the latter, the intelligibility of an object's form compels us to postulate an intelligence responsible for the form, although we admit that the object might have arisen by accident. Similarly, certain objects in their subject matter or content, for one reason or another, cannot be easily conceived of as not having a certain purpose.

Just as there are cases where an object's purposive *form* compels us to suspect that there is a purpose underlying the object (in which case we can reflect upon the object's pure beauty by considering the form alone, without specifying the object's purpose), there are cases where an object's *content* compels us to ascribe a purpose to the object. In such cases, if we were to attempt to judge the object's pure beauty, we would find ourselves constrained by the simultaneous acknowledgement that the object cannot easily be regarded as not having a specific purpose, once it is recognized what sort of object it is. In the case of human beings, for instance, it is almost impossible to see people as being mere objects, so in such cases, judgments of adherent beauty are practically unavoidable. With respect to people, judgments of pure beauty verge on being immoral, for such judgments must ignore, rather than respect, the humanity in people.

In reference to human beings, then, Kant consequently subordinates pure beauty to adherent beauty, claiming that it is morally inappropriate to treat the human body as the subject of free beauty, as when one decorates it with visually-attractive, spiralling tattoos that obscure the perception of facial expressions and the human purpose in general.[10] Appropriate to the human being is thus a concept of beauty which adheres to the human being's moral purpose.

Given the centrality of morality within Kant's philosophy as a whole, it can only be an interpretive error to dismiss adherent beauty as an insignificant type of beauty, notwithstanding some of the phrasing Kant uses to characterize this type of beauty that suggests that it is not free and not pure. As we continue to explore Kant's theory, it will become evident that his aesthetics initially focusses on pure beauty in an effort to establish the universal validity of judgments of taste, slowly gravitates towards distinguishing adherent beauty in a positive way, owing to its capacity to respect moral obligations, and ends up symbolically aligning every form of beauty with morality.

Since Kant extensively characterizes pure beauty, it nonetheless remains odd that he refers to two different kinds of beauty, as opposed to acknowledging simply the one pure kind he has labored to characterize. One reason we would not expect Kant to introduce a separate type of beauty is in connection with his argument that judgments of perfection spoil the purity of judgments of (free) beauty, just as do judgments of sensory gratification, as when pure beauty is mixed with charm. When analyzing judgments of sensory gratification, Kant did not introduce yet another kind of beauty – although this could indeed be called unrefined, tasteless, or vulgar beauty – that matches our ordinary claims that the bright colors of sunsets render them beautiful, or that the delicate pastel color and sweet perfume of a rose constitute part of the rose's beauty. So we can ask why he now identifies two sorts of beauty in his exposition.

Kant states that, strictly speaking, perfection does not gain by beauty, nor does beauty gain by perfection; they are independent considerations. This provides another motivation to maintain that there is only one essential sort of beauty – pure beauty – and that pure beauty can be rendered impure by being amalgamated with either sensory or conceptual components. His decision not to use such phrasing indicates that it is not as easy to dismiss the theory of beauty-as-perfection as is the theory of beauty-as-sense-gratification, and that the former theory carries more weight than the relatively implausible position that a well-cooked meal or a cold drink of water on a hot day could be reasonably or tastefully described as "beautiful," although some people do speak this way.

To clarify the theoretical situation when conceptual components are introduced into judgments of pure beauty, we can identify three factors operating in the distinction between free and adherent beauty. The first is a disinterested satisfaction in a judgment of pure beauty that is not grounded upon a concept of what the object being judged ought to be. The second is a satisfaction in a judgment of perfection that arises upon perceiving that an object measures up to what it ought to be.

These two sorts of satisfaction are of different kinds, and they correspond to the two main types of judgment that constitute the respective themes of the two parts of the *Critique of the Power of Judgment*, namely judgments of pure beauty and teleological judgments. Broadly speaking, the former involves a purposiveness without purpose; the latter involves a purposiveness with purpose. The former involves the form of purposiveness; the latter involves the content of purposiveness. In the case of the human being, moreover, the content of purposiveness – morality – is universal and unconditional, and matches the universality and necessity of judgments of pure beauty. This allows for a compatibility between pure beauty and perfection that is not possible in the mixture of pure beauty with sensory gratification.

The third factor is how to understand the amalgamation of the above two sorts of satisfaction in a judgment of adherent beauty. There are two main options for understanding how this beauty is constituted:

(1) We could recognize the presence of two sorts of satisfaction within their own respective spheres, recognize that the object's purpose needs to inform our consideration of the object's beauty, but disregard any satisfaction arising from the apprehension of the object's perfection. The resulting judgment of beauty would be a judgment of adherent beauty in that we would restrict our attention to reflecting only upon those purposive forms in the object that do not contradict the object's purpose. For instance, we would disregard the graffiti on a church's door when judging the architectural beauty of the church *per se*, and we would also disregard any satisfaction in appreciating how well the purpose of a church was fulfilled in

the design. The church's purpose would be taken into account, but only to narrow down the sorts of purposive forms that can legitimately enter into the disinterested judgment of the church's purposive configuration, considered nonetheless as an abstract form.

(2) We could recognize the presence of two sorts of satisfaction within their own respective spheres, and combine the satisfaction in the object's perfection with the more limited disinterested satisfaction in the object's beauty described above in (1). This yields a situation where the satisfaction in an object's perfection is combined with the disinterested satisfaction arrived at through a contemplation of a subset of object's purposive forms – regarded simply as abstract designs – that do not contradict the object's purpose.

Kant's exposition is clear about two points: (a) the object's purpose, if recognized as a positive constituent of the judgment, restricts the sorts of purposive forms that are appropriate to contemplate aesthetically, and (b) judgments of adherent beauty damage the purity of judgments of beauty, just as the combination of sense-gratification damages the purity of judgments of beauty. Kant makes the latter comparison in the fourth paragraph of §16.

Option (1) preserves the purity of the judgment of beauty – it does not allow any admixture of alien types of satisfaction to enter into the judgment, and one would still be disinterestedly contemplating only the object's purposive form. The difference is that we would not be disinterestedly reflecting on all of the object's purposive forms, but only upon the subset of them that is consistent with the object's purpose. This restriction does not render the judgment of beauty impure in the sense that factors other than disinterested contemplation would be involved.

Option (1) therefore does not preserve any systematic parallel with how judgments of sensory gratification would analogously render a judgment of beauty impure. Speaking generally, impurity in judgments of beauty arises – if we follow the example of the introduction of sensory charm – because alternative modes of satisfaction mix into the content of the judgment itself and blend with the satisfaction that is unique to pure beauty. If we interpret the impurity of judgments of adherent beauty in this latter way, then the amalgamation of the satisfaction in the object's perfection with the satisfaction in pure beauty will need to be part of the judgment of adherent beauty.

Of the two options, (2) is consequently the more plausible alternative to explain how judgments of adherent beauty are both impure and adherent. They adhere to a concept with respect to both their form and content: the object's purpose restricts the set of purposive forms that one can legitimately contemplate disinterestedly, and the satisfaction in the object's perfection introduces an additional pleasurable (or displeasurable) content to the judgment, thus grounding it upon two different sorts of satisfaction. If the notion of impurity is understood in reference to there being two grounds of the judgment that are present side-by-side, then judgments of adherent beauty can be characterized in a fashion that parallels the introduction of sensory gratification into judgments of pure beauty.

A judgment of adherent beauty would thus be an impure judgment insofar as a non-aesthetic satisfaction mixes with the specific aesthetic satisfaction related to beauty. A judgment of vulgar beauty, in both comparison and contrast, would involve mixing two different sorts of aesthetic satisfaction, viz., that of pure beauty and that of sense-gratification. The latter mixture yields a "pure" or exclusively aesthetic judgment (in the broad sense of "aesthetic"), which is nonetheless not a judgment of pure beauty. Both judgments of vulgar beauty and judgments of adherent beauty are thus impure with respect to pure beauty, but judgments of vulgar beauty nonetheless remain purely aesthetic judgments, whereas judgments of adherent beauty do not.

One reason why Kant is more positively disposed towards judgments of perfection as opposed to judgments of sensory gratification is that judgments of perfection include moral judgments. An action's moral content is measured in terms of how well it satisfies the ideal conditions of rational behavior. This association between judgments of perfection and judgments of pure beauty thereby allows Kant to introduce one of the foremost themes of the *Critique of the Power of Judgment*, namely, how the spheres of beauty and moral goodness work in sympathy with each other. As we continue with Kant's exposition in the *Critique of the Power of Judgment*, we will see that moral themes will become increasingly salient.

In §16, Kant claims initially that although the satisfaction in an object's perfection is independent of the satisfaction in the object's pure beauty, the combination of the two satisfactions (as in option (2) above) allows beauty to act positively in the service of goodness. This is because the subjective universality, or generalized public quality (a public quality related to the conditions for scientific knowledge, or to cognition in general) of the satisfaction in beauty can be matched with the universality of moral demands.

The disinterested satisfaction that grounds judgments of pure beauty introduces a reference to a public, objective, and shared world that is expressive of the harmony of the cognitive faculties of the understanding and imagination. This is a validity that is an abstracted and indeterminate version of the more definitive objective validity, universality and necessity that Kant associates with space, time, and the categories insofar as they are the conditions for scientific knowledge. The validity associated with cognition in general is simply the idea of a necessarily structured public world without any further specification.

Once this sort of satisfaction that is related to pure beauty is linked with a presentation that has a moral content, as is true in the case of a beautiful human body, we have a situation where we project upon a moral context from the sphere of the beautiful, the generic form of the universality and validity associated with scientific judgments. This gives the moral contents an aesthetic (i.e., subjective) support that carries the persuasive weight of scientific knowledge, if only in a formal and generalized sense. Hence, adding a beautiful quality to an object that has a moral content gives an added presentational power to the moral content that the object is embodying, and presents the idea that science and morality are not inconsistent with each other. Specifically, the addition of beauty lends a stronger sense of spatio-temporal reality to a given moral content. For moral purposes, people are better off looking as beautiful as they can, speaking generally.

In the end, although Kant refers rhetorically to two different kinds of beauty, there is only pure beauty whose disinterested satisfaction can be amalgamated with other sorts of interested satisfaction to produce impure – but more importantly, *augmented* – expressions of this single kind of beauty. It is not as if feelings of disinterested satisfaction combine with other sorts of satisfaction to change the nature of the disinterested satisfaction itself. If this were the case, one could in fact speak of a new, emergent sort of beauty that arises through the combination of disinterested satisfaction with the satisfaction of apprehending an object's perfection. As intriguing as the idea might be, Kant does not describe a dynamic and genuinely dialectical interaction between sorts of satisfaction that would generate a new kind of beauty (i.e., as copper and tin amalgamate to constitute brass). For him, the satisfaction that grounds judgments of pure beauty is always due to the harmony of the cognitive faculties in a disengaged condition of free play.

One of the issues concerning Kant's distinction between free and adherent beauty concerns the apparently negative valuations of the terms "dependent," "accessory," "adherent," and so on that are used to describe the opposition to free beauty. What is easily overlooked, however, is that these terms describe not only how a judgment of beauty depends, or is conditioned by, some concept of the object's purpose. They describe the evaluation of the beautiful component of an object considered with respect to acknowledging the overriding importance of the object's purpose. That is, if one believes that the moral purpose of human being is unconditional, then the human being's beauty will be an accessory, or adherent, to that paramount purpose. How people behave is far more important than how they look, and their beauty is a secondary matter.

This is exactly how Kant uses the term "dependent" (*anhängend*) at the end of §16, when he mentions how in view of positively valuing an object's purpose, the object's beauty becomes a secondary matter. The beauty of adherent beauty depends upon a concept of an object's purpose, but its quality is not so-called because the object's purpose interrupts one's attention from its free beauty. The purpose is not an accessory to the beauty. Rather, the beauty is an accessory to the purpose. The beauty's adherent quality is so-called because the beauty itself adheres to, is subordinated to, and gives an added reality to, the object's purpose.

Such reflections on Kant's use of the term "dependent" or "adherent" directly show how the larger and central theme of the third *Critique* concerns morality, how beauty and teleology are accessories to realizing the purposes of morality, why Kant immediately follows §16 with a discussion of human beauty, and why some aspects of the theory of beauty-as-perfection fit more closely with Kant's wider philosophical interests. The main point is that when considered in connection with human beings, where the moral purpose involved is *unconditional*, adherent beauty locates what was formerly free beauty within a moral context that augments beauty's significance, as it constrains its inherent aimlessness to adhere to and respect an unconditional human content.

Adherent Beauty (II): Ideal Human Beauty as Moral Expression in a Generically-formed Human Body

[**§17: "Concerning the ideal of beauty"**] It is a challenge for Kant to coordinate the traditional theory of beauty-as-perfection with his account of disinterested satisfaction in connection with the harmony of the cognitive faculties. The difficulty of achieving this is evident in §17, whose topic is the "ideal of beauty." Kant recognizes that there are models or idealized exemplars of beautiful things, and this rationally suggests that at the highest level there is some single, ideal presentation of beauty towards which all of the models aspire and converge. To create a beautiful thing, one could do well by imitating some of the existing exemplars, even though a slavish imitation would display no sense of taste, and even though the creation of an original model is different from copying an already-existing one. Beautiful models exist, but if the satisfaction in beauty is independent of determinately applying concepts to objects, there is a problem about how the models of beauty can fit into Kant's account at all, if a model suggests ideal conditions, and if ideal conditions are defined by concepts of some sort, as is the case with ideals such as Platonic Ideas (e.g., perfect circles and the like).

With respect to models of beauty, Kant believes that one thing is sure: these models are formulated neither as a matter of logical implication from general principles, nor as a matter of directly applying some given determinate rule to a given object or situation. The feeling of approval that grounds judgments of pure beauty arises independently of categorizing objects as things of this or that kind. Whatever the source of the models of beauty happens to be, we know that they cannot derive from a science of beauty. They must derive from the application of taste itself.

Now in reference to models of beauty, Kant introduces a mode of judging an object's beauty that differs noticeably from his canonical account where we reflect disinterestedly upon an object's purposive form and experience a certain degree of satisfaction that results in relation to cognition in general. Instead, he describes a mode of judging that resonates more closely with the beauty-as-perfection view:

> . . . the highest model, the archetype of taste, is a mere idea which each person must bring into being for himself, and in accordance with which he must judge everything that is an object of taste, or that is an example of judging through taste, even the taste of everyone.
>
> (§17, Ak 232 (54), G 116–17, P 79, M 75–76, B 68–69)

According to the above description, each person produces for himself or herself an ideal representation of what an object with the highest degree of beauty would be like. This would be an ideal representation that, if realized, would set the faculties of imagination and understanding into a perfect cognitive attunement. With such an ideal in mind, the person would then judge all other cases in reference to this ideal. So Kant is importing the model of judgments of perfection into his account of beauty, and is trying to fit his canonical format of disinterestedly judging an object's purposive form for the purpose of ascertaining the object's beauty, into the format where we consider some individual in light of its ideal condition.

Such an archetype of taste can only be a product of imagination and, as instantiated in each person, will also vary from person to person, since we are only imagining some hypothetical object that has the most intense presentation of purposive form and that sets the cognitive faculties into swing at the most effective level imaginable – in a sort of optimal attunement between them. The situation is open-ended in terms of what each person will specifically imagine to fit this description (presumably, though, it will be a systematically-organized presentation that has the highest imaginable unity combined with the highest imaginable diversity). Degrees of purposive form are difficult to measure and specify, and we can refer to intensities of the free play of the cognitive faculties only vaguely and generally.

With respect to beauty in general, then, Kant believes that it is impossible to delineate any archetype of taste, and he maintains that the model of judgment according to the beauty-as-perfection view consequently does not apply. The sort of beauty that can be understood more effectively in terms of measuring up some individual to an ideal image, however, makes better sense when we can be more exact about what sort of thing we are judging. This invites the introduction of a conception of the sort of thing at hand that can set some constraints on its configurational possibilities, but even with this, it can be difficult to form an image of the most beautiful type of this or that sort of thing.

Kant, noting this fact, and then taking a position at the opposite extreme, maintains that it is impossible to form an ideal of beauty regarding anything whose essence is not knowable *a priori*. This is to say that he believes that it is impossible for us prescriptively to delineate the form of the most beautiful oak tree, or the most beautiful church, in reference to which we would judge the beauty of any given oak tree or church.

One reason Kant mentions for the impossibility of formulating an image of the most beautiful residence, beautiful tree, beautiful gardens and the like is because the purposes of these things are supposedly too vague to prescribe how the objects ought to look. This is different from saying, though, that such an ideal cannot be formulated because the concepts are empirical (which is the relevant contrast to *a priori* concepts). So a stronger reason is required for restricting ideals of beauty to those things (there turns out to be only one group of them) whose essence can only be known *a priori*.

At first sight, the judges at a cat show have exact criteria for how perfect cats of various sorts ought to look and, given their definitions, it is reasonable to suppose that the judges construct fairly determinate ideals of beautiful cats of this or that species as an aspect of their judging. Such examples, moreover, would be paradigm cases of judgments of adherent beauty. We will see in a moment why these do not count as appropriate ideals of beauty, however. Turning to the positive side of things, Kant states the following:

> Only that which has the purpose of its existence in itself, the *human being* – who through reason determines his purposes himself, or, where he must derive them from external perception, can nevertheless compare them to essential and universal purposes and in that case also aesthetically judge their accordance with them – is alone capable of an ideal of *beauty*, just as the humanity [*Menschheit*] in his person, as intelligence, is alone capable of the ideal of *perfection*, among all the objects in the world.
>
> (§17, Ak 233 (55–56), G 117, P 81, M 76–77, B 69–70)

This remark expands upon the initial §16 references to the combination of moral goodness and beauty, and it is clear that Kant is interested in continuing this reference through a discussion of human beauty and moral expression. Unlike ideals of beautiful Siamese cats and such, only the ideal of human beauty is neither contingently nor arbitrarily defined. It is therefore is the only sort of ideal that can introduce universality and necessity and demand the assent of others who judge in reference to it.

Just as everyone similarly grounds the universal satisfaction that attends judgments of pure beauty and the harmony of the cognitive faculties, and just as this universal satisfaction can be brought into the service of morality such as to coordinate two sorts of universality – a subjective aesthetic universality and an objective moral universality – Kant's restriction of the ideal of beauty to human beings fits with his interest in coordinating beauty and goodness. To preserve the universality of the satisfaction that can be involved in judgments of perfection so that it can match the universality of the satisfaction involved in judgments of pure beauty, the ideal of beauty can refer only to human beauty. The ideal beauty of species of cats, even though in some cases the species might be defined in reference to natural biological kinds, is ultimately grounded upon empirical considerations and cannot therefore require a necessary and universal agreement amongst people. Kant's intention, in effect, is to describe a situation where two sorts of universal feelings of approval are amalgamated in a more powerful experience of adherent beauty that demands agreement for two reasons at once, and where the predominant reason of the two is a moral one.

Having established that only the ideal of human beauty can ground a universal satisfaction in the associated judgment of perfection (i.e., when judging that some human being exemplifies well how a human being ought to present itself aesthetically), Kant proceeds to characterize the structure of the ideal of human beauty. Its elements involve an empirically-derived aesthetic delineation of the human being in its physical perfection that is informed and restricted by the idea of the human being as a moral being that is knowable *a priori*. In this characterization, Kant imagines the standardized physical form of a human being, insofar as this can establish the parameters within which the beauty of any particular person can be judged.

To formulate the ideal of human beauty, i.e., a model of the perfected human spatio-temporal form, Kant combines a flatly generic conception of the human structural appearance with a generic conception of the essence of human beings as moral beings. This combination takes the form of a judgment in general, where an intuition (in this instance, an aesthetic image of the human's standardized physical contours) and a concept (considered generally, which in this instance is the idea of morality) are fused together in the "*S is P*" logical format. This, to recall, is the logical format also reflected in the harmony of the cognitive faculties where the imagination (the faculty of intuitions) is subsumed under the understanding (the faculty of concepts) and radiates thereby a universal satisfaction related to cognition in general.

In the case of the ideal of beauty, the structure is logically the same, except that the two components that enter into the judgmental format are neither entire faculties nor determinate concepts and intuitions, but are peculiar sorts of intuition and concept. Specifically, both the intuition and the concept involved are indeterminate.

The effect of this combination is to introduce not a harmony between the cognitive faculties of imagination and understanding, but a harmony between the imagination and reason, for the indeterminate concept involved is the idea of morality:

> But there are here two components: *first*, the aesthetic *normal idea*, which is an individual intuition [*Anschauung*] (of the imagination) that represents the standard for judging it as a thing belonging to a particular animal species; *second*, the *idea of reason*, which makes the purposes of humanity insofar as they cannot be sensibly represented into the principle for judging of its figure, though which, as their effect in appearance, the purposes are revealed.
>
> (§17, Ak 233 (56), G 117–18, P 81, M 77, B 70)[11]

The ideal of human beauty is consequently neither a microcosm of the harmony of the cognitive faculties nor a structure that reflects the nature of free beauty. Rather, it represents the amalgamation of moral content with aesthetically disinterested content and expresses a logical fusion of goodness with beauty following the form of judgment in general. It exemplifies adherent beauty (*pulchritudo adhaerens*) wherein the beauty adheres to a moral idea.

Kant's notion of an aesthetic normal idea – the empirical component of the ideal of beauty – might easily be overlooked as an eccentric aspect of his account of this ideal, for he states that the most beautiful stature of the human being must be consistent with the mathematically average human stature, that the most beautiful nose must be consistent with the averagely-sized nose, and so on, independently of the exercise of either idealization or taste.

In the wider context of Kant's aesthetic theory, however, his notion of an aesthetic normal idea assumes a greater significance in light of one that, as we shall see, is central to his theory of artistic beauty. This is the conception of an "aesthetic idea" that will be discussed in Chapter 3 (§49), which bears a close resemblance to that of an "aesthetic normal idea" developed here in §17. Kant will later state that beauty, both natural and artistic, is the expression of aesthetic ideas.

As mentioned, the ideal of beauty involves the combination of a generic image of the human being in its spatio-temporal contours with a generic moral idea that defines the essence of the human being. The generic image of the human being – the image of the human being in general that reflects its universality in a physical form – is arrived at through a process of averaging and generalizing the diversity of human linear forms. It is a reduction of human contours to the least common denominator, with the intention of arriving at a normalization, standardization or regularization of how people typically look. It aims to reflect *the bodily plan that nature had in mind* in the production of human beings. Reasonably illustrative approximations to this plan, Kant believes, are classical Greek sculptures that convey a universal image of the human being. He mentions as an example Polycleitus's famous Doryphorus. He also mentions Myron's idealized sculpture of a cow to indicate how aesthetic normal ideas are not unique to the human species, but can be defined for many natural kinds.

Despite the beauty of Polycleitus's masterpiece, the aesthetic normal idea's form which lies at the sculpture's basis is not in itself particularly attractive; it is simply regulative and generic. One considers the average size of the human being, the average ear, the average head, and so on, and imaginatively amalgamates these to construe the natural pattern that underlies the human being's bodily form.[12] The aesthetic normal idea is simply a textbook diagram of a "standard human being" as one might find in a book on general anatomy. Since aesthetic normal ideas are not unique to the human body and can be formulated with respect to many different species of things, the aesthetic normal idea does not constitute the ideal of beauty by itself.

Only when the human being's generic physical delineation is combined with the *a priori* conception of the human being as a moral being do we have an ideal of beauty in the sense that universalistic content is introduced. The addition of the moral content defines the purpose of the human being that is knowable *a priori*, in reference to which we interpret the purposiveness of the human body's generic contours. The theoretical elegance of the situation is that both moral ideas and the spatio-temporal forms relevant to the generic image of the human being are considered independently of sensory gratification, are both associated with types of universal feelings of approval, and are brought together according to the structure of the most basic form of logical judgment, "*S is P*."

Since neither the moral ideas nor the aesthetic normal idea are in themselves beautiful, though, Kant's discussion of the amalgamation of moral ideas with aesthetic normal ideas in the ideal of beauty should be seen as establishing only the necessary conditions for the most beautiful representation of a human being. One needs further to modify this generic presentation through artistic genius and taste (e.g., add some gracefulness to it, as Polycleitus did in his Doryphorus) to produce a beautiful representation of a human being that approximates to the ideal.

Having thus set forth some initial relationships between beauty and morality that will be developed in later parts of the *Critique of the Power of Judgment*, Kant concludes the Third Moment by stating "*beauty* is the form of an object's *purposiveness*, insofar as this is perceived in the object *without the representation of a purpose*." This characterization is less precise than it might have been, since the form of an object's purposiveness is equivalent to the object's purposiveness without purpose, and there is no other way to perceive this form of purposiveness except without the representation of a purpose. His main idea, though, can be expressed by saying that beauty is the form of an object's purposiveness (*Form der Zweckmäßigkeit*), insofar as this is perceived in reference to the object's purposive form (*zweckmäßige Form*) (to which he refers in the note accompanying this definition).

THE FOURTH LOGICAL MOMENT: THE UNIVERSAL FEELING OF APPROVAL THAT GROUNDS JUDGMENTS OF PURE BEAUTY CARRIES THE FORCE OF NECESSITY (§§18–22)

Scientific Universality, Moral Universality, and the Universality of Cognition in General

[§18: "What the modality of a pure judgment of beauty is"] The Fourth Moment returns to the core characterization of judgments of pure beauty and addresses their relationship to the modal concepts of possibility, actuality, and necessity. The focus is specifically upon the kind of necessity associated with the feeling of approval that grounds judgments of pure beauty, for in such judgments we feel that everyone ought to agree with us. Kant has already explained how the universality of this satisfaction rests on the universality of cognition in general, and in this section he elaborates on the nature of that aesthetic universality insofar as it contrasts with alternative types that arise in connection with science and morality.

With respect to scientific judgments and their associated *a priori* conditions (viz., space, time, and the categories of the understanding), Kant refers to a "theoretical objective necessity." This strong sense of necessity entails that every person must experience things in exactly the same way, e.g., that every human experience must be at some time or other, and that there is no such thing as a timeless experience. A theoretical objective necessity related to feeling would assert that according to universally-prescribed, actual circumstances, everyone will feel a particular way.

Kant contrasts such a theoretical objective necessity with moral necessity. The latter is the "consequence of an objective [moral] law and signifies nothing other than that one absolutely . . . ought to act in a certain way." It does not follow that anyone necessarily acts morally, or that anyone in fact acts morally, but only that each person ought to act morally. A moral necessity related to feeling would assert that everyone ought to be in tune with the moral law, and that anyone who is properly in tune with it will have certain types of feelings (viz., related to self-respect).

In judgments of pure beauty, the kind of necessity involved stems from the identical way in which the faculties of understanding and imagination are assumed to resonate with each other in any person, if the person were to apprehend some given object disinterestedly and aesthetically. The necessity is "exemplary" (*exemplarisch*) insofar as each person would (ideally) apprehend a purposiveness without purpose in the objects' form, or a universal rule that cannot be specified. This inability to specify the universal rule is precisely because the object's purposiveness is apprehended without ascribing any definite purposes to the object.

[§19: "The subjective necessity that we ascribe to the pure judgment of beauty, is conditioned"] Owing to its grounding upon the basic structure of cognition in general, the necessity that attends judgments of pure beauty is associated primarily with scientific necessity. One could call it a necessity related to the mere "form" of scientific necessity, for if there were no harmony of the cognitive faculties in general (i.e., independently of whether that harmony is free or determined), then there could be no definite application of concepts to objects, and hence, no scientific necessity at all. The satisfaction in pure beauty is essentially a cognitively-grounded necessity; it is a feeling that radiates from the activity of the general conditions for empirical knowledge. Such disinterested satisfaction, however, is not always (if ever) present in one's experience in a pure form. This is to say that the disinterested feeling of approval in the apprehension of pure beauty is understandable at least, and possibly at most, as an ideal condition.

This ideal condition is also akin to the necessity that accompanies the moral law for several reasons. First, although we ought to instantiate the moral law in our action, we may or may not instantiate it, so this instantiation remains only a possibility, rather than a necessity. Second, even if we believe that we are acting out of the pure respect for duty, and if our action is indeed in accord with what duty requires, it remains an open question whether we are in fact behaving out of a pure respect for duty, since we might have selfish motives that we fail to recognize in ourselves that are driving the behavior. Moreover, perhaps we are never absolutely free from selfish motives. The last difficulty parallels that which affects supposed judgments of pure beauty.

Kant refers to the necessity associated with judgments of pure beauty as demanding the assent of others in principle, but in actual cases of such judgments a demand that others agree with one's judgment can arise only *conditionally*, namely, on the assumption that one's judgment of pure beauty is itself completely disinterested. One can never be sure, however, that such conditions are being met, either in oneself or in others. Neither is there any obligation to try to make judgments of pure beauty.

Such uncertainties further locate judgments of pure beauty midway between scientific and moral judgments. Their universality abstractly and subjectively expresses the conditions of cognition in general, which is itself necessary to express the universality and necessity of scientific judgments. As is true for moral judgments, though, judgments of pure beauty need not be realized well in actual experience.

[§20: "The idea of a common sense (*Gemeinsinn*) is the (pre)condition of the necessity that is alleged by a judgment of pure beauty"] Kant recognizes that there is a universality and necessity associated with judgments of pure beauty and he has identified this *a priori* quality in connection with the rigidities of our shared cognitive structure. These are, namely, that in all judgments there is a union of intuitions with concepts and hence, a union of the two faculties of the mind (viz., the imagination and the understanding) that are geared respectively and individually towards the production, and interactively towards the unification, of intuitions and concepts.

Maintaining and recognizing that this necessity is based on a satisfying feeling of the free play of the cognitive faculties, but also noting that no definite rules for the cognition of this or that object are applied during such free play, Kant concludes that this disinterested feeling of approval can be defined in reference to a *common sense* that people have. He adds that this common sense is "the effect of the free play of our cognitive powers" (i.e., it is a feeling). Kant has already argued that a necessity is associated with judgments of pure beauty and that this directly concerns cognition in general and the free play of the cognitive faculties, so his reference to a common sense at this particular juncture simply offers a different, more summary, angle from which to refer to what he has already characterized. In the sections to follow, however, this common sense will play a larger role.

As a first approximation for understanding Kant's notion of common sense, we can notice initially that it is a "sense" or is related to a type of feeling. Secondly, we need to keep in mind that it is "common," which implies that everyone has the capacity for similarly experiencing the feelings involved. Unlike senses that depend on the structures of the eyes, ears, nose, tongue, and surface of the skin, all of which structures can vary from person to person, the "common sense" depends upon what all human beings share identically. For Kant, this is the structure of cognition and its specific interplay between the understanding and imagination.

Prior to Kant, the "common sense" was sometimes (e.g., in the Aristotelian tradition) understood as the faculty where the various inputs from the five senses would converge. The postulation of this common sense was necessary to explain how, for example, we can *see* a cup, *feel* a cup, *taste* the tea in the cup, and *smell* the tea's aroma, with the awareness that all of these diverse sensory inputs are stemming from and are referring to the "same" cup of tea. In Kant's characterization of the harmony of the cognitive faculties as holding between understanding and imagination, there is no specification of the kinds of intuitions that the imagination includes. It would thus be the place where all of the sensory inputs from the five senses initially converge. It would also be where, in relation to the concepts of the understanding, the concept "cup" (as in the above example) could be applied to the intuitions entering in from the various sense modalities as a way to integrate one's experience of the cup.

The Perfection of Cognition and the Harmony of the Cognitive Faculties

[§21: "Whether one has grounds to presuppose a common sense"]
Kant elaborates on his notion of the harmony of the cognitive faculties by describing in further detail what happens when an object's purposive form occasions that harmony. He notes that objects have a variety of sensory presentations and that in reference to their amenability to being comprehended as best as possible, they each differ with respect to the sort of attunement they require between the imagination and the understanding. Generalizing from this claim, he states that there must accordingly be an idea of a maximal, most effective attunement of the imagination and understanding. Kant maintains that this idea of perfect attunement – a conception towards which he was moving in his §17 discussion of the ideal of beauty – is the cognitive condition to which judgments of pure beauty refer, adding that the disinterested feeling of approval that grounds judgments of pure beauty expresses this idea of perfected cognition. Kant also refers to common sense as the ability to experience this feeling of optimal attunement.

It is unclear whether Kant has in mind a single, actual attunement that would stand constantly as the ideal for every apprehension of an object in an effort to comprehend it – one that would be exemplified in a pure and unqualified ideal of beauty, if such an ideal were possible – or whether more plausibly, he is thinking rather that in every apprehension, case-by-case, there is a specifically optimal attunement between understanding and imagination suitable for maximally comprehending the given object. Either interpretation serves Kant's purpose of identifying something common between people when judgments of pure beauty relative to some given object are being made.

Speaking generally, then, when making a judgment of pure beauty, one presupposes an optimal attunement between the imagination and understanding, either in general, or relative to the structure of the object in question. This optimal attunement would be the condition, judging in reference to one's common sense, that one would aim to experience in an attempt to apprehend the object's pure beauty. Most importantly, it is the same condition towards which one would expect others to aim, judging with their common sense, in their own efforts to reflect disinterestedly upon the object's purposive form.

A motivation for Kant's reference to a common sense can be seen in his implicit recognition that with respect to any given object, various attunements between the imagination and understanding are possible, not only between objects, but between people who are nonetheless perceiving the same object in a disinterested fashion. Some could experience a free play of the cognitive faculties relative to the object, but in a less intense way than might be possible under a better attunement between the imagination and understanding.

To standardize the experiences of the harmony of the cognitive faculties, Kant consequently hypothesizes an ideal attunement between the imagination and understanding to which judgments of an object's pure beauty would be coordinated. This mutual convergence upon a single attunement would provide a necessary condition for ensuring that the feeling is the same between people who are perceiving the object disinterestedly. This, in turn, would ensure that it will make sense for one to expect someone else to have the same feeling with respect to the object when one judges that the object is beautiful to such and such a degree. In general, then, the condition of disinterestedness removes the factors of sense-gratification and conceptualization, and the condition of common sense removes the remaining variations in attunement between the imagination and understanding that can arise, even when two people are reflecting upon the object disinterestedly. This is all done in an effort to standardize the judgment.

With respect to the purpose of cognition in general, the idea of optimal attunement and common sense also represent how the faculties of understanding and imagination would in fact be related to each other, if the object were to be known in the most comprehensive manner. It therefore represents additionally a condition for the perfection of cognition, since if we were disinterestedly to contemplate an object in accord with this ideal to appreciate the object's beauty, and if we were afterwards to shift our mode of interpretation to a scientific one, then the imagination and understanding would already have been set in the best position to comprehend the object in reference to applying concepts. In this sense the free play of the imagination and understanding would lead to a concept, although to which concept it would lead would remain undetermined.

Kant's idea of a common sense, that is, of a capacity to feel what the optimal attunement of the cognitive faculties of imagination and understanding would be in relation to some given object, can be seen as yet another effort to give due respect to the alternative theory of beauty-as-perfection. Although in the case of optimal attunement there are no applications of empirical concepts to the object, there is nonetheless operating at a higher level a definition of what the purpose of the joint operation of the understanding and imagination happens to be (viz., to accumulate and systematize empirical knowledge). Realizing the purpose of cognition is exactly what the achievement of a properly disinterested attitude towards an object helps facilitate. So although the appreciation of pure beauty does not involve the application of concepts to objects and does not produce empirical knowledge, the very appreciation of pure beauty produces a mental condition – one, owing to its disinterestedness, that fosters the classical image of the scientist as a completely detached and objective observer – that facilitates the optimal realization of the purpose of cognition. This is to say that scientists would do well to develop an appreciation for pure beauty, since this generates the mental condition required for the best determinate and systematic comprehension of nature.

When the cognitive faculties are in free play, no concept is being applied to the object. For this reason it can be said that the free play of the cognitive faculties is "noncognitive." However, the attunement of the cognitive faculties is itself an expression of "cognition in general," and for this reason, it can be said more directly that the free play of the faculties is "cognitive." The latter characterization is more central, since the very relation of the faculties to the purpose of cognition accounts for why their attunement is pleasurable. As an expression of cognition in general, the free play is itself geared towards the specific realization of cognition. It is consequently a generic precondition for scientific knowledge, whether or not it can be experienced independently and in abstraction from sensations and conceptual determinations, as judgments of pure beauty prescribe.

To sum things up, one could say that the concept of perfected cognition in general subsumes the optimal free play of the cognitive faculties (which is the optimization of the power of judgment), and that the optimal free play of the cognitive faculties subsumes the object that is judged to be beautiful.

[§22: "The necessity of the universal agreement that is thought in a judgment of pure beauty is a subjective necessity, which under the presupposition of a common sense, is represented as an objective necessity"] In relation to his reflections on the optimal attunement of the cognitive faculties, Kant adds some reflections about the reliability of our actual judgments of pure beauty. He is clear that judgments of pure beauty are grounded in our disinterested attention to an object's purposive form and that if we could attend perfectly to the object in such a way, a disinterested feeling of approval would result, viz., the harmony of the cognitive faculties in their becoming exactly attuned to comprehending the object. The satisfaction in pure beauty thus amounts to the optimal experience of the power of judgment in general. This also implies that that very experience of the power of judgment identifies a precondition for achieving scientific knowledge in the most effective manner possible. It is not, however, that optimally knowing an object entails the experience of beauty. Kant's thought is rather that if the particular attunement between the imagination and understanding in such circumstances could be fully detached and abstracted in order to be experienced on its own in relation to the well-known object, then a feeling of beauty would result.

Kant observes, though, that there is no guarantee that any judgment we assert to be a judgment of pure beauty is indeed one that instantiates the demanding and ideal criteria of such judgments. We could believe that we are judging disinterestedly but in fact be judging under the influence of desires and interests. Moreover, since desires and interests virtually permeate our consciousness, it could be that pure judgments of pure beauty are rarely attainable, if ever.

Kant states accordingly that the common sense – the capacity to experience the optimal free play of the harmony of the faculties without any admixture of interest – is only an ideal norm (bloße idealische Norm) that regulates our efforts to make judgments of pure beauty. Whether judgments of pure beauty are realizable remains an open question, for it could be that we might only be able to approximate the ideal of making a judgment of pure beauty without any influence by charm, practical interests, or external considerations. It could be that in almost all, if not all, cases, alleged judgments of pure beauty are always impure to some extent, either through an admixture of sensory gratification or though an admixture of conceptually-grounded interests, or through an admixture of both. If this were so, however, it would nonetheless remain necessary to recognize at the basis of the judgment of pure beauty, the ideal norm of a common sense as that which accounts for the possibility of agreement in such judgments. This is because even among a set of perfectly disinterested people, their respective attunements between the understanding and imagination can vary, not because the object varies, but because individuals' inner cognitive dispositions can vary.

One can imagine, for instance, two people who are judging the beauty of a snowflake, one of whom is a mathematician whose understanding is extraordinarily active, the other of whom is a poet whose imagination is extraordinarily active. The idea of common sense, or optimal attunement, would serve to adjudicate between their differing cognitive dispositions and remaining differences in judgment, after the two have successfully abstracted from interests related to concepts and sense-gratification.

This leaves Kant in a situation where he suspends his opinion about whether the common sense refers to actual experiences or to merely an ideal attunement between the understanding and imagination and an associated ideal optimization of the power of judgment. It could be the case that judgments of pure beauty never actually occur. Even if this were the case, however, we would still require the assent of other people to the degree that we believed that we were approaching the ideal of making a judgment of pure beauty. This indicates that it is plausible to interpret Kant's entire canonical account of judgments of pure beauty in §§1–22 as a characterization of an idealized and standardized approach to beauty that, in practice, is never fully realized.

The Perfection of Cognition and the Ideal of Uniformity Amidst Diversity

["General Remark"] In a summary reflection on §§1–22, Kant highlights the importance of the imagination's creative play in the (ideal) experience of pure beauty. He focuses strongly on the imagination's activity *per se*, rather than on the free play of the imagination and understanding in conjunction, and mentions that the imagination's creative activity in the experience of pure beauty simply should not "offend" the understanding. One motivation in this emphasis is to argue against Francis Hutcheson's view that regular forms such as circles and triangles are paradigms of pure beauty. As alternative examples, given his own theory of beauty, Kant is more disposed to refer to birdsongs, flowers, complicated designs, and all sorts of intelligible presentations that stimulate one's imagination. In this concluding remark, there is even the impression that intense beauty arises when a form's diversity is elaborated as much as possible, almost to the point where one reaches the edge of comprehensibility. This privileging of the imagination-side of the harmony between the imagination and understanding introduces some tension into Kant's account.

A more consistent alternative would be to maintain that both unity (the organizing factor of understanding) and diversity (the creative factor of imagination) should be intensified equally in an intensely beautiful presentation, such that the most beautiful presentation would not be akin to a baroque flourishing of forms whose diversity challenges the bounds of understanding, but would involve forms that are highly diversified, as well as being maximally organized and systematic. This is closer to the scientific ideal and what the perfection of cognition would dictate.

A god-like comprehension of a perfectly rational world in its infinite detail would produce such an image as well, and would also reflect the leading idea of perfected cognition and a satisfaction related to cognition in general. This would give a balanced weight to both the understanding and imagination in the feeling of satisfaction associated with the harmony of the cognitive faculties, and would coincidentally coincide with the prevailing traditional formula for beauty as expressing a "uniformity amidst variety," not to mention Kant's own emphasis upon how purposive forms impress us with a compelling intelligibility. In minor segments of his theory of artistic genius, as we will see, Kant's account will nonetheless retain this disposition towards the more romantic, more baroque, factor, where the creative power of imagination prevails over the power of understanding.

One curiosity of Kant's emphasis upon flourishing imaginative forms in this appendix to the first main section of the *Critique of the Power of Judgment* is that it creates some friction with his discussion of the ideal of human beauty, where well-proportioned, classical Greek statues are the paradigm, and where complicated ornamentation to the human body such as facial tattooing is set aside on moral grounds. This suggests a basic tension in Kant's discussions from the very start between offering an account that maximizes the free play of the imagination to guarantee liveliness in the experience of beauty, as opposed to emphasizing the role of understanding to accentuate that the pleasure in the beautiful is nonetheless a pleasure related to cognition.

It is not as if only the latter part of the Critique of Aesthetic Judgment (which focusses on art) sometimes emphasizes imagination over the understanding in the theory of genius, and that the former part (which focusses on pure beauty) is exclusively classically-oriented in terms of how Kant organized his text. Although the weight of Kant's theory of beauty is formalistic, neoclassical, rationalistic, and cognition-centered in spirit, it is evident from his general remark at the end of this first section that he sometimes expressed a strong preference for highly imaginative forms, even in the midst of a discussion that focusses on more classical forms.

Kant's general remark nonetheless highlights the importance of "play" in the experience of pure beauty (this is a concept which, in later years, has a central role in the aesthetic theories of Friedrich Schiller and Sigmund Freud). As examples and analogies, Kant mentions how in the appreciation of beautiful landscape scenery, the indistinctness of the far-away objects inventively stimulates our imagination, and how watching a charming brook with its bubbling water, or the changing shapes of a fire in a hearth, similarly sustain the imagination's free play.

THE DEDUCTION (LEGITIMATION) OF JUDGMENTS OF PURE BEAUTY (§§30–40)

The Deduction and Our Sensus Communis

The term "deduction," in Kant's usage, is a legal term that refers to a justification or legitimation of a claim or principle. In the present situation, there is a need to justify how a judgment of pure beauty can make a claim to necessity, since it is based only on feeling and is not a cognitive judgment that provides empirical knowledge. At first sight, it would seem that no such justification is possible, since "subjective" usually implies contingency, privacy and variability from person to person.

Kant rejects such a relativistic notion of subjectivity, of course, but he does try to explain precisely how a judgment that is based on feeling alone, that is not provable, that remains uncertain whether in fact we are even meeting the criteria of such judgments in any particular case, could nonetheless carry a claim to necessity. He aims to show, in other words, how one person's feeling of approval could be upheld as the rule for everyone else, even if no proofs are available that could force the individual's judgment on anyone.

Some of the themes arising now in the deduction (§§30 – 40) are familiar from the first four logical moments of the judgment of pure beauty (§§1–22). There is a separate expository section on the deduction of pure judgments of beauty, however, since methodologically Kant's aim in §§1–22 is only to describe analytically the features of judgments of pure beauty, rather than engage in justifications and legitimating considerations. The expositions in the four moments nonetheless provide the source materials for the justification of the universal validity of pure judgments of beauty that will now be addressed, and we find that his discussions in §§30–40 significantly repeat some of the points made in §§1–22. Despite this repetitiousness, Kant advances some new considerations in the deduction and he brings the justification of the universal validity that attends judgments of pure beauty to a noticeably more fundamental theoretical level.

The problem of the deduction concerns whether there are any feelings that are universal, non-empirical, and do not have a basis in determinate concepts. In his moral theory, Kant identifies the feeling of the respect for law as a universal feeling whose ground is *a priori* (i.e., non-empirical), but is based on concepts. This example from morality suggests that there could additionally be universal feelings that are not based on concepts and that could serve as the ground of judgments of pure beauty.

In the case of pure beauty, the universal feeling is necessarily coordinated with the purposive structure of some given (usually empirical) object, and this introduces a paradox into the situation. Although the feeling of beauty is coordinated with a given object's purposive structure, this feeling is not itself a sensory feeling whose attractiveness varies from person to person, as do the tastes of foods, the textures of surfaces, and the scents of perfumes.

As we have seen, the universal feeling associated with pure beauty – the feeling of approval that we know Kant believes radiates from the harmony of the cognitive faculties – is thus in an intermediary theoretical position between moral feelings and sensory gratifications. Unlike moral feelings, feelings of beauty are not based on concepts. They nonetheless typically require an empirical object's given structure to stimulate them, although neither are they sensory gratifications that vary from person to person.

The essence of the deduction is as follows:

> This pleasure (*Lust*) [in pure beauty] must necessarily rest on the same conditions in everyone, because they are subjective conditions of the possibility of a cognition in general, and the proportion of these cognitive faculties that taste requires is also required for the common and healthy [i.e., basically given, not yet cultivated] understanding that one may presuppose in everyone.
>
> (§39, Ak 292–93 (155), G 172–73, P 159, M 150, B 135)

> To be justified in claiming universal agreement for judgments of the aesthetic power of judgment that rests merely on subjective grounds, it is sufficient to grant only: 1) the subjective conditions of this faculty are one and the same in all people, as far as is concerned the relation of the cognitive powers thus set into activity for a cognition in general. This must be true, because otherwise people could not communicate their representations and even cognition itself. 2) The judgment has considered merely this relation . . . and is pure . . .
>
> (§38, footnote, Ak 290 (152), G 170, P 155, M 147, B 132)

The leading idea is that all human beings obtain empirical knowledge in exactly the same fundamental way, namely, through judgments of the "*S is P*" form that express the application of concepts to individual things. In Kant's terminology, all human beings obtain empirical knowledge through an interrelationship between the understanding and the imagination. When someone's cognitive capacities are working in their basic way, there is a fundamental attunement, or proportion, between the understanding and imagination that we can suppose is the same in everyone, since everyone's elementary structure of cognition is knowable *a priori* in reference to the operation of the categories of the understanding and the forms of space and time in relation to some given empirical content that they organize.

Kant believes that as a consequence of this common cognitive structure, we have a capacity for judging objects in a way that highlights, or has as its ideal, a fundamental attunement between imagination and understanding that is necessary for comprehending things in each and every case. He refers to this here as a common sense or *sensus communis*. It is a capacity we can suppose in everyone, since we are all cognitively constituted in the same way. We can all therefore judge an object using this *sensus communis*, and reflect upon on object solely in reference to its capacity to stimulate an ideal harmony of the cognitive faculties. To apply this faculty, Kant states that we should consider the object by leaving out everything related to sensory gratification and conceptual content and attend simply to how the object affects the formal qualities of one's cognitive state. This is only to say that, as here characterized (i.e., more generically, in contrast to §§20 – 22[13]), the *sensus communis* is coordinated with the disinterested attitude that we would adopt when making a judgment of pure beauty. Central to the deduction, then, is the presupposition that we are all cognitively constituted in an identical way.

The Phenomenology of Cognition in General

In the above excerpts from Kant's deduction of judgments of pure beauty, it is stated that the satisfaction in pure beauty rests on the subjective conditions of the possibility of cognition in general. What Kant means here by "subjective" is simply those conditions that are understandable *a priori*, in abstraction from any given object of experience. This sense of the term "subjective" does not refer to feelings that are experienced, but refers to structures, principles, concepts, faculties, and the like. As applied to structures, principles, and so on, that are known *a priori*, "subjective" means having to do with the mind's operation independently of experience, purely theoretically and not experientially or phenomenologically.

The crucial issue of Kant's deduction, however, does not involve this sense of the term "subjective," but a different sense of the word. This is a phenomenological sense of the word that refers to experiences of one sort or another. One could say, for example, that objectively my hand is on the table for others to see, and that subjectively, I can feel the inside of my hand, and that no one else feels this. In this example, what is subjective is an experiential correlate to an objective situation, structure or object.

There is a sense in which the structures of the human mind – the understanding, the imagination, judgment, and so on – are all objective in that everyone has these structures and that they can be referred to without referring at all to the feelings anyone happens to experience. Indeed, since these structures define the universal and necessary conditions for human experience, they have to be describable in detached, impersonal, and neutral terms.

The deduction of judgments of pure beauty can therefore be formulated in a more perspicuous way that reveals the depth of the problem at hand. Specifically, the deduction involves hypothesizing that *the quality of the subjective experiences associated with the operation of the objectively-describable cognitive structures that everyone shares, matches the universality and necessity of the cognitive structures themselves*. It is one thing to argue theoretically that human empirical knowledge is constituted in a certain abstract and logical way, viz., as the fusion of concept and individual (i.e., the fusion of concept and "intuition" or what Kant calls an "*Anschauung*"), or as the fusion of understanding and imagination, and quite another to postulate, firstly, that there are human experiences that correspond to these necessary structures and, secondly, that the corresponding human experiences are the same in everyone, simply because the structures are the same.

This hypothesis is akin to asserting that if, at some moment, the brain states and bodies of two people are atom-for-atom identical (i.e., aside from their location, are indiscernibly identical from a physical standpoint), then the two people must be thinking exactly the same thoughts. Framed in this manner, the problem is straightforwardly philosophical and not obviously soluble.

Much debate surrounds this type of issue and it is fair to say that the answer is inconclusive, when stated in the above terms. What can be asserted with more confidence, though, is that Kant's deduction of judgments of pure beauty is grounded on the assumption that the *phenomenology of cognition* (i.e., the supposedly universal feelings involved in the operations of cognition) in general matches, or can in principle match, the *theoretical structures of cognition* (viz., the harmony of understanding and imagination). Only if this correspondence is possible – and it is difficult to prove that it is impossible – can one develop a theory of judgments of pure beauty along the lines that Kant describes.

This leaves us in the following situation with respect to the guarantee that judgments of pure beauty carry with them a necessity. Kant cannot hold that the necessity of judgments of pure beauty is guaranteed because he can prove that the universal harmony of the cognitive faculties is matched with a universal feeling that phenomenologically or subjectively corresponds to that objective harmony.

It can only be said that since cognition is structured in the same way for each person, then it is not contradictory, and is even quite reasonable, to assume that people feel this structure's operations in the same way. Since the presence of such feeling is neither provable nor disprovable, its philosophical reality is closer to a matter of faith than it is a fact. But it can nonetheless serve as – as Kant states – an ideal norm to which we can refer our attempts to make judgments of pure beauty, not to mention our art-critical and nature-critical aesthetic discussions. What we have, then, is a theory whose foundations cannot be disproven and which suggests fairly plausibly that if the objective conditions are identical in two objects, then the subjective conditions, if any, will also be the same.

It is interesting to reflect that the reason why we so easily accept aesthetic disagreement in matters of food is exactly because we acknowledge that the structures of people's taste buds can differ. If, in any particular case, we knew that the sensory and brain structures were exactly the same between two people, the presence of disagreement would make far less sense. Kant believes that the same would follow in the case of identical cognitive structures. If the cognitive structures are identical in any given situation, and if a judgment were based exclusively upon that identity, then disagreement would be unlikely.

Finally, from a less basic philosophical level and speaking more from within the contours of Kant's own theory, the deduction of a universal feeling associated with the harmony of the cognitive faculties can be understood as a generic form of a more specific satisfaction associated with ordinary cognitive judgments. These judgments are either determining or reflective, and they amount either to fitting an object to a concept or fitting a concept to an object. If there is a satisfaction in, for example, starting with the concept "rose" and then finding some flower in the garden that fits the concept, or in starting with some apprehension of a flower and then ascertaining that the flower is a rose (or any such example), then there is a basic satisfaction in making individual cognitive judgments.

One can expand upon this by supposing that if there is a satisfaction in making any and every individual cognitive judgment, and if there are consequently no exceptions to the process, it is reasonable to expect an associated satisfaction related to "cognition in general," viz., a satisfaction in the operation of the general mental operations that structurally match this process of making any cognitive judgment. This would be, namely, the fitting (or attunement, or harmonious accord) of the understanding with the imagination or vice-versa. Along such lines, one can hypothesize a satisfaction in the harmony of the cognitive faculties that expresses the idea of a fit or attunement between concepts and intuitions in general.

2

THE SUBLIME AND THE
INFINITE (§§23–29)

SUBLIMITY IS SUBORDINATE TO BEAUTY

[§23: Second Book. Analytic of the Sublime. "Transition from the capacity for judging the beautiful to that for judging the sublime"] Kant initiates his discussion of the sublime with a revision in terminology that characterizes judgments of sublimity and beauty in reference to a more generalized taxonomy of judgments. There are different ways to formulate this taxonomy, but the most consistent array locates the distinction between cognitive judgment and aesthetic judgment at the taxonomy's most generic level.[1] Cognitive judgment can be either determining or reflecting, and aesthetic judgment can be either sensory or reflecting. Aesthetic judgments of reflection include judgments of pure beauty and judgments of the sublime. The arrangement is as follows:

I.   Cognitive Judgment (based on conceptual application)
    A. Determining Cognitive Judgment
    B. Reflecting Cognitive Judgment
II. Aesthetic Judgment (based on feeling)
    A. Sensory Aesthetic Judgment

B. Reflecting Aesthetic Judgment
  1. Judgments of Pure Beauty
  2. Judgments of Sublimity

All judgments related to cognition are based on the elementary fusion of concepts with individuals (i.e., they follow the elementary form, "*S is P*"), and the difference between determining and reflecting judgment depends, as noted in the previous chapter, simply on whether we begin with a concept and find some object that fits the concept, or whether we begin with some object and find some concept that fits the object. To begin with a concept and then to find an appropriate object is to make a determining cognitive judgment; to begin with an object and then to find an appropriate concept is to make a reflecting cognitive judgment. In the former case, we determine an object's quality through the application of the concept; in the latter case we reflect upon an object's presentation and apply a concept in view of that presentation.

Judgments of pure beauty and judgments of the sublime are a species of reflecting aesthetic judgment, for in both cases we are presented with an object, and follow this presentation with some conceptual activity that is appropriate to the object. These judgments are singular and they claim universal validity. They are not reflecting *cognitive* judgments, however, for the reflection on a given object does not issue in the application of a determinate concept to the object to produce empirical knowledge. Reflecting cognitive judgments and reflecting aesthetic judgments are consequently important to distinguish, since beauty and sublimity concern only the latter.

The conceptual activity involved in reflecting aesthetic judgments is a higher-order activity, for we do not complete the judgment by applying some concept to a given object, but associate the object, via the imagination, with entire faculties of concepts, viz., either with the understanding (the storehouse of determinate concepts) or with reason (the storehouse of indeterminate concepts). In the case of pure beauty, we refer a given object to a harmony between the imagination (through which the object is presented to begin with) and the understanding; in the case of the sublime, as we shall now see, a given object stimulates a tension between the imagination and reason, which is the storehouse of rational ideas such as those of morality, God, freedom, the world, and the immortal soul.

To characterize the sublime, Kant employs the style of analysis he used in the analysis of beauty, since the sorts of judgment related to each are the same insofar as they are aesthetic reflecting judgments. As we know, Kant referred to three main divisions of the mind in his analysis of beauty – understanding, imagination, and reason – having analyzed the satisfaction that grounds judgments of pure beauty in reference to a feeling of harmony between the cognitive faculties of imagination and understanding. He also drew some relationships between beauty and reason in the context of the ideal of beauty. Kant develops similar sorts of relationships between imagination, understanding, and reason within the context of sublimity.

Given the nature of sublime feelings – which we will explore presently – Kant will claim that whereas the faculties of imagination, understanding, and reason operate consistently with one another in the experience of beauty (both free and adherent), the imagination *conflicts* with both understanding and reason in the experience of sublimity. The experience of the sublime will provide some satisfaction, but this will be accompanied by displeasure.

Kant's account of the sublime continues by outlining differences between the beautiful and the sublime in connection with the idea of purposiveness, which we have seen play a major role in the apprehension of beauty. In one type of sublimity, for instance, we are presented with extremely powerful objects that are sometimes disorganized, wild, and unruly. These defy comprehension, and they do not display a purposive form that strongly suggests that some plan or intelligent design is at their basis. They consequently do not lead us to wonder whether nature has an underlying plan or design, and they frustrate the quest for intelligence and moral meaning within nature itself.

Kant consequently subordinates sublimity to beauty with respect to his more fundamental philosophical theme of ascertaining whether there is any suggestion in nature itself, that our moral demands can have an effective influence on the external world:

> For the beautiful in nature we must seek a ground outside of ourselves, but for the sublime merely one in ourselves and in the mode

of thinking that introduces sublimity into the representation of nature; a very necessary preliminary remark, which completely separates the idea of the sublime from that of a purposiveness of *nature*, and makes of the theory of the sublime a mere addendum [*einen bloßen Anhang*] to the aesthetic judging of the purposiveness of nature, because this means no particular form is represented in nature, but there is developed only a purposive use that the imagination makes of its representation.

(§23, Ak 246 (78), G 130, P 100, M 93, B 84–85)

Kant does not say that the theory of sublimity is an addendum to the theory of beauty *per se*; he states that the theory of sublimity is an addendum to the judging of the purposiveness of nature. This reveals how his interest in writing the *Critique of the Power of Judgment* is not only to explain what beauty is, but to complete a broader project of analyzing judgments that are directed towards ascertaining the purposiveness of nature. Underlying the *Critique of the Power of Judgment* as a whole are questions of human meaning, God's existence, and matters concerning the confidence we can reasonably have in the establishment of a moral reality on earth (i.e., in space and time). Related to these questions is the issue of how much resistance nature presents to the actualization of moral demands, given that from the scientific standpoint nature is understandable as a merely mechanical entity with no moral content at all. In his analysis of the sublime, Kant will associate a moral content with the feeling of the sublime (which is nonetheless different from a moral feeling), but mostly absent from the account will be reflections on how the empirical world itself embodies moral contents. To this extent, the analysis of the sublime applies to Kant's deeper practical goal of rendering the world a more moral place by attending mainly to the reinforcement of moral awareness within the individual.

The upshot of these reflections is to conceive of the sublime as a feeling that, unlike the satisfaction in pure beauty, does not issue in a universalistic projection of a quality called "sublimity" upon an object akin to how we ascribe a size, shape or weight to the object. Very large or very powerful objects stimulate certain feelings in us, and Kant refers to these feelings themselves as sublime. An objective link to the external world, similar to the projection of necessary intersubjective agreement that arises in judgments of pure beauty, is mostly absent, for the feeling of the sublime is not based on a satisfaction related to cognition in general and accordingly, the universality of judgments of the sublime is not grounded in the nature of cognition. If anything, objects that cause feelings of the sublime frustrate the drive towards comprehension. Kant explains:

> But one sees from this immediately, that we express ourselves completely incorrectly if we call some or other *object of nature* sublime, although we can quite rightly call very many of them beautiful; for how can we designate with an expression of approval, that which is apprehended as being in itself counter-purposive [*zweckwidrig*]? We can say no more than that the object is fit for the presentation of a sublimity that can be found in the mind; for what is actually sublime cannot be contained in any sensible form, but concerns only ideas of reason. These, though no presentation adequate to them is possible, are provoked and called to mind precisely by this inadequacy, which does allow of sensible presentation. Thus the wide ocean, enraged by storms, cannot be called sublime. Its visage is horrible; and one must already have filled the mind with all sorts of ideas if by means of such an intuition it is to be put in the mood for a feeling which is itself sublime, in that the mind is incited to abandon sensibility and to occupy itself with ideas that contain a higher purposiveness.
>
> (§23, Ak 245 (76), G 129, P 99, M 91–92, B 83–84)

This lengthy excerpt captures the essence of Kant's theory of the sublime, and we can see at the outset how he continues to discern purposiveness in whatever phenomena he is addressing. In the case of the sublime, however, he finds this purposiveness only within the mind itself in relation to its moral ideas, rather than outside of it in the spatio-temporal configurations of objects in the external world. Indeed, he adds that experiences of the sublime have the effect of turning a person inward and away from the external world, since the latter is experienced as inadequate for expressing the infinity-related contents of the sublime with any completeness.

[§24: "**Concerning the division of an investigation of the feeling of the sublime**"] Kant officially organizes his investigation of the sublime in terms of the same four logical moments that structure his analysis of pure beauty. In the following excerpt, he elegantly summarizes the results of his analysis of beauty, which he now aims to reiterate in connection with the sublime:

> For the satisfaction in the sublime, just like that in the beautiful, as a judgment of the aesthetic reflecting power of judgment, must be represented as universally valid according to its *quantity*, as without interest according to its *quality*, as subjective purposiveness according to its *relation*, and as a necessary subjective purposiveness according to its *modality*. Thus the method will not depart from that in the preceding section . . .
>
> (§24, Ak 247 (79), G 130–31, P 100, M 93, B 85)

If we recall the first lines of the *Critique of the Power of Judgment*, we will remember that Kant referred to the alternative ways a given representation can be interpreted. There were either objectively in reference to the knowledge it represents, or subjectively in reference to the pleasure or displeasure it stimulates. In his theory of beauty he extended this mode of analysis, outlining various ways in which a given representation can be held up for aesthetic contemplation in view of the purposiveness of its form, either in reference to powers of cognition in general (in which case the universal satisfaction in a judgment of pure beauty may result), or in reference to the powers of reason (in which case we regard the representation aesthetically in light of its moral content).

In the theory of the sublime, the basic situation is the same. The difference is that the sort of objects that stimulate sublime feelings do not exhibit any purposiveness of form, and as a result, the subjective effects of holding up such a non-purposive representation, respectively, to the faculties of understanding and reason yield different types of feeling. They also yield different types of the sublime, namely, the mathematically (*mathematisch*) sublime that arises when the non-purposive representation is held up to the faculty of understanding, and the dynamically (*dynamisch*) sublime that arises when the non-purposive representation is held up to the faculty of reason. The former leads to a feeling of respect; the latter, to a feeling of freedom. The type of non-purposiveness that the object exhibits is different in each case, and depending upon the type of non-purposiveness, either the understanding or reason plays the leading role in the experience of the sublime. The mathematical sublime concerns objects of extremely large numerical magnitude that defy our understanding; the dynamically sublime concerns objects of overwhelming power that underscore the fragility of our physical existence.

THE INFINITE MAGNITUDE OF THE MATHEMATICALLY SUBLIME

[§25: "Nominal explanation of the sublime"] Kant offers three definitions of the mathematical sublime which he considers to be interchangeable with each other:

1. "We call that *sublime* which is absolutely large." (§25, Ak 248 (80), G 131, P 103, M 94, B 86)
2. *"The sublime is that in comparison to which everything else is small."* (§25, Ak 250 (84), G 134, P 105, M 97, B 88)
3. "The sublime is that, which in the very ability to think of it, demonstrates a mental capacity that surpasses every measure of the senses." (§25, Ak 250 (85), G 134, P 106, M 98, B 89)

The third of these has the most import, and it is based on the first definition, which contains an implicit contrast between that which is large and that which is absolutely large. To illuminate this distinction, Kant begins with some reflections on ordinary statements that refer to the sizes of things, since size is the relevant feature of mathematically sublime objects. The statement "that is big" suggests that, at least relative to the sort of thing in question, there is nothing bigger. If we reflect further, though, in appreciation that we are considering some physical thing, it becomes evident that such a judgment can only be comparative, since for any given large thing relative to its kind, there is always some other kind of thing that is even larger.

Any small thing can appear to be large when it is set against even smaller things; any large thing can appear to be small when it is set against even larger things. The earth is small in comparison to our galaxy, and the earth is large in comparison to a tree growing on its surface. Every ascription of the term "large" to a finite object can only be a conditional ascription, since no finite object can be absolutely large or absolutely great in size. Since every object of the senses that we can concretely imagine is finite, no such object of the senses can be absolutely large, and there are consequently no such objects of the senses that fit the definition of the sublime. Kant curiously never discusses the infinite size of space itself in this respect, which in the *Critique of Pure Reason* (A25 / B40) he states is represented by us as an infinite magnitude.

From this Kant concludes that the very thought of the sublime directs our attention *away* from the world of sensory experience towards purely conceptual entities that can more adequately represent infinite totalities. He adds that very large sensory objects nonetheless stimulate our imagination to expand in the direction of the infinite, and that this imaginative expansion produces an aesthetic satisfaction. At some point during the expansion, there is nonetheless a frustrating moment when one's imaginative powers become exhausted (i.e., as in trying impossibly to complete an infinite sequence of numbers, 1, 2, 3, 4, . . .). This frustration is accompanied by the realization that objects of this kind *can* be comprehended, not by adding unit to unit, but from the rational standpoint of summing the sequence in a more idealizing way (i.e., as when we put set brackets around the numerical sequence to represent the closure of a set such as (5, 10, 15, 20, 25, . . .)).

[§26: "Concerning the estimation of the magnitude of natural things that is required for the idea of the sublime"] In principle, every finitely-sized object in our experience can be comprehended within the field of perception, simply because the object is finite and a standpoint from which we could take in the object in a single survey is at least conceivable. In this abstract respect, no finitely-sized object would be expected to stimulate feelings of the sublime. There are many occasions, of course, when we are not in an optimal perceptual situation to be able to comprehend some given finitely-sized object, and feelings of the sublime can be stimulated by finite objects under such conditions. The experience of the Great Wall of China would be an example, which is possible to experience only in small segments of its close-to-incomprehensible length, when one is situated on the ground. The experience of the earth's sphere is yet another example, which is comprehensible as a whole only from a distant standpoint in outer space.

Kant's analysis of the mathematical sublime focuses on the experiences of extremely large objects – objects that, although not infinitely large themselves, nonetheless suggest the idea of infinity – and he reveals some surprising psychological dynamics that arise in the course of our attempts to comprehend such objects. As the benchmark for the analysis of all objects that stimulate the feeling of the mathematical sublime (e.g., the expansive ocean, the starry sky, an apparently endless desert, etc.), Kant focuses on the mental processes involved when attempting to comprehend an object that is so large that it exhausts our imagination.

In such situations, he notices two main dynamics. The first has been mentioned above, where no matter how we try to measure the size of an inexhaustibly extensive object, the units eventually diminish in magnitude such as to become useless. For example, we could start measuring a line extending out into space in miles, then progress quickly to light-years, but then imagine the universe as being so large, that even the measure of light-years reduces to the significance of centimeters as a way to measure a field as large as we can possibly imagine. In due time, we reach a steady-state condition where no matter how large we make our finite units, they end up being reduced to useless infinitesimals. The effort to measure what is inexhaustibly large eventually puts us on a treadmill, where we end up standing conceptually still.

The second sort of dynamic is more experientially relevant and is grounded in the phenomenology of perception. Kant states that when surveying items of an extremely large size, we reach a point in our imagination where we can retain only so much, and what we add on in our imagination at one end to further comprehend the object is lost at the other. An example would be trying to take in a large city in a single perceptual sweep as one walks quickly through the city. After awhile, one gains as much as one loses. The same would be the case in trying to comprehend the Egyptian Pyramids if one were standing too close to them. Such cases express a kind of steady-state, treadmill-like condition where progress in comprehension comes to a standstill. One walks or visually surveys, but one does not go anywhere in terms of increasing one's comprehension.

These steady-state mental processes associated with the imaginative efforts to comprehend an extremely large object signify to Kant that the imagination is simply not equipped to comprehend physical objects that suggest the concept of infinity. We try to absorb the entire object, and soon have a sense that either we could continue forever with our effort, or that our effort is simply making no progress. He writes:

> Nature is thus sublime in those of its appearances, whose intuition brings with them the idea of their infinity. Now the latter cannot happen, otherwise than through the inadequacy of the greatest effort of our imagination in the estimation of an object's magnitude.
>
> (§26, Ak 255 (93), G 138, P 112, M 103, B 94)

We thus have an expansion of the imagination in the presence of an extremely large object. The expansion is initially pleasurable, but it continues only to a point when one realizes that the object cannot be comprehended in the sense of its being grasped all at once. One's imagination is at that point frustrated, but in this experience of frustration, the very awareness of the totality for which we strive reveals the activity of a different mental faculty – the faculty of *reason*, which is the seat of morality – whose very role is to comprehend infinite totalities. The totalities that reason comprehends, however, are only ideals that no experience can instantiate. They nonetheless importantly represent an aspect of our nature that is supersensible and free of mechanical determination. The experience of the sublime thus draws our attention to what lies supersensibly, and in this case introspectively, beyond nature.[2]

Judgments of pure beauty, as we know, are made in reference to the purposive form of an object and stimulate a harmony between the imagination and the understanding. In contrast, judgments of pure mathematical sublimity are made in reference to the immense and non-purposive size of an object. This size initially stimulates an expansion of the imagination, but it also eventually brings one's imagination to a frustrating treadmill-like activity that fails to comprehend the object fully. This frustration, however, is answered by the presence of reason and its capacity to comprehend infinite totalities. The purposiveness, or intelligible directedness, in this experience does not therefore reside in qualities of the extremely large object itself, but in how the large object stimulates one's imagination to advance towards infinity. Kant concludes:

> Thus, just as the aesthetic power of judgment in judging the beautiful relates the power of the imagination in its free play to the *understanding*, in order to agree with the understanding's *concepts* in general (without determination of them), so is the power of the imagination related to *reason* in judging a thing to be sublime, in order to correspond subjectively with its *ideas* (to which ones remains indeterminate), i.e., to produce an attunement of the mind that is in conformity with them and compatible with that which the influence of determinate (practical) ideas would produce on feeling.
>
> (§26, Ak 256 (94), G 139, P 112–13, M 104, B 94–95)

[§27: "Concerning the quality of the feeling of approval in the judging of the sublime"] Let us now consider the above-mentioned attunement of mind that is associated with the mathematical sublime in more detail. One of Kant's interests in attending to the nature of sublimity is in setting forth the relationship between moral consciousness and the experience of sublime feelings. He states that a feeling of respect emerges when we find ourselves in a position where, as a matter of fact, we cannot attain a level of comprehension or realization that we feel that we ought to be able to attain, but can nonetheless apprehend that the condition can be realized in principle. We consequently have a feeling of respect towards the realization of that ideal condition. For instance, we might feel that we could become more accomplished than we presently are at this or that activity, and consequently have a feeling of respect towards someone who seems to have attained, or who has come much closer to, the ideal condition for which we aim.

The unique feature of the experience of sublimity is that these two conditions reside within ourselves: one part of us cannot realize what we ought to, and yet another part of us can. One aspect of ourselves consequently ends up having a feeling of respect towards the other. Specifically, our sensory, finite, bodily aspect ends up having a feeling of respect towards our purely rational aspect. This feeling of self-respect is the overall effect of the experience of the sublime. It is analogous to, although it is not identical with, our feeling of self-respect that arises in the context of moral awareness.

In the experience of the mathematical sublime, an overwhelmingly large object challenges our imaginative effort to comprehend it completely, and this imaginative effort eventually fails when it arrives at the treadmill-effect described above. Reason, however, enters into the activity and completes the comprehension of (what amounts to, for all practical purposes) the infinite. It does this only by stepping into the non-sensory, purely rational realm where infinite totalities can indeed be comprehended. The idea of humanity that resides in the purely rational realm is thereby in a position to be associated with the experience. The overwhelmingly large objects that cause the imagination to reach for the infinite and that indirectly produce an awareness of our purely rational aspect become themselves the objects of admiration insofar as they have this capacity to induce moral awareness, but ultimately Kant states that the feeling of the sublime in nature is not about the large objects themselves, but is about a feeling of respect for our own rational vocation.

It should be added that when we project a feeling of respect towards the overwhelming objects, this does lead us to regard them as being analogous to persons. This lends a more anthropomorphic guise to nature, despite the comprehension-defying qualities that overwhelming objects possess. The experience of the sublime thus has the indirect effect of projecting a human-friendly intelligence into nature, even in its most overwhelming and incomprehensible aspects. As we shall see in later sections, Kant believes that such an underlying intelligence needs to be assumed if our moral obligations are to be met, so in this small respect the experience of the sublime assists in Kant's project of coordinating nature and morality.

THE OVERWHELMING POWER OF THE DYNAMICALLY SUBLIME

[§28: "Concerning nature as a power"; §29 "Concerning the modality of the judgment on the sublime in nature"] It is tempting to assume that in the feelings of the mathematically sublime and the dynamically sublime the content is essentially the same, but there is a significant difference between the two. Both feelings do involve initial displeasures that issue in a higher level of awareness, but the kinds of displeasures are different in each type of the sublime: feelings of the mathematically sublime involve a frustration of the imagination in an effort to comprehend an object, but no element of fear; feelings of the dynamically sublime are grounded upon an initial fear of a threatening object. The dynamically sublime thus fits more closely with Edmund Burke's 1757 characterization of the sublime, described famously in his *A Philosophical Inquiry Into Our Ideas of the Sublime and Beautiful* (Part IV, §7) as a "tranquillity tinged with terror." Kant himself states the following:

> . . . nature is judged as sublime in our aesthetic judgment, not insofar as it arouses fear, but rather because it calls forth our power (which is not nature) to regard those things about which we are concerned (goods, health and life) as minor, and hence to regard its power (to which we are certainly subjected in regard to these things) as not the sort of dominion over ourselves and our authority to which we would have to bow, if it came down to our highest principles and their affirmation or abandonment.
>
> (§28, Ak 262 (105), G 145, P 121, M 111, B 101)

In the experience of the dynamically sublime, a powerful physical object or phenomenon – bold cliffs, towering storm clouds, lightning and thunder, volcanoes, hurricanes, a raging ocean, a lofty waterfall – is acknowledged as being seriously fearsome, even though when we contemplate the object we might not happen to be fearing it at the time. Kant maintains that, in the face of such threatening phenomena, we can consider them disinterestedly and thereby realize that there is a component to ourselves that remains immune from their physical threat. Upon such a realization, we apprehend with some satisfaction that even the overpowering forces of nature can do nothing to undermine our rational principles, since those principles are of an altogether different, nonphysical order. An effect of this is to enhance one's inner strength of character. There is a certain character-building effect associated with having experiences of the dynamically sublime, and a moral benefit to putting ourselves in some physical danger, as long as we can maintain a disinterested state of mind.

To recall, in feelings of the mathematical sublime, every possible unit of measure, however relatively large it might be as a finite unit, is transformed into an infinitesimal magnitude once it becomes compared to what is absolutely large. Light years quickly shrink into centimeters as we enlarge the scope of our conception of the physical universe's size. In feelings of the dynamically sublime the mental process is comparable, except that what diminishes into an infinitesimal quantity is, more profoundly, the meaning of all worldly interests that depend on our physical constitution. The meaning of happiness, as Kant defines it as the satisfaction of worldly desires, is made small in the face of reason and made utterly insignificant when it stands alone. Feelings of both the mathematically and dynamically sublime consequently stimulate an awareness of a supersensible and privileged aspect of our being in comparison to our perishable fleshly condition. Both bring reason and, hence, moral reality into view.

Kant gives a list of physical phenomena that stimulate feelings of the dynamically sublime (e.g., bold cliffs, etc., as mentioned above) and although natural objects and phenomena are usually recited as the paradigm examples of the sublime, Kant soon gravitates into a discussion of the sublime human character to give his discussion a deeper moral import. His example is worth quoting:

> For what is it, that even to the uncivilized person is an object of the greatest admiration? It is someone who is not frightened, who has no fear, and thus does not shrink before danger but energetically goes to work with complete deliberation. And even in the most civilized circumstances this exceptionally high esteem for the warrior remains, only now one demands additionally that he also show all the virtues of peace, gentleness, empathy and even proper care for his own person, exactly because the incorruptibility of his mind by danger is recognizable in this manner.
>
> (§28, Ak 262 (106), G 146, P 121, M 112, B 102)

Kant celebrates the incorruptibility of character as an expression of the sublime, and in league with his outstanding warrior who has a moral conscience, we can add those religious, scientific, nationalistic, and community-minded people of all types who die for their convictions and face their executions without fear, or who even willingly sacrifice themselves fearlessly for their convictions. Within Kant's view, it is essential to emphasize that such convictions need to be universal, necessary, and rationally-grounded, but the quality of sublime character to which he refers is recognizable in many different contexts. In Kant's view, a sublime character is someone who regards no physical obstacle as unconditionally standing in the way of the realization of moral principles. A society of sublime characters would therefore go a long way towards realizing such principles in their community, as opposed to groups of weaker-willed people who are more easily intimidated by danger or whose behavior is dominated by sensory gratification.

Kant believes that the feelings of the dynamically sublime are in principle universally-grounded, since they are based on the supposition that every human being has the same moral constitution. He is less confident, though, that there will be as much actual agreement in judgments of the dynamically sublime as there is agreement in judgments of pure beauty. His own view is that a more extensive cultural background is necessary for experiencing feelings of the dynamically sublime, and he gives the example of a Savoyard peasant who simply believes that mountain climbers are fools who risk their lives needlessly. Kant explains such differences in attitude as a matter of cultural refinement, but one can wonder whether the differences reside more directly in whether or not a person is more easily overcome by fear and is more or less interested in self-preservation. Presumably, there have been many naturally-courageous people who were uncultured and who were also naturally reflective with an upright moral sensibility, and who it could be supposed reasonably had experienced feelings of the dynamically sublime as well.

["General Remark"] Kant concludes his account of the sublime with a few clusters of comments on various themes, some of which reiterate earlier discussions. One of the non-repetitive discussions continues a brief treatment of religious themes from the preceding

§28. In that preceding section, Kant noted that some of the more superstitious religious attitudes towards God regard divine power as being not much different from a threatening natural force – a force whose actions are unpredictable and that can strike a person down at any moment. Here, the typical religious attitudes involve not exactly respect, but a "submission, dejection, and a feeling of complete powerlessness that is the appropriate disposition of the mind to the appearance of such an object." Kant believes that this is a morally insensitive and primitive conception of God, since it overlooks how human beings themselves have a moral nature and how this moral nature is *itself* akin to the divine. He thus uses his theory of the dynamically sublime to distinguish between highly superstitious religions and more enlightened ones.

In his concluding general remark Kant continues this theme, mentioning how Judaism and Mohammedanism are well situated in the sphere of enlightened religions:

> Perhaps there is no more sublime place in the Jewish law than the commandment: you should make neither any image, nor any likeness of that which is either in heaven, or on the earth, or yet under the earth, etc. This commandment alone can explain the enthusiasm that the Jewish people during its civilized epoch, felt for its religion when it compared itself with other peoples, or the pride that Mohammedanism inspired. The very same thing also holds of the representation of the moral law and the tendency to morality in us.
>
> (General Remark, Ak 274 (124–25), G 156, P 135, M 127, B 115)

Kant's theory of the sublime has an undercurrent of religious content, and in this context we can observe two further associations to traditional arguments for God's existence. The first of these is how Kant's definition of the mathematically sublime as "that which is absolutely large" resonates with the more abstract and generalized definition of God that initiates the traditional ontological argument for God's existence, namely, "God is a being than which no greater can be conceived." In both cases we have, as Kant would state, an idea of reason that represents an absolute standard against which everything else is rendered finite.

The association between that which is absolutely large and "that than which no greater can be conceived" might at first be regarded as somewhat attenuated, because quantitative magnitude and the concept of God are not synonymous. Kant, however, moves swiftly from his analysis of the rational idea of the absolutely large, to a reference to the realm of rational ideas in general, and introduces moral content into the experience of the mathematical sublime via the conception of the respect we have for anything that represents an ideal for us. Given his remark in §28 that aligns morality with God in connection with the dynamically sublime, the connection between God and the sublime is evident. He states:

> . . . the right frame of mind to admire the greatness of God, for which one requires a mind-set of calm contemplation and a completely free judgment. Only if he is conscious of his upright, God-pleasing disposition do those effects of power serve to awaken in him the idea of the sublimity of God's being, insofar as he recognizes in himself a sublimity of disposition suitable to God's will, and is thereby raised above the fear of such effects of nature, which he does not regard as outbursts of God's wrath.
>
> (§28, Ak 263–64 (108), G 147, P 122–23, M 113–14, B 103)

Not only does Kant's overall discussion of the sublime reflect the definition of God that initiates the ontological argument for God's existence, the specific experience of the mathematically sublime reflects the thought-process that defines another traditional argument for God's existence, namely, the cosmological argument. As is known to many, this argument begins by observing that contingent things exist at present, and that these contingent things have themselves been generated from other previously-existing contingent things. The argument asserts that this sequence cannot be extended backwards forever, since this only leaves us with an infinite sequence of contingent things that itself remains contingent and without explanation. Hence, we need to postulate some non-contingent, or necessary, being, to explain the presence of the things right now.

This argument structure mirrors how Kant describes the experience of the mathematically sublime: our imagination expands in the direction of infinity, fails to encompass it, and then arrives at a comprehension that is non-imaginative, purely rational, and situated on another conceptual dimension. As noted in the connection to the ontological argument above, the endpoint of the imaginative process brings us to an awareness of a mode of unconditional being akin to the divine.

It could be said that the experience of the mathematical sublime is an aesthetic and phenomenological version of the cosmological argument, with of course the qualification that the God that emerges turns out to reside exclusively in us, rather than in nature.[3] When Kant's theory of sublimity is interpreted in this way, the religious and moral components become more salient and the underlying infinite meaning and unconditional ground of the sublime becomes more clear. Kant maintains that the theory of sublimity is only an appendage to the project of ascertaining purposiveness in nature, and in reference to this project, the contributions of the sublime are limited to projecting a feeling of respect on overwhelmingly large and powerful objects. However, in view of his ultimate view that we need to suppose God's existence to render nature and morality compatible in a genuinely effective way, the avenue towards moral awareness that the experience of sublimity provides does significantly underscore the primary, unconditional moral interests of Kant's outlook.

3

THE FINE ARTS AND CREATIVE GENIUS (§§41–54)

ARTISTIC BEAUTY VS. NATURAL BEAUTY

[§41: "Concerning the empirical interest in the beautiful"] After completing his legitimation (i.e., deduction) of the universality of the feeling that grounds judgments of pure beauty (§§30–40), Kant returns to his general theme of how other sorts of satisfactions can be combined with the disinterested satisfaction peculiar to judgments of pure beauty. We have already seen one instance of such a doubly-grounded combination in judgments of adherent beauty, where the satisfaction in an object's perfection combines with the satisfaction in its pure beauty. Another instance has been when sensory gratification combines with the satisfaction in an object's pure beauty, as when charm and emotion enter into the judgment.

There are further ways to associate other sorts of satisfaction with beauty, and Kant notes that there can be direct (as in the cases above) and indirect ways of introducing such satisfactions into the situation. In the indirect modes, the judgment of pure beauty is presupposed as already having been successfully made without the admixture of either conceptual or sensory satisfaction. An interest is introduced afterwards that associates this satisfaction in pure beauty itself with other kinds of satisfactions, and these latter satisfactions can either be empirically-derived or have *a priori* grounds. The situation is roughly comparable to the difference between drinking pure water mixed with sugar and obtaining a sensory satisfaction from the sweet and clearly refreshing sensation of the complex mixture, as opposed to drinking pure water alone, obtaining a sensory satisfaction from the refreshing and unsweetened water, while also obtaining an added practical satisfaction from having done something useful to maintain one's health.

Among the satisfactions related to empirical interests that can be added to the satisfaction in pure beauty, Kant mentions the natural interest of people to be sociable. This is closely connected to the appreciation of beauty, since our intrinsic (i.e., natural, but not supposedly *a priori*) social awareness inevitably leads us to conceive of our universal capacity to appreciate beauty in relation to communicating our feelings to other people. Kant believes that when people are altogether disengaged from society, as one might be when stranded upon a desert island, the disposition to beautify oneself and one's surroundings would fade.

Kant mentions the above example of the desert island in passing, for his main concern is in identifying how *a priori* interests can be linked with the satisfaction in pure beauty. The objects of our experience typically present us with an amalgamation of *both* sensory (i.e., colors, tastes, textures, etc.) and spatio-temporal qualities, and since in judgments of pure beauty we abstract away from the sensory qualities and the gratification they produce, Kant regards the capacity to appreciate pure beauty as itself an important way to detach ourselves from, and elevate ourselves above, sensory gratification. If, however, in addition to this detachment and elevation, pure beauty can be associated with *a priori* interests – and for Kant these are mainly moral interests – then the capacity to appreciate beauty could serve as an intermediary and transitional point between raw sensory gratification and rational moral awareness.

[§42: "Concerning the intellectual interest in the beautiful"] To understand Kant's discussion of the intellectual interest in beauty.

it is important to recall that judgments of pure beauty altogether disregard the origins of the object whose beauty we are estimating. We estimate only how the object's purposive form makes us feel, and consider it unimportant whether we happen to be contemplating a dream object or an actual object, natural object or a work of art. None of the latter considerations matter in the judgment of pure beauty. Only the quality of the apprehended design matters, and reflection upon where this design in fact happens to originate is not part of the judgment.

At the outset, then, we must distinguish between (1) judging an object's pure beauty in reference to its abstract design alone (i.e., no matter where it came from),[1] (2) judging an object's pure beauty as in (1), but then taking the supplementary step of associating this pure beauty with an additional satisfaction related to the object's origin as a natural object, and (3) judging an object's beauty insofar as we reflect upon its abstract design in view of our recognizing it as a work of art, i.e., as having originated through someone's intentional action. Judging the beauty of an object *as* a work of art, and therefore as having a definite purpose, clearly entails that we form a judgment of adherent beauty that highlights what sort of thing the object is. Judging an object *as* an actual natural object (i.e., believing it to be such) also involves adding an interest to the situation. This marks a difference between aesthetically judging an object as an abstract design *simpliciter*, as opposed to judging it aesthetically as a natural object, i.e., as something that actually has a public existence, but which is not a work of art.

This threefold distinction emerges in recognition of Kant's canonical example of the imaginary palace that illustrates his core conception of disinterestedness in §2. This is an imaginary image, or representation of the imagination, that the mind can produce spontaneously, and which is judged neither as an objective natural product nor as an intentional product of art. Kant introduces the example precisely because he wants to emphasize that it is irrelevant to making a judgment of pure beauty, whether or not an actual object corresponds to the representation that we are reflecting upon.

Kant's numerous references to natural beauty thus need to be disambiguated in reference to whether he is referring simply to a judgment of an object, where the "object" is merely some mental representation considered only as such, or whether he is referring more complexly to a judgment of an object, where the mental representation involved is viewed additionally as having been produced objectively by nature and hence, as referring to an actual natural object. We will refer to "pure beauty" as opposed to "natural beauty" to distinguish the former, simple situation from the latter, complex one. Judgments of natural beauty – and these are of primary moral concern in the Critique of Aesthetic Judgment – are neither judgments of adherent beauty, nor are they examples of paradigmatic and theoretically foundational judgments of pure beauty.

Kant emphasizes the difference between appreciating an object's beauty as a natural object as opposed to appreciating it as a work of art in reference to making character assessments of people who are interested in beautiful things. He reports that within social circles of art connoisseurs, one often encounters vain, obstinate, and spoiled characters. For Kant, this supports the view that having an interest in beautiful works of art does not provide evidence of good moral character (i.e., taking an interest in beautiful art is neutral with respect to the issue of character). In contrast, he maintains that taking an interest in natural beauty and actively wishing to preserve naturally beautiful things is indeed evidence a good moral character. He goes so far as to say that if one has a good moral character, a less intense example of natural beauty will be more satisfying than a more intense example of artistic beauty, thus underscoring how those with good moral characters are more interested in the significance of natural beauty.

The explanation of this difference in attitude resides in the nature of moral interests themselves. If one has a good moral character and tries to do what one unconditionally ought to do, and hopes thereby more generally that everyone will someday do what they morally ought to do, there is an underlying disposition to search in nature for evidence that nature *itself* is supportive of our moral activity. It is therefore a rational interest to search within the field of nature for morally-supportive phenomena.

Beautiful natural objects fit this description insofar as the disinterested attitude required for assessing the morality of an action is analogous to the disinterested attitude required for judging the pure beauty of an object. When making a moral judgment, for instance, we do not consider ourselves privately, but regard ourselves as a person in general, whose maxim of action would be applicable to anyone in the same situation. Moreover, since objects of pure beauty themselves dispose us to adopting a disinterested standpoint in general, they are therefore resonant with moral awareness as well. Kant consequently believes that if one has a good moral character to begin with, then objects of natural beauty will be especially attractive, owing to how their purposive structure resonates with one's own generally disinterested mind-set. Such kinships are the theme of §59, "Beauty as the Symbol of Morality."

Kant maintains that at the foundation of a good moral character, there is an interest in the ultimate purpose of human existence, so in its universal and practical significance the good character's interest in natural beauty surpasses merely localized interests. This is one of the reasons why, in certain respects, Kant subordinates artistic beauty to natural beauty in the *Critique of the Power of Judgment* and why he subordinates the theory of the sublime to the theory of beauty. He is mainly interested in the conditions for successful moral activity, and this motivates him to ask how closely morality, beauty, and sublimity are related. Since moral activity takes place within nature itself, a prime moral concern is thus whether nature gives us any signals of its own compatibility with what our rational nature defines as our ultimate purpose. Kant discovers strong signals in the presence of natural beauty, and somewhat weaker signals in the presence of the natural sublime. With a moral purpose in mind and with a positive attention towards natural beauty, Kant then develops an account of fine art.

[§43: "Concerning art in general"] Kant defines art (*Kunst*) as a type of productive activity that is grounded in rational deliberation. This sense of the term "art" approximates that of the Greek word "*technê*" (τέχνη) which signifies a craft, a type of know-how or skill, or more abstractly, the general idea of making or doing something according to plans with some technical expertise. Kant's use of the term "art" is more generic than what is ordinarily meant by "fine art," but fine art is included within the realm of art as one of the species of art. Just as aesthetic judgment divides into several species, art divides into several species.

In merely generic or ordinary art, Kant maintains that there is a prior plan along with an outcome that realizes the plan, and that this sort of rational activity distinguishes works of art from animal productions such as beehives and the like. With respect to the discussions of fine art in the sections below, this underscores how it will be supposed that some plan, either determinately definable or vague, is at the basis of every work of art, whether it is fine art or any other type of art. Judgments of fine art are thus judgments of adherent beauty, and if one is self-consciously discussing or judging *art*, then rules, plans, concepts, and purposes are constitutive aspects of the subject at hand. It is consequently impossible to make exclusively a judgment of pure beauty that is also a judgment of artistic beauty.

[§44: "Concerning beautiful art"] The generic quality of Kant's use of the term "art" becomes evident when, following his distinctions between determinate cognition, sensory gratification, and pure beauty, he continues to distinguish the various species of art. If one formulates a plan to make an object and then simply realizes the object by following the plan, then this is a mechanical style of art (*mechanische Kunst*). If the plan has the goal of stimulating sensory gratification, then this is an art of enjoyment or is merely pleasurable art (*angenehme Kunst*). If the plan has the goal of disinterested satisfaction, then this is an art of beauty. Kant refers to this as "fine art" or as "beautiful art" (*schöne Kunst*).

In this section we find Kant's well-known remark that there is no science of beauty. As discussed above, he maintains that the feeling of pure beauty arises without any need to know what sort of object we are aesthetically judging. Consequently, concepts of such kinds cannot be used to prove that an object is beautiful. Moreover, since we reflect only upon the rational quality of a representation's abstract design in making a pure judgment of beauty, and since the judgment is aesthetic (i.e., it is based only on feeling), then logical proofs are out of place.

[§45: "Beautiful art is an art, insofar as it appears to be nature at the same time"] Before describing the contents of §45, we can note briefly the following as a preliminary consideration. Since an object's pure beauty is due to its purposive form, then every beautiful thing is beautiful because it suggests the presence of a designer of the purposive form, whether or not there happens to be, or happens to have been, an actual designer. To appreciate an object's pure beauty, we also need either to remain ignorant of, or disregard, the exact plan that the hypothetical designer had in mind, since the purposive form needs to be apprehended independently of any particular purpose.

In the case of an object that we *know* was designed (i.e., a work of art), we must initially disregard this fact to appreciate the object's pure beauty. We need to consider the object's form only with respect to the abstract suggestiveness of the design itself, independently of what we happen to know about its origins. These origins are only subsequently brought into consideration when we judge the work as art.

In contrast, in the case of natural beauty that we recognize as such, we do *not know* that the object was designed. Our reflection upon the object's form only with respect to its abstract suggestiveness of an underlying intelligibility is consequently made that much easier, since there is no concept that we could confidently project upon the form to define its purpose. Since we are abstracting away from all purposes, this situation with natural beauty is similar – although it is not identical – to the case of judging the object in reference to its pure beauty. The difference is that in the case of natural beauty, our knowledge of the object as a natural item additionally satisfies a moral interest, or interest of reason.

The moral interest in natural beauty arises as follows. When appreciating an object's pure beauty, we are led to postulate a designer for the object. In the case of imaginary objects, such a postulated designer could be located outside of ourselves or we ourselves could be the (unconscious) designer. In the case of natural beauty, though, the situation is different. Although the postulation of a designer for the natural object arises exclusively from our reflection on the object's purposive form (i.e., moral considerations are not taken into account), the postulation of such a designer locates that designer clearly outside of ourselves. This presence of natural beauty thereby acknowledges an intelligible force underlying nature's productions. Since the structure of the beautiful object is rational and suggestive of a purpose, and since the foundations of morality (for Kant) reside themselves in pure rationality, then the presence of natural beauty signifies that nature's intrinsic being is compatible with our moral interests.

Now Kant states in §45 that nature is beautiful because it looks like art. This is to say that it looks beautiful because it looks like the product of a designer. This is true for anything that is beautiful. The problem in referring to a work of art as beautiful is that we already know that it is the product of design, so its purposive form comes as no surprise. Since the apprehension of pure beauty involves an appreciation of an object's purposiveness without purpose, rather than a purposiveness with purpose, the appreciation of the beauty of a work of art as such poses a dilemma.

One horn of the dilemma is to apprehend the object's purposive form in complete abstraction from the fact that it was designed. We would then regard the work of art, not as art at all, but as either a natural object or as a pure constellation of forms. The other horn is to apprehend the artwork's purposive form, since we are contemplating a work of art with a design, as exhibiting a purposiveness *with* purpose and fail, consequently, to appreciate the artwork's beauty. With works of art, we seem to gravitate into either judgments of pure beauty or judgments of perfection with no room for appreciating beautiful art as such.

With respect to representational art, Kant's solution to this problem issues from his appreciation of how art can represent the actual things in daily life and yet have an illusory quality. Let us take as an example an artist's painting of a flower that represents the flower faithfully and accurately. Both the painting and the flower, considered in the abstract as pure designs, could both be beautiful and perhaps the same judgment of pure beauty would be given in relation to each configuration. When we judge the flower's beauty, taking into account that it is a natural object, then its pure beauty becomes an object of moral interest, since there is a significant difference between apprehending some form whose origins are left indeterminate, as opposed to apprehending some form that we know arose naturally and outside of the forces of human production.

When Kant states "art can only be called beautiful if we are aware that it is art and yet appears to us like nature," it follows that art can only be called beautiful if it looks like the natural objects that automatically become objects of moral interest on account of their purposive form. Another way to express this is to say that beautiful works of such art *represent* the satisfaction of moral interests. When an artist paints a picture of a beautiful flower or, more interestingly, when an artist paints a picture that has more beautiful flowers in it than would ever occur naturally, the satisfaction of the interests of reason is being artistically represented. By painting natural things as beautiful, it is as if the artist is expressing the hope that the world will conform to moral demands. The beautiful flowers in the painting are only artificial, so they do not actually satisfy the interests of reason. They more abstractly speak to reason itself and reinforce its interest in discovering naturally-occurring beautiful things.

This interpretation arises if we emphasize the meaning of judging an object's beauty as a natural object *per se*, as opposed to judging its beauty as a pure abstract design, independently of any consideration of its origins. In the preceding sections, Kant draws such a distinction, so it makes sense to employ it in his claim that art can be called beautiful only if we are aware of it as art and yet looks to us like nature.

Natural objects appreciated as such, along with presentations that we regard as pure abstract designs, exhibit the same sort of purposiveness without purpose, and Kant's prescription about how to reflect upon artistic beauty further indicates that we must somehow appreciate a work of art's beauty in light of our knowledge that the work was designed. We must also, however, appreciate the work of art in a way that judges its purposive form independently of any definite purposes the work might have.

As noted above, this creates a dilemma on the face of things, and one solution within the context of representational art has been to appreciate the work of art as if one were appreciating a natural object, with the knowledge that one is having this appreciation within an imaginary context. The awareness of the work as art as such would produce the imaginary context, and the appreciation of the work's representational content as nature (but only fictionally so, since the beautiful flower in the painting is only a representation of an actual flower) would undercut the problems in knowing that the work was designed. For instance, if we were reflecting upon an idealized portrait of a person, we would make believe that we were looking at the actual person and appreciate the idealized forms in the portrait as if they were the product of nature, rather than the intentional product of the artist.

A second way to resolve the problem presented by beautiful art – one also found in Kant's texts and which is arguably the leading solution he offers – is to emphasize the distinction in §44 between mechanical art and beautiful art. As we have seen, Kant defines mechanical art as an art involving a plan that is realized straightforwardly in the product and is presumably evident in the product. In mechanical art, we see the product as a purpose and can easily discern the purpose's underlying intent. Beautiful art has the contrasting aim of stimulating a disinterested satisfaction, however, and the only way to do this is to create an object whose form does not immediately suggest a definable purpose and that lends itself to the apprehension of the object's purposiveness without purpose.

In the case of natural beauty, an object presents a form and the purposiveness of the form compels the perceiver to hypothesize an intelligent designer that created the object, while remaining uncertain either of the presence of the designer or, most importantly, of what the purpose (if any) happens to have been. In the case of artistic beauty, the situation is almost identical, except that we know that there was a designer. The beauty of the work of art can therefore only reside in the mystery of what the designer intended. This is to say that the intelligibility that we apprehend in an art work's purposive form must surely reside in some rule, but in a rule that we cannot define or pin down with a set of exact formulas. In this way, the beautiful work of art will present a purposiveness without purpose of an intermediate sort. Kant describes this in the final sentence of §45 by saying that for a work of art to be beautiful, its academic form should not show through, and it should not seem as if the artist had some definite rule in mind that constrained his or her imaginative powers.

KANT'S THEORY OF GENIUS

[§46: "Beautiful art is the art of genius"] Kant asserts that the type of intellectual power that we hypothesize as the teleological cause of natural objects' beauty is akin to that which produces the beauty of art works. In the apprehension of purposiveness without purpose, we reason back to the same type of intellectual force, namely, to one that presents objects whose form has a compelling but indefinable rationality to them. We apprehend beautiful nature "as art," and when Kant considers the actual forces within an artist that produce beautiful works of art, he interprets the artist's productive powers as akin to the intelligibility we ascribe to nature's productive powers when it produces beautiful things. This amounts to a power to produce purposive forms whose intelligibility is mechanically incomprehensible. It is also the power of the artistic genius.

Since artistic beauty depends upon apprehending an artwork's form as purposive but without any determinate purpose, while yet acknowledging the form as the actual product of a human, artistic intelligence, we postulate a rule that underlies the purposive form. The rule, however, cannot be a determinate rule, lest the beautiful art work be reduced to a work of mechanical art. The rule must be an indeterminate one that withstands our attempts to encapsulate it into a set of scientific procedures or formulas. So when Kant defines the artistic genius as "the talent (natural gift) that gives the rule to art," he has in mind the creation of indeterminate rules that cannot be explicitly formulated.

This account of creative genius captures the common opinions that artistic greatness is not a teachable matter, and that the productions of great artists are original exemplars for others to emulate. Since there is no science of beauty, a great artist cannot explicitly explain what inspires the beauty of the art works he or she produces; it is only possible to display the works as examples of artistic greatness to allow others to discern aesthetically the rule that underlies the works. The new, genius-created examples emerge from past tradition, while they break new ground in the way new metaphors do: they make sense within their surrounding language and traditions, but add previously unimagined associations.

The philosophical ingenuity of Kant's theory of artistic genius, however, does not reside in the easy association of genius with the ability to create new metaphors. It resides rather in his pregnant characterization of genius as a natural talent or natural gift. This seems to be a simple matter, but its implications are extensive. Since the genius's talent for producing beautiful works of art is a natural talent, the forces of nature themselves produce the beautiful works of art in the very manifestation of the artistic genius. Kant writes:

> Since the talent, as an inborn productive capacity of the artist, belongs itself to nature, one could also express it as follows: *Genius* is the inborn mental predisposition (*ingenium*) *through which* nature gives the [indeterminate] rule to art.
>
> (§46, Ak 307 (181), G 186, P 174, M 168, B 150)

An implication is that if objects of natural beauty stimulate our speculations that a supernatural intelligence underlies those beautiful products, and if the power of artistic genius is itself the expression of a natural force, then the underlying intelligence of nature that produces beautiful natural objects would also be considered as working through the artistic genius when beautiful works of art are being produced. Natural forces produce beautiful things, and these beautiful things suggest an underlying intelligence behind nature, so it is easy to hypothesize that it is one and the same intelligence that underlies both artistic genius and beautiful natural objects. Kant does not express the position in such bald terms, but his position resonates with the view that great works of art are divinely inspired and that God speaks to us inspirationally through both the artistic genius and through nature.

Now if the same intelligent and creative force underlies both artistic genius and beautiful natural objects, then the very existence of an artistic genius would satisfy the interest of reason or morality, since the latter is an interest in apprehending the presence of beings that suggest that nature is compatible with moral demands. If the artistic genius is itself expressive of the same intelligence that underlies beautiful natural objects, then beautiful artistic productions would satisfy the interests of reason as well, not because they represent the objects of natural beauty, but because these artistic products themselves can be regarded as natural products whose underlying intelligibility suggests the compatibility of nature with moral demands. With respect to the origin of their beauty, snowflakes and beautiful works of art are essentially the same. Moreover, the stronger the artistic genius's moral awareness happens to be – the more the products of artistic genius have a moral content that has been given a beautiful appearance – the stronger the confirmation of nature's compatibility with morality will be, quite beyond the confirmation that snowflakes and tulips offer.

The artificiality of beautiful works of art resides in their determinate plan, but according to Kant's theory of artistic genius, their beauty is a natural occurrence. This suggests that as far as their respective beauties are concerned, as noted, artistic products and natural products are not significantly different from each other, and that the indeterminate rules that each embodies are subject to the same sort of analysis. The result is that Kant's analysis of the genius's production of indeterminate rules will be applicable both to natural beauty and to pure beauty considered in abstraction from the specific origins of the objects at hand. We will see this below in Kant's account of what he will call "aesthetic ideas."

[§47: "Explication and confirmation of the above account of genius"] The emphasis so far has been on the beautiful aspect of beautiful art, but Kant adds that beautiful "art" as such also requires a determinate plan and an academic correctness that provides the technical basis for the art work's beauty. In the absence of such a determinate plan, which would leave only the genius's indeterminate rule, Kant does not conclude that the work of beautiful art would reduce to an object of natural beauty, since it would then be the mere product of natural forces working through the artist, minus the deliberative component (i.e., like a cough). Instead, he refers to the powers of genius in a different way than before, suggesting that the power of genius in the absence of determinate rules yields only confusion:

> Genius can only provide rich *material* for beautiful artistic products; its elaboration and *form* require an academically trained talent, so as

to make use of it in a way that can bear examination by the power of judgment.

(§47, Ak 310 (186), G 189, P 178, M 171–72, B 153)

There is a questionable peculiarity in Kant's above characterization, for it contradicts his earlier description of genius as the talent for prescribing the form or (indeterminate) rule to art. To say that genius can only provide rich *material* for art, and that this intrinsically unorganized material must be tempered by academic technicalities, determinate plans, and the like, ignores how genius itself has the power to prescribe rules. It also ignores how an object's form, not its material, is responsible for its beauty. As Kant himself states, the power of genius prescribes indeterminate rules whose embodiment is beautiful to apprehend. Granted, when there are no determinate rules there indeed can be no use, or purpose, that can be associated with the genius's purposive presentations and the product could not be apprehended as art *per se*. This fact alone, however, only provides the technical basis for the work of art, and does not account for its beauty.

One way to understand the philosophical motivation for Kant's characterization of pure genius as the source of inspired, but essentially disorganized, material is to consider how there are always determinate rules operating in the production of all natural objects, namely, the laws of nature. In the beautiful products of nature we have the determinate natural laws that govern the form of the objects, but have in addition the mysterious quality of the purposive form that, for Kant, defies comprehension in mechanical terms alone. One could call this mysterious quality the "life" or "spirit" of the beautiful natural object.

Products of artistic genius can be considered to have the same basic structure as beautiful natural objects, where the determinate academic rules and plans play a role analogous to the laws of nature. Without the natural laws, there would indeed be not much more than sensory chaos, and in his reflections on the nature of artistic genius, Kant seems to be reasoning similarly in his assertion that genius without academic form would also lead to incoherence.

[§48: "Concerning the relation of genius to taste"] When reflecting upon the difference between taste and genius, Kant draws on the distinction between mechanical and beautiful art, associating taste with the former and genius with the latter. Suppose, for instance, a person were to paint a picture of a flower whose beauty has been copied directly from nature (i.e., a situation comparable to taking a non-artistic snapshot of a beautiful flower). In such a case, the representation's beauty would derive exclusively from the natural beauty of the flower and there would be no artistic inspiration that enhanced the representation. Nonetheless, someone could look at the representation, exercise their taste, and judge that the flower portrayed is beautiful.

With this observation, Kant concludes that taste does not imply genius (i.e., that taste is a merely judging rather than a productive faculty), and that mechanically-produced artifacts can be beautiful, although they will not count as beautiful (i.e., fine) art. Amongst such mechanically-produced works of art Kant includes uninspired poetry, accurate but boring stories, and all "correct" works that fit into the standard descriptive categories of art, but that are lacking in inspiration. For Kant, there is a wide difference between beautiful art and academic or merely "correct" art, and this corresponds to the distinction between taste and genius.

In the case of fine art, the inspiration of genius is necessary and the result will never be mere copies of natural beauties. Artistic genius has the capacity even to beautify objects and subject matters that are often aesthetically and morally repulsive, such as the devastations of war. Hence Kant refers to the beauty of art as "a beautiful representation of a thing," since the represented things might not be beautiful at all in their natural condition.

As a critical observation, it is worth noting that Kant's definition of beautiful art is difficult to generalize, since there are many instances of non-representational, abstract, purely configurational art that are nonetheless beautiful. Such works of art manifestly "represent nothing" (as in the §4 reference to pure beauty). This would not imply, though, that these works of art are therefore free, or pure beauties of an artistic sort. "Representing nothing" is only a necessary, and is not a sufficient condition for being an object of pure beauty. There is also the necessary condition of not being judged "under a definite concept" (also as in the §4 reference to free beauty) and this latter condition precludes any work of art (when judged as art) from being the subject of a judgment of pure beauty. Here, in §48, Kant states clearly that if an object is presented as a work of art, then this introduces a concept of what the object is supposed to be. The perfection of the object must therefore be taken into account and the appropriate aesthetic judgment will be a judgment of adherent beauty.

AESTHETIC IDEAS AND THE BEAUTY OF FINE ART

[§49: "Concerning the capacities of mind which constitute genius"]
Kant's elaboration of how the activities of genius produce beautiful works of art constitutes one of the more complicated segments of his aesthetic theory, for he needs to account for artistic beauty – which is an instance of adherent beauty – as opposed to the simpler, more abstract and self-contained phenomenon of pure beauty. Nonetheless, he preserves at the foundation of his account of artistic beauty the core principle that beauty is grounded in a feeling of disinterested satisfaction that radiates from the logically-structured harmony of the faculties of imagination and understanding. We will keep this in view throughout the exposition.

As opposed to a mechanically produced work of art that lacks inspiration, Kant refers to the more inspired and animated works as having "spirit" (*Geist*). Artistic beauty, spirit, and genius all coincide. When this artistic spirit is embodied in an object, the animated object becomes artistically beautiful, and the manner in which this animation stimulates the harmony of the cognitive faculties in the perceiver, matches and communicates the very quality of the original artistic spirit that was in the artist. "Spirit" is what the artistic genius adds to a work of otherwise academic art. This spirit is what constitutes the artistic beauty of the work and is that which, in principle, stimulates the harmony of everyone's cognitive faculties.

Kant claims more specifically that a given subject matter becomes animated by artistic genius when the genius produces "aesthetic ideas" (*ästhetische Ideen*) in connection with that subject matter and combines these into the work of art expressive of that subject. For instance, an artist can begin with the theme of love, and then produce an aesthetic idea in connection with love that, with a certain attunement, animates the work of art whose basic subject matter is love. Some complications arise, though, upon considering how Kant characterizes aesthetic ideas and upon explaining how they produce the harmony of the cognitive faculties that is characteristic of pure beauty in general.

Kant gives two characterizations of aesthetic ideas:

> ... by an aesthetic idea, I understand that representation of the imagination that stimulates a great deal of thought, without there being, however, any determinate thought, i.e., *concept*, that can be adequate to it, and that consequently, no language can fully attain or make intelligible. – One easily sees that an aesthetic idea is the counterpart (pendant) of a *rational idea*, which conversely, is a concept to which no *intuition* (representation of the imagination) can be adequate.
>
> (§49, Ak 314 (192–93), G 192, P 182, M 175–76, B 157)

> In a word, the aesthetic idea is a representation of the imagination that is attached to a given concept, which is bound together with a manifold of partial representations in the free use of the imagination,[2] such that no expression demarcating a determinate concept can be found for it. Much that is unnameable is therefore allowed to be added to the concept, the feeling of which enlivens the cognitive faculties[3] and binds language in its merely literalistic meaning together with spirit.
>
> Therefore, the mental powers whose union (in a certain relation) constitutes *genius*, are imagination and understanding.
>
> (§49, Ak 316 (197), G 194, P 185, M 179, B 160)

It is clear from these excerpts that an aesthetic idea is not a rule or concept (*Begriff*), determinate or indeterminate, but is a "representation of the imagination" or intuition (*Anschauung*). An aesthetic idea is a sensory presentation that is combined with the ordinary and literalistic presentation of some concept. A simple example would be when we have the concept "cup" along with an ordinary cup that stands as the purpose of the concept, and then artistically modify the cup's presentation to enlarge the concept of the cup. For instance, we might cover the cup with fur to suggest a contrast between the thoughts of liquid and dryness in relation to the liquids that would typically be in the cup. It is difficult to say what is exactly intended by covering the cup with fur, but it stimulates one's imagination in relation to the concept "cup." Structurally speaking, we have a definite concept, an item that fits the concept and an artistic modification of the item's presentation that stimulates the imagination in relation to the definite concept's meaning.

Judgments of adherent beauty fit this structural arrangement, for consider the judgment of a church's adherent beauty. We have the concept "church," an instantiation of the concept in the presence of some actual building that is intended to be a church, and then, in relation to that instantiation, the particularly artistic way that the architect sets out the building's forms. We have a perfection-related satisfaction insofar as the building fits the concept "church" combined with a disinterested aesthetic satisfaction insofar as the specific forms of the church exhibit a purposiveness without purpose.

In the case of an aesthetic idea, we have a perfection-related satisfaction in seeing how the work of art fits its theme, and a disinterested aesthetic satisfaction in apprehending how the aesthetic idea incorporated into the work elaborates on the given theme in an expansive but indeterminable manner. The purposiveness without purpose of the church's architectural form is comparable to the purposiveness without purpose of the aesthetic idea's elaboration of the given theme in a manner that defies definite formulation.

In this model, the work of art's beauty is essentially due to the presentation of the aesthetic idea that imaginatively elaborates the core meaning of the work. The work of art's core meaning and the academically correct features of the work are also necessary, but they stand only as the determinate foundation to which the work of art's beauty then adheres. This beauty arises upon apprehending how the aesthetic idea expands the work of art's subject matter in a way that suggests an underlying intelligibility – the perceiver apprehends and resonates with the "genius" of the artistic presentation – but this is an intelligibility that does not support any mechanical understanding or any attempt to explain it in terms of any formula. One apprehends the purposiveness of the aesthetic idea's semantic form and marvels at that form's intelligibility in connection with the subject matter it aims to expand. In this sense of marvel, one feels a satisfaction in the harmony of the cognitive faculties.

Kant offers a fairly specific account of how aesthetic ideas are constituted. At the basis are the "aesthetic attributes" (*ästhetische Attribute*) of an object. These are typically symbolic or metaphorical images that can be clustered around a given object or theme, and that can stimulate one's imagination to expand the object's or theme's meaning. For example, if the theme were a sunrise, then a possible aesthetic attribute could be a further comparison between the rising sunlight and the way tranquillity issues from virtue. Similarly, if the theme involved calm and retrospective reflections at the end of one's life, then a possible aesthetic attribute could be a further reference to how the sun leaves a soft afterglow after it sets. A cluster of such associations around a given object or theme constitutes the respective aesthetic idea.

Kant's account of genius and artistic beauty does not end with the judgment of adherent beauty and the harmony of the cognitive faculties. There is a supplementary relationship to reason and moral interests that accompanies the experience of aesthetic ideas. We can begin to discern this relationship by noting how Kant refers to aesthetic ideas as "ideas" (even though they are intuitions and not concepts) because they expand one's imagination in the direction of infinity. From the standpoint of some given purpose, an aesthetic idea associated with that purpose expands the purpose's meaning inexhaustibly. Kant writes:

> One can call such representations of the imagination *ideas*: on the one hand, because they at least strive toward what lies beyond the borders of experience, and thus seek to come close to a presentation of rational concepts (of intellectual ideas), which gives to them the appearance of an objective reality; on the other hand, and indeed mainly, because no concept can be fully adequate to them as inner intuitions.
>
> (§49, Ak 314 (193–94), G 192, P 182–83, M 176, B 157)

Owing to their expansive quality, aesthetic ideas generate associations with moral concepts in how they formally stretch our imagination in the direction of reason. It follows that moral themes are appropriate subjects for beautiful works of art, since then the given moral purpose would be reinforced by the aesthetic idea's expansive form. Any aesthetic idea will set the faculty of intellectual ideas (reason) into motion and will thereby generate not only a logically-structured harmony of the imagination and understanding but, in a manner reminiscent of the experience of the mathematical sublime, generate a relationship between the imagination and reason.

The harmony between imagination and reason in the experience of artistic beauty is different from, and is more internally consistent than, the relationship between those faculties in the experience of the sublime. In the latter, the role of the imagination is primarily negative in its frustrated effort to express the idea of infinity in a finite sensuous form. Aesthetic ideas, in contrast, do not primarily aim to express the idea of infinity itself, which, as in the case of the sublime, would lead to frustration; they aim productively to expand the meaning of a determinate purpose beyond its given limits, and this is a task at which they can be successful.

From within the standpoint of a given determinate purpose, the aesthetic idea adheres to the given purpose but, while doing so, it also introduces a kind of boundlessness. So when the aesthetic idea suggests ideas of reason in its expansion of some determinate purpose's meaning, it does so in a context different from the sublime effort to embody the infinite in a finite form. Aesthetic ideas and the experience of the sublime are comparable to some extent, but the way that aesthetic ideas lead to reflection on ideas of reason differs. Specifically, it does not entail the subordination of imagination to reason where one abandons the contents of imagination for the purpose of contemplating rational ideas in a self-sufficient manner.

Aesthetic ideas in the experience of beauty therefore characterize the more philosophically integrative of the two modes of reflective aesthetic satisfaction so far examined, viz., beauty and sublimity. Judgments of sublimity involve imagination, understanding, and reason, but portray the imagination and understanding in tension-ridden relationships with reason. Aesthetic ideas involve imagination, understanding and reason, but involve a feeling of beauty that radiates from the harmony of the cognitive faculties, while also producing a positive harmony between imagination and reason whereby moral ideas can be given the positive appearance of an objective reality.

This payoff is not surprising in light of Kant's claim that the powers of genius are none other than the powers of nature. If there is an intelligibility that underlies nature, then this is what produces aesthetic ideas. So it is nature itself as embodied in the artistic genius that is responsible for creating the resonant artistic images that suggest ideas of reason through their purposive form. More broadly, nature itself thereby suggests moral ideas in the production of beautiful things in general, no matter what the subject matter happens to be, and this is itself a powerful confirmation of the compatibility between nature (either acting objectively in the production of natural beauty or subjectively through the artist in the production of fine art) and morality.

To top things off, when the works of artistic genius are specifically works that represent natural objects as beautiful (i.e., an idealized landscape), we have nature (conceived of as being directed by an underlying intelligence) portraying itself in a manner whereby moral ideas are represented as being embodied in nature. This amounts to nature representing its own moral goal through the artistic genius, in content (insofar as the portrayal is of a natural scene) as well as in form (insofar as the aesthetic ideas involved formally expand one's attention in the direction of reason).

[§50: "Concerning the combination of taste with genius in products of beautiful art"] In §48 Kant distinguishes between artistically beautiful art and mechanical art that is nonetheless beautiful, associating genius with the former and taste with the latter. The beauty of mechanical art derives from copying either the beauty of natural objects or the artistic beauty derived from genius that "gives the rule to art." At the end of §47, Kant also mentions that genius in the absence of taste would produce only chaos and that, for beautiful art, an academic foundation is required to give a solid form and a determinate purpose to the work of art. Creating some confusion and contradicting the statement from §46 that "genius is the talent (natural gift) that gives the rule to art," Kant states in §47, as noted, that:

Genius can only provide rich *material* [*Stoff*] for beautiful artistic products; its elaboration and *form* require an academically trained talent, so as to make use of it in a way that can bear examination by the power of judgment.

(§47, Ak 310 (186), G 189, P 178, M 171–72, B 153)

The above excerpt suggests that all beautiful form is provided by taste and academic rules, and that genius only supplies the material to be tempered and rationalized by taste. In §50 Kant reiterates this non-rule-generating conception of genius, stating that in reference to beautiful art, the inspiration of the work is due to genius, but that the beauty requires taste. He is careful to say that taste is only a necessary condition for artistic beauty, but he adds nonetheless that without taste, all the richness of content that genius produces in its lawless freedom is nothing but nonsense. In light of such statements, there is consequently a difficulty in deciding how much power genius actually has to "give the rule to art" on its own.

The only way to prevent Kant's theory of genius from falling apart is to maintain that taste is requisite for the determinate foundations of artistic beauty, but that genius is responsible for the enlivening inspiration and, hence, for the artistic beauty *per se*. Kant's identification of genius with the lawless creation of material that taste then organizes conflicts too directly with a series of central claims: (1) that genius gives the rule to art, (2) that aesthetic ideas have an inner intelligibility, (3) that the power of genius is the same intelligent power of nature in its creation of beautiful things, and (4) that aesthetic ideas themselves have an inner directedness or intelligibility that leads us to search for a maximum and therefore to contemplate rational ideas. A significant degree of rationality and intelligibility is contained in the very ideas of genius and aesthetic ideas to begin with, in other words. So Kant's claim that genius only supplies the material that taste then organizes has the effect of undermining his theory of artistic genius as nature's favorite.

One reason why Kant might have characterized artistic genius in this limited way is because he seems to have noticed that the semantic resonance of an aesthetic idea might not always match what is commonsensically characterized as beautiful. For instance, he states here in §50 that being rich and original in ideas is not the main consideration in connection with beauty. This is often true, but it is not the sort of richness that is distinctive of genius as Kant has defined it. What characterizes genius is the capacity to produce a rich and resonant aesthetic idea (i.e., a set of aesthetic attributes) that has in addition, an expansiveness that exhibits a purposiveness without purpose. It is the formal intelligibility of the semantic richness that is paramount, not the richness itself. This intelligibility, however, is not due to taste; it is due to the inspiration of genius. So it seems as if Kant did not characterize the artistic genius in the above excerpt from §47 with the completeness that his original definition required.

AESTHETIC IDEAS AND NATURAL BEAUTY

[§51: "Concerning the division of the beautiful arts"; §52: "Concerning the combination of the beautiful arts in one and the same product"] Kant begins an inquiry into the taxonomic division of the fine arts with what seems to be a straightforward and non-controversial assertion:

> In general, one can call beauty (whether it is natural or artistic beauty) the *expression* of aesthetic ideas: however, in beautiful art this idea must be occasioned by a concept [i.e., purpose] of the object, and in beautiful nature, the mere reflection on a given intuition without a concept of what the object ought to be, is sufficient for the awakening and communicating of the idea [*der Idee*] of which that object is considered as the *expression*.
>
> (§51, Ak 320 (204), G 197, P 189, M 183–84, B 164)

Although we have had a glimpse of Kant's detailed account of how aesthetic ideas operate within the context of artistic genius and beautiful art, he has said little to explain how natural beauty can be conceived as the expression of aesthetic ideas. For the most part, this account needs to be constructed independently and we can take as our guide Kant's account of pure beauty and his explicit account of aesthetic ideas to see how the two can be coordinated.

As we know, Kant maintains that pure beauty concerns the disinterested apprehension of an object's purposive form and that the satisfaction that grounds judgments of beauty radiates from the harmony of the cognitive faculties. One can reasonably, but also crucially, add that the disinterested apprehension of an object's purposive form leads to the postulation of a summary or unifying rule that underlies the object's purposive form, that lends to that form its intelligibility, but that remains undetermined. The apprehension of an object's pure beauty thus involves not only the apprehension of an object's purposive form, but the postulation of some indeterminate concept that serves as the rule that underlies the purposive form.

If we conceive of pure beauty in this manner, then it becomes clear how the underlying rule postulated as the ground of a beautiful natural object's intelligibility could be referred to as an aesthetic idea, or more accurately, as an indeterminate principle of intelligibility that underlies the aesthetic idea expressed by the object. In a natural object, the purposive form stimulates a harmonious activity of the cognitive faculties that adheres to no determinate subject matter or purpose, so whatever mental contents are involved in the harmony of the cognitive faculties in this case remain unspecified.

In the case of aesthetic ideas related to artistic beauty, the mental contents involved in the harmony of the cognitive faculties are more specifiable and more circumscribed. These are the widespread associations that an aesthetic idea produces in connection with the purpose, or artistic theme, it intends to expand upon. The situation is the same as in pure beauty, except that in the latter case there is no specification of what the mental contents are that enter into the harmony of the cognitive faculties, whereas in the case of adherent beauty there is a specification with respect to the artistic theme involved.

This implies that the nature of artistic beauty can only reside in how the aesthetic ideas expand *stylistically* upon a concept as opposed to involving constitutively what the particular meanings within the expansion happen to be. The network of semantic relationships appreciated with respect to their formal structure, in other words, would be the focus when judging a thing's artistic beauty. This is where the formal intelligibility of the aesthetic idea resides.

Kant's general claim that beauty is the expression of aesthetic ideas helps bring forth the idea that the same sort of intelligibility is apprehended as underlying both objects of natural beauty and works of artistic beauty. What inspires the artistic genius is hypothesized as the same intelligent force that inspires nature's production of beautiful natural objects, and this reinforces the idea that there is a rationality within the powers of artistic genius itself.

THE DIVISION OF THE FINE ARTS

As is true for most aesthetic theories of the time immediately before and after Kant, we find in the *Critique of the Power of Judgment* a taxonomy of the fine arts. It is best represented initially in the form of an outline, as a summary of Kant's verbal characterizations to be described below:

I.   Arts of Speech
     A. Rhetoric
     B. Poetry
II. Pictorial Art
     A. Plastic Arts (Arts of Sensible Truth)
         1. Sculpture
         2. Architecture
     B. Painting in the Broad Sense (Arts of Sensible Illusion)
         1. Art of the Beautiful Depiction of Nature
             a. Painting Proper
         2. Art of the Sensible Arrangement of Natural Products
             a. The Art of Pleasure Gardens
         3. Interior Decoration
III. Art of the Play of Sensations
     A. Music (Artistic play of Hearing)
     B. Artistic Play of Colors
IV. Hybrid forms:
     A. Drama: the fusion of rhetoric and a painterly presentation of its subjects and object

B. Song: the fusion of poetry and music
C. Dance: music and the play of shapes

In formulating this taxonomy Kant is guided by two factors. The first is an analysis of communication – and he believes implicitly that art is fundamentally about the communication of aesthetic ideas – that divides human expression into word, gesture, and tone. He aligns this threefold division with the philosophically foundational concepts of thought, intuition, and sensation, and thereby grounds the taxonomy of the fine arts in the structure of communication and in some basic epistemological elements. The arts of speech communicate thoughts, the pictorial arts communicate intuitions, and the arts of the play of sensations communicate self-evidently via sensations.

In the course of providing details to his taxonomy, Kant mentions importantly in a more general theoretical mode that:

> However, in all beautiful art what is essential consists in the form [*in der Form*], which is purposive for our observation and judging, where the pleasure is at the same time civilizing [*Cultur*] and disposes the spirit to ideas . . .
>
> (§52, Ak 325–26 (214), G 203, P 195, M 190–91, B 170)

This reinforces the above, primarily formalistic, interpretation of aesthetic ideas in reference to the sort of intelligibility they exhibit. With respect to their content, however, Kant adds that if the beautiful arts are not combined with moral ideas, then the result is ultimately superficial, and beautiful art stands in danger of degenerating into mere (and, for Kant, essentially meaningless) enjoyment. He believes that moral content is indispensable to beautiful art.

[§53: "Comparison of the aesthetic value of the beautiful arts with one another"] To elaborate on his taxonomy of the fine arts and to conclude the first major segment of his analysis of judgments of beauty and sublimity, Kant adds some reflections on the hierarchy of the fine arts. These are not complete and systematically organized, but they do provide a glimpse into the respective values Kant places on the various arts. His reasons for locating this or that art in its place in the taxonomy are revealing as examples of his aesthetic theory in a more practical application.

Kant maintains that poetry is the most valuable art, as the most free, as offering the purest display of the power of genius, and as therefore an art that stimulates the imagination to the greatest extent. Part of this celebration concerns poetry's conceptual medium and Kant's belief that fine art in general requires an association with moral ideas, if it is not to become superficial. As a conceptual art, poetry's medium is immediately closest to moral ideas, while it remains defiant of formulas, definitions, and unimaginative rigidity. It thus stands as a strong vehicle to raise one's attention beyond the realm of determinate conceptual forms to that of reason, morality, and the indeterminate concepts associated with the latter.

With respect to poetry as a vehicle for moral expression, Kant observes that poetry has a noticeable independence from raw sensations and formulaic conceptual forms, and also conveys perspectives that nature in its given spatio-temporal forms does not offer. That is, nature itself does not produce science fiction or fantasy, except through the powers of the artistic genius. Insofar as poetry has the power for presenting nature in alternative conditions that include among them visions of a morally perfected world, it has the power to serve in the interests of reason as a "schema" or intermediary for reason's instantiation in the world.

With an anti-Sophist attitude of which Socrates and Plato would be proud, however, Kant states squarely that the art of rhetoric is not worthy of any respect. This is owing to its power to distract attention from the truth. The following quote puts his view in a nutshell:

> I must confess that a beautiful poem has always given me a pure satisfaction, whereas reading the best speech of a Roman popular speaker or a contemporary speaker in parliament or the pulpit has every time been mixed with the uncomfortable feeling of disapproval of a deceitful art, which understands how to move people like machines, to a judgment in important matters which when considered in quiet reflection, must lose all weight for them.
>
> (§53, footnote, Ak 327–28 (217), G 205, P 198, M 193, B 172)

After attending to poetry and rhetoric, Kant considers the value of music, which impresses him highly from one perspective, while from another, leads him to locate it as the least valuable of the fine arts. On the positive side, Kant's theory of music is insightful, for he associates it directly with language and communication. He notices that when people speak, their voices have a cadence that abstractly matches the meanings expressed, and that music is like language, except that it abstracts away from the determinate meanings and provides a general form of meaning that stimulates our imagination. If there were a set of abstract forms that underlie all of language, music could have the capacity to express these forms and even constitute a universal language.

Although one can draw the above account from Kant's characterization of music, he does not develop the idea that musical forms express underlying linguistic structures considered generally. He focusses rather on the connection between music and emotional expression through language, and is more suggestive of a theory of music as expressive of emotional forms relative to the core emotions that all humans share. This gives us the foundation of considering music as the expression of emotions in a manner detached from the specific contexts in which they arise, so as to be able to contemplate them in a distanced and disinterested aesthetic manner.

The sensory quality of music as constituted by sequences of sounds, however, induces Kant to temper his praise of music. Insofar as music is grounded in raw sensory qualities, there is a strong connection to non-reflective, simple enjoyment, and this explains for Kant why music needs constantly to change and why, for him, it becomes tiresome with excessive repetition. He thus presents a polarized account of music, for while it appeals to our sense of abstraction and formality, it is also grounded in the naturally enjoyable qualities of sound. This reinforces the idea that within Kant's aesthetics music needs to be appreciated formalistically to preserve its beautiful quality.

With further respect to his fundamental view – one where the satisfaction that grounds judgments of pure beauty radiates from the harmony of the cognitive faculties – Kant ends up locating music on the lowest rung of the fine arts:

If, on the contrary, one estimates the value of the beautiful arts in reference to the culture that they provide for the mind, and takes as one's standard the enlargement of the capacities that, for cognition, must come together in the power of judgment, then in this respect music occupies the lowest place among the beautiful arts (just as it might occupy the highest place among those that are appreciated in terms of their agreeableness), because it merely plays with sensations.

(§53, Ak 329 (220), G 206, P 199–200, M 195, B 174)

This characterization brings music closer to cooking, since cooking similarly plays with sensations (of a gustatory sort), albeit in a more desire-stimulating manner. Kant does not mention cooking, but he does compare the sensory aspect of music with perfume-making, since both sounds and scents can be pervasive and cannot easily be ignored when they touch the ears or nose. Music is often described as a sublime and transcendent art, and some metaphysical views even consider the core of the universe to be musical, but we do not encounter this attitude in Kant's explicit treatment of music in §§53–54 (although we can discern it at a deeper level, as the conclusion to this study will note). Kant clearly and officially associates music with charm, sensory satisfaction and enjoyment, mentioning its more formalistically elevated qualities as being weighed down, quite unlike poetry, by music's vulgar entrenchment in the field of sensation.

In passing, Kant states that the pictorial arts offer a more concept-filled content that stimulates the understanding in a more determinate fashion, thus locating the pictorial arts midway between the arts of speech and the arts of the play of sensations. What we see in general is a foundational schema that is constructed along the spectrum that ranges from pure sensation to pure conception, where at the top he locates the more conceptually-based media, and at the bottom, the more sensation-based media. *Prima facie* the arts are organized along this continuum, with added reflections and provisos that temper the location of each art. Rhetoric, for instance, is diminished in quality and music is raised in quality, given the added details of the arts themselves.

[§54: "Remark"] Kant's extended attention to music in his discussion of the hierarchy of the arts, in conjunction with the failure to consider some of the other arts he mentions at any length at all, indicates that he is not primarily interested in discussing each art in sequence, but has other interests that are guiding his discussion. The account of music and what follows in his concluding remark in the analytic section of the Critique of Aesthetic Judgment reveals a wider interest in assimilating his theory of beauty into a broader consideration of aesthetic experience in general (which includes sensory gratification) and the promotion of health.

At first sight, Kant's concluding remarks appear to be a mere collection of observations concerning minor arts of enjoyment, such as telling jokes and playing light-hearted games. The length at which Kant discusses jokes seems strange, peripheral and mostly irrelevant to his aesthetics, given that there is no fine art of joke-telling. This would be a misinterpretation, though, for there is a good reason for him to reflect on the nature of jokes and to offer an account of the nature of laughter. To him, music and materials for laughter are similar in the following way:

> . . . music and material for laughter are two kinds of play with aesthetic ideas or even representations of the understanding, through which in the end nothing is thought, and which can please us in a lively way merely through their change; by which they make it rather clear that in both cases, although it is occasioned by ideas of the mind, the enlivening is merely corporeal and that the feeling of health through such a movement of the viscera corresponding to that play constitutes the whole gratification in a lively party . . .
>
> (§54, Ak 332 (224), G 208, P 202, M 198, B 176–77)

Kant stated in §1 that in aesthetic judgment in general, a representation of an object in an aesthetic judgment is related to one's "feeling of life." It was emphasized earlier how important it is not to confuse the term "judgments of taste" (i.e., judgments of pure beauty) with the term "aesthetic judgment," since the later is a generic category that includes three types of judgment, namely, judgments of pure beauty, judgments of the sublime, and aesthetic judgments of sense. In this concluding remark to the analytic of aesthetic judgment, Kant considers aesthetic judgments of sense and judgments of pure beauty in their joint connection to the feeling of health or life. He recognizes that both beauty and sensory gratification can stimulate our feeling of health and now considers music and laughter as examples of activities that clearly involve sensory gratification, but in a manner that is consistent with the satisfaction that beauty provides.

Evidence of this broader interest in beauty, sense-gratification, and feelings of health resides in how Kant's begins and ends this section with a reference to Epicurus, who maintained that everything reduces to sense-gratification, that sense-gratification is an animal function, and that all gratification aims to support bodily well-being and health. The problem Kant faces is to explain how sensory gratification does not always conflict with beauty, since there is a level at which it can and does conflict: satisfaction in pure beauty is disinterested, whereas satisfaction in sense-gratification is fundamentally interested. If Epicurus were correct, then the claim that "everyone has his own taste" would be true, and Kant's universalistic theory of beauty could not get off the sensory ground.

Throughout the *Critique of the Power of Judgment*, though, Kant is careful to acknowledge that formal and sense-gratification qualities can be (and typically need to be) present in the same object. For a judgment of pure beauty, we need to ignore the sense-gratification qualities to provide a universal ground to our judgment. The problem concerns how we are prohibited from saying that an object is beautiful on account of its sense-gratification qualities and how to acknowledge nonetheless that these qualities cannot be avoided, and, indeed, frequently present themselves in thematic combination with an art work's formal qualities.

Kant believes that Epicurus was correct to emphasize the importance of maintaining bodily well-being and health, but Kant disagrees that only sense-gratification works towards this end, since the satisfaction in pure beauty appears to foster health as well, and the latter is not a sense-gratification. What he adopts from Epicurus, though, is the idea that beauty and sense-gratification are compatible with respect to the furtherance of moral interests. And this is the point of Kant's lengthy discussion of laughter, which he defines as an effect that results from the sudden transformation of a heightened sensation into nothing.

The definition of laughter sounds peculiar without putting it into the context of Kant's view that the satisfaction in pure beauty is disinterested. When a joke transforms some subject-matter "into nothing," the effect is to negate the theoretical and practical interests in the joke's subject-matter, thus rendering the pleasure in the laughter detached from such interests. It is comparable to how music detaches itself from determinate concepts and expresses emotions in a disinterested manner. The result is an instance of sense-gratification that has a resemblance to beauty and that does not necessarily threaten moral interests as other forms of sensory gratification might do. We can thereby appreciate one of the few jokes in the *Critique of the Power of Judgment* in light of Kant's interest in explaining how both the satisfaction in pure beauty and some forms of sensory gratification can contribute to our feeling of life. He states:

> Suppose someone tells the story that an Indian, who at the table of an Englishman in Surat, expressed his great amazement with many exclamations upon seeing a bottle of ale being opened and all the beer, transformed into foam, spill out. And in response to the Englishman's question "What is there here to be so amazed at?" answered, "I am not amazed that the foam is coming out, but by how you could get it all in," we laugh, and it gives us a hearty pleasure. This is not because we find ourselves more clever than this unknowing person, or because of anything else that is entertaining that the understanding allows us to notice, but because our expectation was heightened and then suddenly disappeared into nothing.
>
> (§54, Ak 333 (226), G 209, P 203–4, M 199–200, B 178)

The disappearance of our expectation "into nothing" (*ins Nichts*) amounts to an elevation of the sense-gratification into a relatively disinterested condition. So although Kant associates music with perfumery and although one can associate music with cooking on the same grounds, the stronger analogy is between music and laughter, since both have a disinterested relationship to sensory gratification that perfumery and cooking have to a lesser degree.

4

BEAUTY'S CONFIRMATION OF SCIENCE AND MORALITY (§§55–60)

THE ANTINOMY OF TASTE

[First Part, Critique of Aesthetic Judgment. Section II. Dialectic of Aesthetic Judgment. §55] In this second division of the Critique of Aesthetic Judgment which concerns the "dialectic" of aesthetic judgment, Kant initiates an inquiry into the foundations of his aesthetic theory by asking an important question: Is there any contradiction in the theory of beauty at the level of basic principles? If there is such a contradiction, then any attempts to formulate a universalistic theory of beauty will be fruitless. It is therefore important for Kant to show that his own account stands on consistent ground, despite what appears to be a threatening tension at the basic level and an impediment to all theories of beauty. In particular, he observes a conflict associated with the claim that judgments of pure beauty have a universal validity.

With respect to the alleged universal validity of judgments of pure beauty, Kant admits that people often disagree in their aesthetic judgments. This could suggest that there might be no single principle of judgments of pure beauty that everyone ought to observe and that would precipitate universal agreement. That

actual disagreement exists is not itself deeply problematic, however, since Kant's theory can resolve many differences of opinion
by distinguishing between judgments of pure beauty, judgments of
sensory gratification and judgments of perfection, and by distinguishing pure beauty from adherent beauty. A person could be
making a judgment of beauty that is more influenced by sensory
gratification or by an interest in an object's purpose, for instance,
and this could explain why the person disagrees with others.

[§56: "Representation of the antinomy of taste"] Kant's more
substantial worry is that, at their core, theories of beauty might
suffer from an internal and irresolvable conflict of doctrines that
would yield contradictory bases for the judgments of pure beauty
themselves. This would undermine the philosophical attempts to
formulate a general theory altogether. He is ultimately confident
that there is no such conflict or "antinomy" whose recognition
would undercut his theory of beauty, but to put this issue to rest,
he formulates the strongest version of such a theory-breaking conflict that he can philosophically imagine. To do this, he reaches initially into the field of general proverbs about beauty and extracts
two commonplace beliefs that contradict his conclusion that judgments of pure beauty have a universal validity. These are the rela-
tivistic sayings that "everyone has his own taste" and that
consequently "there is no disputing about taste."[1]

From these proverbs Kant unfolds an antinomy of taste that sets
their relativistic import against a more universalistic and non-rela-
tivistic alternative. On the one side, then, we have the claim that
there is no disputing about taste, where "dispute" entails strin-
gently that one or the other side's position could be logically
proven. To assert that there is no disputing about tastes is to maintain that no logical proofs can be advanced to ground judgments of
beauty. Now if such judgments *were* conceptually-based, so the
reasoning proceeds, then they would be open to proof, so if we
assume that there is no disputing about tastes, then judgments of
beauty cannot in any sense be conceptually-grounded.

Even if everyone does not always argue about matters of beauty
with the explicit assumption that a logical proof will emerge to
conclude the disagreement, it remains that we do in fact have serious disagreements about matters of beauty. This raises the question

of how it is possible to disagree at all reasonably and vociferously, if judgments of beauty have no conceptual basis and altogether defy rational discussion. The very presence of serious debate – as is also the case for philosophical disputes – suggests that there is *some* objective basis to judgments of beauty, and if postulating a conceptual basis to the judgment is the only way to account for this objectivity, then judgments of beauty would need to have a conceptual basis of some sort.

In actual fact, people disagree about matters of beauty as they do in philosophical matters, and never seem to be able to bring forth logical proofs to substantiate their opinions with some conclusive reasoning. So the nature of such disagreements about beauty remains unclear, since proofs would seem to be required, if only in principle. It is peculiar that for centuries, people have been arguing with each other over judgments of beauty and philosophical matters, but despite all of the argumentation, the conclusive proofs never seem to materialize. We thus seem to stand at an impasse and face the following conflict in the basic principles of taste:

1. **Thesis**. The judgment of pure beauty is not grounded on concepts, because otherwise it would be possible to dispute (*disputiren*) about it (decide through proofs).
2. **Antithesis**. The judgment of pure beauty is grounded on concepts, because otherwise, its variety notwithstanding, it would not even be possible to have any controversy (*streiten*)[2] about it (to demand the necessary agreement of others to this judgment).

(§56, Ak 338 (234), G 215, P 211, M 206, B 183–84)

[§57: "Solution of the antinomy of taste"] Kant believes that he can easily resolve the antinomy of taste by revealing an ambiguity in the meaning of the term "concept" (*Begriff*) as it appears in the thesis and antithesis. The thesis and antithesis immediately become compatible if (1) the thesis is interpreted as asserting that judgments of pure beauty are not based on *determinate* concepts, and therefore are not susceptible of being decided by logical proofs, and if (2) the antithesis is interpreted as asserting that judgments of pure beauty are based on *indeterminate* concepts, thereby preserving the possibility for establishing a universal conceptual ground for the judgments and, hence, a reference for serious disagreements, since their general conceptual basis is retained.

After having resolved this ambiguity in the antinomy's thesis and antithesis, Kant introduces the required indeterminate concept that – so he maintains – serves to ground the universality of judgments of beauty. This is where some complication and controversy of its own enters into the interpretation of Kant's theory of beauty, since the indeterminate concept he introduces is not the concept one would expect him to refer to at this point.

In this section Kant speaks generically about the distinction between determinate concepts and indeterminate concepts, stating that whereas every determinate concept can be adequately instantiated in the field of sense experience, every indeterminate concept defies exact correspondence with any set of sense experiences. He adds that the most generic and foundational indeterminate concept is the transcendental, rational idea of the supersensible (i.e., the idea of an unconditional being, or unconditional mode of being) that grounds all sense experience, or all sensory intuition. In the broadest sense, this is the objective reality that cognition in general ideally aims to know. This idea of the supersensible is the indeterminate concept Kant introduces to resolve the antinomy of taste.

This generic idea of the supersensible, if it is not the immediate ground, nonetheless must be the ultimate ground of judgments of beauty, insofar as they rest on indeterminate as opposed to determinate concepts, following Kant's dictates. His reason is that this generic idea of the supersensible is at the basis of not only the universal validity of judgments of pure beauty, but is additionally at the basis of the universal validity of *all* judgments. It grounds the universal validity of cognition in general, in other words, and this is the key point. His assertion is that if our judgments are to have universal validity in the strongest sense, we need to suppose that their intersubjective content is directed towards and based on reality as it is in itself, and not only on how we need to experience things.

Kant's reference to the idea of what lies behind all sensory appearances, however, does raise some interpretive questions about the status of his earlier account of the universal validity of judgments of beauty, viz., his deduction of those judgments. The present §57 reference to the idea of the supersensible comes somewhat unexpectedly, since the deduction in §38 is presented as being sufficient (*genug*) to establish the universal validity of judgments of pure beauty. Assuming that §38 was written before §57 and that the Critique of Aesthetic Judgment is consistently composed,[3] then either Kant is now representing the contents of the §38 deduction from a different angle, or he is contradicting its alleged sufficiency, or he is expanding upon it by simply drawing implications from what he has already established in §38. The third of these alternatives seems to be the most plausible, as can now be explained.

Earlier in the Critique of Aesthetic Judgment, Kant characterized the disinterested and universal satisfaction that grounds judgments of pure beauty in reference to his §9 claim that nothing can be universally communicated "except cognition and representation insofar as it belongs to cognition." This developed immediately into his canonical rendition of the harmony of the cognitive faculties as accounting for the judgment of beauty's universal validity, since the judgment issues from a basic harmony between the understanding and imagination that can be assumed to be the same in everyone.

Now presently, in the resolution of the antinomy of taste and in the resultant need to specify an indeterminate concept upon which the universal validity of judgments of pure beauty is based, one would expect Kant to turn directly to the harmony of the cognitive faculties, since according to his earlier exposition, we know that this harmony grounds the universality of judgments of pure beauty and remains independent of conceptual proofs. A reference to the harmony of the cognitive faculties seems to be exactly that for which the resolution of the antinomy of taste calls.[4]

The harmony of the cognitive faculties in connection with judgments of pure beauty is characterized by a free play between those faculties through which the power of judgment in general is expressed. Specifically, this free play involves an indeterminate harmony between the faculties of imagination and understanding. The logical form of this harmony reflects the elementary "*S is P*" form of logical judgment without any further specification – that is, the harmony is generically conceived – and this generic quality also reveals how the harmony is indeterminate, since no particular state of either faculty is specified in their condition of free play and mutual attunement.

In Kant's initial account of the universality of judgments of taste in §§1–22 and §§30–40, we can thus identify several references to indeterminacy and can straightforwardly identify a concept that grounds the universal validity of judgments of pure beauty in direct reference to the harmony of the cognitive faculties. This is the concept of "cognition in general" that refers to the free harmony of the faculties and it is what one could also expect Kant to recall at this point as the indeterminate concept that resolves the antinomy of taste. Kant's note to §38, moreover, also quoted above in Chapter 1, is explicit about how the free harmony of the cognitive faculties is sufficient to establish the subjective universal validity of judgments of beauty:

> To be justified in claiming universal agreement for judgments of the aesthetic power of judgment that rests merely on subjective grounds, it is sufficient [*ist genug*; note that Kant states "sufficient," rather than "necessary"] to grant: (1) the subjective conditions of this faculty are one and the same in all people, as far as is concerned the relation of the cognitive powers thus set into activity for a cognition in general. This must be true, because otherwise people could not communicate their representations and even cognition itself. (2) The judgment has considered merely this relation . . . and is pure . . .
>
> (§38, footnote, Ak 290 (152), G 170, P 155, M 147, B 132)

In his solution to the antinomy of taste and in his quest for a concept that grounds the universal validity of judgments of beauty, Kant does not, however, directly refer to "cognition in general" and let the matter rest as having already been established in earlier discussions. He instead introduces the indeterminate concept mentioned above, namely, the concept of a being that underlies all phenomenal appearances, or what can alternatively be described generally as the idea of the supersensible "thing-in-itself."

It is thought-provoking that here in §57 Kant maintains that if judgments of pure beauty are not grounded on the indeterminate concept of what underlies all phenomenal appearances, then we could not "save" (*retten*) the universal validity of such judgments. This wording suggests that the universal validity of judgments of pure beauty has in fact been established to a significant degree, but that now, in light of some further considerations or previous omissions, it faces a threat from which it needs to be saved. It does appear that the deduction was "easy" (*leicht*) and that it was completed earlier in §38 with the assertion that in all human beings the subjective conditions of the faculty of judgment are identical with respect to cognition in general. §38 states explicitly that assumptions (1) and (2) in the excerpt above are sufficient for the deduction. It does not state that the two assumptions are merely necessary, which would imply that something more would be needed to complete the deduction. So what we read in §57 calls for some interpretation.

The following questions consequently arise. What is the threat that Kant perceives? Why does he believe that he needs to invoke the idea of the supersensible to alleviate it? What, if any, is the relationship between the idea of the supersensible and cognition in general?

To approach some answers to these questions, it helps to recall the meaning of "adherent" in Kant's characterization of adherent beauty: when one is primarily interested in an object's purpose, the object's beauty immediately becomes a secondary matter that adheres to that main interest. To take Kant's prime example, if some object has an unconditional purpose (as does the human being), then whatever beauty it has will be a secondary matter that adheres to that predominant purpose. Given some object that is considered in reference to some overriding purpose, then, beauty will always take a back seat and will adhere to the purpose.

In the present situation, we are not concerned with the unconditional moral purpose of the human being, but a closely related purpose, namely, the purpose of human cognition. This purpose is to obtain empirical knowledge, since this is the best we can possibly do in an ideal effort to know how things are in themselves. Cognition is fundamentally directed outwards towards objects in space and time, and by extension it is fundamentally directed towards the unknowable that underlies those objects, namely, what Kant calls the supersensible.

If the considered and realistic purpose of cognition is to obtain empirical knowledge, then the harmony of the cognitive faculties can only be geared to that purpose as well, and this implies that all experiences of beauty *prima facie* will direct our attention to what is public and objective.[5] This public quality precisely reflects the nature of the universal validity of judgments of pure beauty, which is an abstracted form of the universal validity that attends our ascriptions of spatio-temporal qualities to objects. So just as the categorical and unconditional purpose of morality forces one to harmonize the satisfaction in free beauty with moral values, the categorical and apparently fixed purpose of cognition forces one to harmonize the satisfaction in pure beauty with epistemological values, and these require a reference to the way the world is in itself.

The very nature of pure beauty consequently requires us to regard every object that is judged to be beautiful "as if" it were an object of natural beauty, whether it happens to be a figment of one's imagination, a work of art, or a natural object itself. This is also to say that every object of pure beauty *represents the satisfaction of the interests of morality* (even though it does not satisfy them in actuality), given that every actual occasion of natural beauty does in fact satisfy those moral interests. Every object of pure beauty is thus like a drawing of a naturally beautiful object: in light of the purpose of cognition, we represent the objects apprehended as purely beautiful, as being natural objects, but this is only a subjective representation, i.e., we represent them only "as if" they were natural objects.

These considerations shine a different theoretical light on pure beauty. Pure beauty is certainly the baseline notion of beauty in Kant's aesthetics, and although the disinterestedness of a judgment of pure beauty requires us to acknowledge that it makes no difference to a representation's beauty whether or not it actually refers to anything actual, the very resonance of the cognitive faculties that that representation produces – since it is a resonance related to *cognition* – requires us to regard that representation as referring to an actual object, even if we know that it is merely a dream image. There is consequently a small tension between the neutrality of the disinterested attitude that suspends our interest in an object's actual existence for the sake of pure contemplation, and the pragmatic purpose of cognition in general – a purpose that accounts for the very satisfaction in such contemplation – that requires us to regard the object as if it nonetheless were actual. This is because the purpose of cognition is fundamentally geared towards what actually exists.

Kant's introduction of the idea of the supersensible can thus be regarded as an explicit recognition that cognition in general is pragmatically directed towards the acquisition of empirical knowledge, even though its purpose is temporarily suspended in the experience of pure beauty. This reference to what is supersensible is implicit in the excerpt from §38 above, so what he asserts in §57 can be regarded as simply the drawing of an obvious implication. Specifically, Kant states in §38 that in the experience of pure beauty, the harmony of the cognitive faculties is "set into activity for a cognition in general," and since the purpose of cognition in general requires that it be fundamentally directed towards actual objects – objects whose ultimate ground is the supersensible – the idea of the supersensible is entailed by the very concept of cognition in general.

This entailment can be appreciated upon noting that to suspend a purpose does not imply that the purpose is completely set aside and forgotten. Even the weight-lifter's flexing of muscles or the revving of a car's engine only makes sense as such in relation to the purpose of lifting weights or the actual driving of the car. Flexing is not itself weight-lifting, but it is done with the weight-lifting in view. Similarly, the experience of beauty is not the experience of knowing anything, but it is experienced with cognition in view, and it is this view towards cognition that introduces the idea of the supersensible, i.e., that which we are ultimately trying to know. The implication is that all beautiful objects be judged as if they were natural objects.

Yet another way to express this is to say that only if the objects judged to be beautiful are regarded as public objects open to everyone's view (i.e., as being made of natural materials) does it make any sense to demand the agreement of others. It is one thing to establish the universal validity of a judgment by noting how everyone thinks alike in a certain respect, and this is what Kant states explicitly in §38, but it remains to point out furthermore that everyone must also direct their common mode of thinking on mutually-perceivable public objects, and this is what the §57 reference to the idea of the supersensible expresses.

Unfortunately, if matters of interpretation were not complicated enough with Kant's introduction of the idea of the supersensible, we encounter in §57, like a small explosion, a series of diverse formulations of this idea of the supersensible within the span of a couple of pages that, although textually close to one another, are not obviously synonymous. Kant will later claim nonetheless that these formulations have essentially the same reference. They are as follows:

Objective Formulations of the Idea of the Supersensible:

[A] A concept of this sort is, however, merely the purely rational concept of the supersensible [*Übersinnlichen*], which lies as the ground of the object (and also the judging subject) insofar as it is a sensory object, consequently as an appearance. (§57, Ak 340 (236), G 216, P 212, M 207, B 185)[6]

[B] . . . the judgment of pure beauty is still grounded on a concept, albeit an indeterminate one (namely, of the supersensible substrate of appearances) . . . (§57, Ak 340–41 (237), G 216, P 213, M 208, B 186)

[C] . . . the judgment of pure beauty is grounded on a concept (of a general ground of the subjective purposiveness of nature for the power of judgment) . . . (§57, Ak 340 (236), G 216, P 213, M 207–8, B 185)

Subjective Formulations of the Idea of the Supersensible:

[D] [the judgment of pure beauty] acquires validity for everyone through this indeterminate concept . . . because its determining ground may lie [*vielleicht . . . liegt*] in the concept of that which can be seen as the supersensible substrate of humanity [*Menschheit*]. (§57, Ak 340 (236–37), G 216, P 213, M 208, B 185)

[E] The subjective principle, namely, the indeterminate idea of the supersensible in us [*in uns*],[7] can only be indicated as the single

> key [*einzige Schlüssel*] to the mystery of this faculty [of taste] . . . (§57, Ak 341 (238), G 217, P 213–14, M 208–9, B 186)

[F] Since the beautiful must be judged . . . in accord with the purposive attunement of the imagination for its agreement with the faculty of concepts in general, it is no rule or precept but only that which is merely nature in the subject, i.e., the supersensible substrate of all our faculties . . . which can serve as the subjective standard of that aesthetic but unconditioned purposiveness in beautiful art . . . (§57, Remark I, Ak 344 (242–43), G 219, P 217, M 212–13, B 189)

We will see that among this crisscrossing array of formulations formulation [C] is at the crux of the discussion. Let us begin, though, with formulation [A] and consider each in sequence. [A] primarily expresses the concept of an unspecified and unknowable supersensible substrate of nature that is assumed to be the ground of some given phenomenal object. This supersensible substrate is also construed in reference to an object considered individually, so [A] suggests the concept of an individual thing "in-itself."

For instance, [A] would refer to the snowflake, tulip, lamp, or any other object, as that object is in itself, i.e., as it is independently of its spatio-temporal and causal dimensions. There is the lamp as it appears to us and there is the lamp as it is in itself, and this lamp in itself is what one might call, loosely speaking, the "transcendental lamp," or more exactly the non-sensory being that we speculate as grounding the appearance of the lamp as an empirically real, phenomenal object. Such a being may have no "lampness" to it at all, as far as we can know. Within the context of judgments of pure beauty, though, [A] is a particularly useful formulation of the idea of the supersensible substrate of nature, since every judgment of pure beauty refers to some individual thing, and we are here considering this or that particular thing as it is in itself.

Formulation [B] is a generalization of [A] and it refers to the unknowable thing-in-itself considered as the supersensible substrate of nature's entirety, and not relative to this or that given thing. [A] is closely akin to [B] and blends into it, since in the realm of the supersensible, internal differentiations are difficult to make sense of, and the two characterizations of the supersensible refer to what is, as far as our knowledge is concerned, an essentially blank mode of being.

Formulation [C] retains the explicit generality of [B], but adds further speculation that the supersensible substrate of nature might be intelligent, since the natural world could be far more disorganized and chaotic than it actually is. Since we conceive of nature's regularities in terms of general and repeatable patterns, since we are not completely responsible for the specific empirical determinacy of the patterns we discover in experience, and since matter itself does not appear to be intelligent, it makes sense to explain the lawlike quality of these patterns by referring to what lies behind nature, i.e., to the supersensible substrate of nature, as having some inherent intelligence.

The presence of empirical laws confirms, although we also more fundamentally have no choice but to assume, that nature acts in sympathy with our efforts to make sense of our experience. This is to say that we have no choice but to assume that nature – or rather, the intelligence that supersensibly underlies it – is purposive for our cognition in general. Such an assumption, viz., the principle of the objective purposiveness of nature, is important within the present context, for it establishes a direct link between the harmony of the cognitive faculties and the reference to the supersensible substrate of nature here expressed in [C]. These in fact represent the subjective and objective poles of a single key to legitimating the universality of judgments of pure beauty, as expressed in §9, and now here in §57.

The subjective harmony of the faculties (§9) can only be possible to any significant degree, if nature's objective presentation is itself assumed to be reasonably coherent (§57). Without presupposing nature's coherence on its own accord, there would be relatively little that could be empirically comprehended, let alone appreciated as beautiful. So the purpose of cognition in general directs us to refer to an objective reality independent of us as the ultimate object of our knowledge, and the more specific need to formulate empirical laws directs us speculatively to ascribe a purpose to that objective reality that is favorable to our cognition. Cognition in general aims to know the world, presupposes thereby the presence of that world, and is further required as a condition for the realization of its aim, to speculate that the world itself is amenable to our cognitive efforts and, hence, that it has an underlying intelligence of its own. The experience of beauty is based on a feeling of approval in apprehending systematically-organized objects, so the experience of beauty aesthetically confirms the principle of the objective purposiveness of nature.

As alternatively expressed, since the harmony of the cognitive faculties expresses the power of "judgment in general" in its "S is P" structuring, Kant's assertion that [C], along with [A] and [B], are the grounds for the universal validity of all judgments, is to assert that [A], [B], and [C] are the grounds for cognition in general and, hence, are the grounds for the harmony of the cognitive faculties. So from this angle, [A], [B], and [C] are objectively necessary for the subjective universal satisfaction that resides at the basis of judgments of beauty.

Just as [A], [B], and [C] represent the objective preconditions for cognition in general, formulations [D], [E], and [F] provide subjective expressions of the supersensible substrate that refer to what is within ourselves, and these can be seen jointly as subjective preconditions for cognition in general. [D] refers to the substrate of humanity. This reference to humanity usually suggests a moral content, since, for example, Kant uses the same term (*Menschheit*) in §17 (on the ideal of beauty) within the context of describing how human beings determine their purposes via reason. He does not always use the term in this way, though, and he sometimes associates humanity simply with universal communicability as in §41 and §60. Within the present context, it is problematic to interpret [D] as referring to morality *per se*, because this interpretation does not cohere with the other five characterizations that are appearing on these two pages, all of which concern the conditions for cognition in general.

Greater consistency arises when we interpret the concept of humanity here as referring not exclusively to morality, but more cognitively to our common human nature – one conceived in relation to how all human beings have the cognitive faculties of understanding and imagination, or perhaps more expansively, how all human beings have the higher level faculties of understanding, judgment, and reason. This renders [D] as essentially the same as [F], which we will discuss further below.

Formulation [E], like [D], is consistent with this more exclusively cognitive interpretation, since it refers only to the supersensible "in us" without further characterization. Formulation [F] is an explicitly broad formulation that refers to the harmony of all of our faculties, and not particularly to our moral nature. All in all, we have a complicated array of overlapping formulations of the supersensible substrate that cover both objective and subjective dimensions, and that are variously specified within each dimension itself. One way to conceive of the entire group of characterizations and to comprehend their subtle differences as bearing on the same basic idea, however, is to regard them all as ways to characterize the necessary conditions for cognition in general. As such, they would stand as necessary conditions for the harmony of the cognitive faculties and, consequently, for the universal validity of judgments of pure beauty.

From this full array of variable formulations of a supersensible substrate, one thing is clear: Kant is adding some content to his §38 deduction of the universal validity of judgments of beauty to include more than the harmony of the cognitive faculties. The principle of the objective purposiveness of nature [C], for instance, is now entering into the discussion. The above analysis suggests that his exposition has now shifted to a more basic level by considering more broadly the necessary conditions, both objective and subjective, that underlie the harmony of the cognitive faculties and the nature of cognition in general. These considerations immediately introduce reflections about the necessary public conditions of the objects whose pure beauty is being judged.

These public conditions lead us to speculate further about the objective source of the purposive form in natural objects such as snowflakes and tulips, not to mention the nature of things in themselves. At the same time, Kant's discussion brings us into more speculative terrain in contrast to the confidently-describable *a priori* conditions for human knowledge, the associated logically-structured harmony of the understanding and imagination and the universal feelings presumably associated with the experience of that harmony. We are now introducing dimensions of the human condition that lead us to refer to, and speculate about, modes of being whose inner qualities are unknowable.

AESTHETIC IDEAS, GENIUS, AND THE SUPERSENSIBLE SUBSTRATE OF NATURE

As we can recall from the previous chapter on artistic beauty, an aesthetic idea is a presentation that expands inexhaustibly upon some given theme in a manner that defies exact formulation. Underlying the aesthetic idea, we suppose an indeterminate rule that accounts for the aesthetic idea's intelligibility; it is the artistic principle through which the aesthetic idea expands coherently upon the given theme. The intelligibility of the aesthetic idea's expansiveness, combined with the dynamic of the expansiveness itself, produces a satisfaction in the aesthetic idea's beauty, and this expansiveness coincidentally directs our attention towards reason or systematic totality. This is, in effect, the moral realm. The aesthetic idea's merely formal expansiveness thus harmonizes with beauty and morality simultaneously.

Since the artistic genius is both a naturally-inspired person and, as a human being in general, an intrinsically moral being, the productions of genius have an added power to express moral ideas. Although the merely *formal* structure of aesthetic ideas expands our imagination in the direction of morality, these formally expansive representations can themselves also have moral *content*. In the artistic genius's expression of aesthetic ideas in the realm of fine art, we can thus have within artistic expression itself, a coincidence between moral interests, natural energies, beauty, natural products, and artistic products. This occurs when the artistic genius creates a work of art that expresses a moral theme.

This account of artistic beauty as the expression of aesthetic ideas also importantly establishes a model for understanding natural beauty. If tulips, snowflakes, and the like are regarded as the expression of aesthetic ideas, then in the very expansiveness of the natural object's purposive form – i.e., in the free play of the cognitive faculties that it stimulates – there is an accompanying expansion of our imagination in the direction of reason, since such a formal expansiveness is characteristic of aesthetic ideas in general. The mental process involved here is comparable to how the mathematically sublime directs our attention to moral ideas.

We have seen above that all of the concepts of the supersensible arising in [A–F] above can be interpreted non-morally as referring primarily to the preconditions of cognition in general. When we characterize beauty, both artistic and natural, more fully as the expression of aesthetic ideas, however, we are led to regard the imaginative expansiveness that naturally beautiful forms stimulate, as suggestive of the moral realm as well. If natural beauty leads us to postulate a supersensible intelligence as the source of the beautiful forms, then the conception of beauty as the expression of aesthetic ideas directs us to postulate a supersensible intelligence with a combination of qualities. Not only would we postulate an intelligence that ensures the purpose of cognition to formulate laws of nature in an economic fashion; we would further postulate that this intelligence is moral as well.

Some added reflections upon Kant's characterization of beauty in general as the expression of aesthetic ideas also help explain why Kant introduces the conception of the supersensible to "save" the universality validity of judgments of pure beauty. To begin with, without a reference to a public object, the notion of universal validity would make no sense in connection with any judgments at all, and, hence, would make no sense with respect to judgments of pure beauty. That is, the initial §38 discussion of how everyone's cognitive structures are the same provides only a subjectively-oriented deduction in the absence of the objectively-oriented, but also necessary, aspect of cognition in general.

We might ask, though, whether anything more specific than a reference to all judgments has been brought forth by Kant's introduction of the idea of the supersensible within the context of legitimating as universal, the satisfaction that grounds judgments of pure beauty. If we examine Kant's theory of aesthetic ideas in this context and ask what this theory provides, some beauty-specific reasons emerge for directing our attention to the ultimate objective grounds of the objects that we judge to be beautiful.

In relation to what supersensibly underlies any object, one of the main upshots of Kant's theory of aesthetic ideas is its reference to an indeterminate rule or principle that supposedly underlies the intelligibility of any given purposive form. In the case of artistic beauty, we can look immediately to the artistic genius's creative energies. This, however, quickly takes us back to the intelligent forces of nature that operate through the artistic genius. In the case of natural beauty, we arrive at the same intelligent forces directly, as they produce beautiful objects such as snowflakes and seashells.

In each of these cases, we are led to postulate an underlying indeterminate rule that is responsible for the intelligibility of any given purposive form, and we project this rule onto natural objects as a consequence of applying Kant's theory of aesthetic ideas to the field of nature, given his definition of the genius as nature's favorite. From the standpoint of aesthetic theory, this indicates a single indeterminate rule that stands behind every beautiful object as the basis of its intelligible form. This single indeterminate rule serves as the explanation of the object's particular aesthetic style, and as the basis of the particular harmony of the cognitive faculties that the object generates in a disinterested perceiver. With respect to the judgment of beauty's universal validity, a common reference to this underlying rule will also contribute indispensably to guaranteeing the universal validity of the judgment. This latter is a second, more specific, reason why Kant's introduction of the idea of the supersensible bears on the question of the universal validity of a judgment of pure beauty.

It is important to appreciate why postulating such an underlying rule – a rule that serves the double-duty of accounting for an object's beauty and for its suggestiveness of moral ideas – is necessary to guarantee the universal validity of a judgment of pure beauty. A main reason is that even abstract designs, which are the objects of judgments of pure beauty, are interpretively *ambiguous*, and it is therefore necessary to stabilize the aesthetic effects of design's presentation on the side of the object itself. This is necessary because it is possible to select one point of an abstract design and apprehend the design's intelligibility from that perspective, but then notice that from a different point of reference the design's organizational quality takes on a new aspect (e.g., as in a duck–rabbit figure or Necker cube).

Appreciating the perceptual and interpretive ambiguity of abstract designs is comparable to interpreting a painting in the absence of knowing the artist's intention. One consequently for-mulates several construals of what the painting's meaning could be. Some aesthetic theories celebrate such open-ended ambiguity, but if we are concerned with the possibility of universal agreement in the painting's interpretation, then there is no choice but to pos-tulate a single meaning for the painting, which can be defined (not without difficulties, however) in reference to what the painter intended the painting to mean.

Whether the postulation of a single meaning for any given work of art is theoretically advisable in the larger scheme of things is a complicated hermeneutical matter. If, however, the possibility of universal agreement is to be established, then it is necessary to prevent the interpretation of the work of art from becoming a rela-tivistic matter that varies from person to person. Now if we trans-fer this problem to the wider context of apprehending the formal intelligibility of an abstract design, it becomes necessary to postu-late as the source of the design some single, indeterminate rule that accounts for the design's style.

In Kant's terminology, we must postulate in the case of natural beauty an intelligible source for the naturally-occurring design that grounds the intelligibility of the aesthetic idea exhibited in the design. Without this, there could arise a relativity of judgments of beauty *even among those who perfectly adopted a disinterested attitude towards the object.* This is a further reason – although this argument is difficult to identify in Kant's text – why both a *subjec-tively*-focussed deduction (concerning the harmony of the cogni-tive faculties) and an *objectively*-focussed deduction (concerning the principle of the purposiveness of nature and the idea of the supersensible) are necessary to establish the universal validity of judgments of beauty.

The abstract design of a natural object is indeterminate in its purpose and this very indeterminacy, when it is coupled with a purposive form, has the power to stimulate the cognitive faculties. At the same time, this purposive form has the power to produce a variety of intensities of the harmony of the cognitive faculties, all of which could be apprehended with a completely disinterested attitude. A single design can be apprehended as an example of many different possible rules, depending upon how one focusses one's perception on the design. So to guarantee the universal validity of the judgment of pure beauty, one needs to postulate that there is a single rule that prescribes the design (i.e., one must regard the object as if it were so produced).

This is to say that by merely adopting an aesthetically disinterested attitude toward the object, the universality of the consequent judgment of pure beauty cannot be guaranteed. If this is the case, then the legitimation of the universality of judgments of pure beauty in the earlier parts of the *Critique of the Power of Judgment* does not succeed by itself. Corresponding to the ideally disinterested attitude, along with the ideal attunement of the harmony of the cognitive faculties in the perception of an object's purposive form, one needs an objective basis for stabilizing the presentation of that form, i.e., a single indeterminate rule or style that underlies the object's aesthetic idea.

This need to coordinate subjective and objective aspects of the aesthetic situation arises also in reference to both empirical knowledge and morality. In each case, Kant specifies some necessary conditions on the side of the subject, and then adds assumptions about how things in themselves must be in order to ensure the actual functioning and real-life application of the subjective conditions.

Specifically, with respect to empirical knowledge, space, time, and the categories of the understanding specify a necessary structure of human experience, but one also needs to suppose the principle of the purposiveness of nature, since there remains the possibility that sensory stimuli could nonetheless present an unmanageable chaos. With respect to moral obligation, the categorical imperative specifies a necessary structure to moral reasoning, but one also needs to suppose that nature is amenable to our moral dictates, since there remains the possibility that our moral obligations could never be realized. With respect to judgments of pure beauty, the harmony of the cognitive faculties specifies a necessary ground for the universal feeling of beauty, but one also needs to suppose that the presentation of the object remains interpretatively fixed, since there remains the possibility that ambiguities in the object's design could preclude an objective ground for universal agreement.

AESTHETIC IDEAS, GENIUS, AND THE SUPERSENSIBLE SUBSTRATE OF THE HUMAN PERSONALITY

["**Remark I**"] In his first remark to clarify his solution to the anti-nomy of taste, Kant recalls and elaborates upon his distinctions between imagination, understanding and reason. He focuses on the notion of an idea, and how the general sense of this term is expressed in both rational ideas and aesthetic ideas. Many of his remarks reiterate his earlier characterizations of aesthetic ideas in §49, but he concludes with a revealing explication of artistic genius, the aim of which is to illuminate the nature of aesthetic ideas. In the context of this explication, Kant adds yet another formulation [F, as mentioned above] of the idea of the supersensible and associ-ates this concept with the conditions for the universal validity of judgments of beauty as well. Using this concept, he offers a com-plementary subjectively-oriented deduction of judgments of beauty that matches the earlier version from §38 closely, notwith-standing its higher level of generality.

As we have seen, the artistic genius has a natural capacity to produce resonant, imaginative presentations that bring the cogni-tive faculties of imagination and understanding into a free har-mony, such as to radiate a feeling of beauty. This capacity of the artistic genius is a natural one that transcends the understanding's merely mechanical functioning. The genius produces imaginative presentations whose intelligibility in each instance derives from an indeterminate, non-formulable rule, expressive of an aesthetic idea. The resonant imaginative presentation, or aesthetic idea, along with the indeterminate rule that accounts for that presentation's intelligibility, thus issue from the artistic genius.

At the subjective foundation of the artistic genius (and at the subjective foundation of every person), Kant postulates [F], viz., a supersensible substrate of all our faculties (*das übersinnliche Substrat aller seiner Vermögen*). This is not identical to any of the individual faculties themselves, but is the ground for the unity of them all. As such, this substrate is the integrative point that ren-ders possible the reciprocal and systematic attunement of each major segment of our mind with every other. Such an idea of a total internal attunement is expressive of an underlying rationality or intelligibility within us that aims for full comprehensiveness. This supersensible substrate of all our faculties that is said to ground the universality of judgments of beauty is a higher-level expression of reason in its quest for total systematicity.

[F] refers us to a generally integrative function of the mind that Kant supposes everyone has, and that operates the same way in everyone, just as the faculties of understanding and imagination are universally shared and operate the same way in everyone. [F] is a broad-based idea and includes the harmony of the understanding and imagination, along with the harmony of imagination and reason, as expressions of the ideal of total self-consistency and harmonious mental functioning. Since [F] includes the harmony of the understanding and imagination described in §38 as grounding the universal satisfaction of judgments of beauty, it can be seen as a more generic concept that, as a necessary condition, grounds the universal validity of judgments of beauty.

This supersensible idea serves as the basis for more than the universality of judgments of pure beauty, however, since it refers to the integrative functioning of every faculty. Reason is therefore included in the account, for instance, as it harmonizes with the imagination and with the understanding, via the faculty of judgment. This idea of the supersensible substrate of the subject is a necessary condition for the harmony of the cognitive faculties, so only upon its assumption is the universal validity of judgments of pure beauty possible. This idea of the supersensible substrate of all our faculties suggests, ultimately, that the expansiveness of aesthetic ideas partially refers to the integration of human personality, and hence to the harmony between what reason dictates in a moral context and what our bodies do in physical activity.

THE UNITARY IDEA OF THE SUPERSENSIBLE

["**Remark II**"] Kant's conception of reason as a principle that strives for totality and his reference to various rational ideas of the supersensible substrate referred to above reaches a powerful climax in this second remark on the antinomy of taste. We have seen how he presents the general idea of a supersensible substrate and then articulates alternative formulations [A–F] that have subjective and objective versions. In the objective versions [A–C], he refers to the unknowable substrate of nature in general, this same substrate considered in relation to some given empirical object, and this same substrate as the ground of our projections of intelligibility onto the phenomenal scenes. In the subjective versions [D–F], he refers to a supersensible substrate within ourselves as the ground of our various mental faculties. The sheer variety of Kant's characterizations indicates the theoretical centrality of the concept of a supersensible substrate, along with the need to draw some subtle distinctions between alternative conceptions of it, depending upon the theoretical context.

In this second remark, Kant proceeds integratively to assimilate these various objective and subjective conceptions of the supersensible substrate into a single thought. This emerges from his recognition that the antinomies referred to in his earlier works (in the first *Critique*, in reference to scientific understanding, and in the second *Critique*, with respect to morality, and now in the third *Critique*, with respect to judgments of beauty) are all resolved if we turn our attention to what lies beyond the world of sense-experience. Whether we are thinking about provable truth, goodness or beauty, the fundamental conceptual tensions that arise in our reflections on those subjects lead us into thoughts about what is supersensible for the sake of preserving consistency.

Kant integrates the various concepts of the supersensible in the following excerpt:

> If it is granted that our deduction is at least on the right path, even if it has not been made clear enough in all of its details, then three ideas are displayed: *first*, that of the supersensible in general without further determination as the substrate of nature; *second*, the very same thing as the principle of the subjective purposiveness of nature for our cognitive faculty; *third*, the very same thing, as the principle of the purposes of freedom and principle of the agreement of freedom with those purposes in the moral sphere.
>
> (§57, Remark II, Ak 346 (245), G 220–21, P 219–20, M 215, B 191)

The coincidence of these three notions of the supersensible establishes a theoretical framework through which to resolve one of the paramount questions in Kant's philosophy, namely, how nature and morality can be sufficiently compatible in order to realize the highest good. We will discuss this further below. For the present, it can be noted that we have arrived at an idea of the unknowable that can admit both scientifically-relevant and morally-relevant projections, and that can be conceived of as a supersensible intelligence that supports both our scientific and our moral efforts. The presence of naturally beautiful objects, regarded as the products of such a divine intelligence, thus provides a cognitively-related yet disinterested feeling that, in an intermediary role, dually reinforces our rational quest to understand the world scientifically as we do what is right.

THE SUBJECTIVITY OF THE *A PRIORI* PRINCIPLE OF JUDGMENT

[§58: "Concerning the idealism of the purposiveness of nature as well as art, as the sole principle of the aesthetic power of judgment"] As he has done in previous sections, Kant now offers a brief, stage-setting taxonomy in review and then continues to develop his main point upon that taxonomic basis. He presently states that aesthetic theories can be empiricist or rationalistic: empiricist theories are based on sense-experience and rationalistic theories are based on *a priori* principles. His refers to his own theory generally as a rationalistic one, but he distinguishes his version of a rationalistic theory from those that are built dogmatically upon determinate concepts. Judgments of pure beauty in the latter cases become logically provable and, as we know, Kant rejects this analysis. His own theory of beauty recognizes an *a priori* conceptual grounding for judgments of beauty, but he identifies this conceptual grounding as an indeterminate one. He has, however, been able to use this indeterminate basis to preserve the subjective universality of the cognition-related feeling that grounds judgments of pure beauty. In this context, the prevailing description of this indeterminate concept is the third [C] of the six concepts of the supersensible mentioned above, namely, that associated with the principle of the subjective purposiveness of nature for our cognitive faculty.

Kant's query here in §58 – the penultimate section of the Critique of Aesthetic Judgment that constitutes the first half of the *Critique of the Power of Judgment* – is whether the principle of the objective purposiveness of nature should be construed realistically or idealistically. He asks whether we should suppose that nature actually has determinate purposes (or, as well, indeterminate aesthetic ideas) in mind such that nature's purposiveness for our cognitive faculty is grounded in actual purposes that constitute the fabric of reality itself, or whether we should suppose that the principle of the objective purposiveness of nature is only an *a priori* projection from the human side of things, much like the forms of space, time, and the categories of the understanding, and that it asserts nothing about the nature of things-in-themselves. As might be expected, Kant opts for the latter, namely, the *ideality* of the purposiveness in the beauty of nature. Some of his justifying rationale, though, is slightly out of synchronization with his key definition of purposiveness.

To recall, Kant defined purposiveness in §9 as involving the perception of a spatio-temporal form whereby we cannot resist postulating that some intelligence produced the form, even though we recognize as a logical possibility that its appearance might have arisen by accident or by purely mechanical causes. It is comparable to encountering a regular hexagon drawn in the sand on an apparently uninhabited island (§64), or to finding a piece of wood in a bog that has a complicated, regular, geometrical shape, as if someone had carved it (§43). The postulation of an intelligence as the source of the object's design is virtually irresistible, and thinking otherwise borders on absurdity.

To undermine the attractiveness of the realistic interpretation of the principle of the objective purposiveness of nature, however, Kant introduces a questionable series of examples of natural beauty – mostly in reference to the production of crystalline forms – where the beauty involved is clearly caused by mechanical means, and where he says that we apprehend "not the slightest reason to suspect" that it requires anything more than nature's mechanism to produce the purposive form. Something is amiss with the examples, though, since according to the definition of purposiveness there should be some difficulty in dismissing the intelligent cause so easily.

Upon further reflection, one might say instead that the beauty of the natural forms leads one to imagine an intelligence, not behind this or that crystalline form, but more globally behind the natural laws that produce the crystalline forms. That the purposive forms can be explained mechanically does not necessarily preclude being astonished by the way merely mechanical laws could, or should, produce such rationally-pleasing products that seem to have been intentionally designed. Moreover, if we follow Kant's definition of purposiveness closely, it could be added that without the strong suspicion of an intelligence behind the forms, one is simply not appreciating the object's beauty.

This slippage in the application of his definition of purposiveness does not do much damage to the overall argument, for after an extensive series of examples of mechanically-produced objects of natural beauty, Kant sets aside the examples and offers a different, and what he believes to be a stronger, argument. He writes:

> The property of nature that provides us with the occasion to perceive the inner purposiveness in the relationship of our mental powers when judging some of its products, and indeed such [an inner purposiveness] as to be explained as necessarily and universally valid on the basis of a supersensible ground, cannot be a purpose of nature, or be judged by us as such: for otherwise the judgment thereby determined would be grounded in heteronomy and would not, as is appropriate for a judgment of taste, be grounded in autonomy and be free.
>
> (§58, Ak 350 (253), G 224, P 224, M 220, B 196)

Kant's point is that if we regard the principle of the objective purposiveness of nature as realistic, then we would postulate determinate purposes (and hence determinate concepts) as the ground for our judgments of beauty. These purposes, moreover, since they would reside outside of and independently of us, would render the judgment of beauty dependent upon empirical considerations. As he states, we would "then have to learn from nature what we have to find beautiful," and this would contradict both the *a priori* ground of judgments of beauty along with the idea that such judgments do not rest upon determinate concepts of what the thing judged ought to be. The postulation of natural purposes involves asserting the presence of determinate concepts that specify what the perfection of the objects would be, however, and this would have the effect of reducing judgments of beauty to judgments of perfection. This represents Kant's stronger reason for rejecting a realistic interpretation of the principle of the objective purposiveness of nature.

Kant concludes §58 with an analogy between the status of space, time, and the categories and the status of the principle of the objective purposiveness of nature, asserting that they are on a theoretical par in an important respect. Just as the objects in space and time do not as such represent how things are in themselves, and just as how no implication can be drawn that things-in-themselves are spatio-temporal, neither do beautiful objects in space and time represent how things are in themselves, and no implication can be drawn that things-in-themselves are actually being designed for our cognitive purposes.

Kant discusses this question in both of his introductions to the *Critique of the Power of Judgment*, and throughout his reflections, the question is always whether or not we should be postulating determinate purposes behind nature. It seems as if, within this context, the choices are to project either purposes onto the supersensible substrate of nature, or to leave it completely undetermined.

In the conception of natural beauty as the expression of aesthetic ideas, however, we need to project an intelligence upon the supersensible substrate of nature that does not operate according to purposes and definite concepts, but operates to produce indeterminate concepts that serve as the stylistic principles of the purposive forms that we apprehend as beautiful. The purposiveness of the form leads to the unavoidable postulation of an intelligence that underlies the form, and the nature of artistic creativity provides us with the analogy for understanding the sort of intelligence that underlies instances of natural beauty. So we are not asserting the behind-the-scenes presence of actual purposes and definite concepts in a realistic way. We are instead postulating – or, in other words, cannot avoid apprehending nature "as if" it had within it – intelligible forces that match the workings of artistic genius.

On phenomenological grounds alone, it is difficult to decide whether this projection is being understood realistically or idealistically. There is a subtle line between asserting the presence of an entity as actual, as opposed to feeling compelled to postulate the presence of an entity with the accompanying awareness that one is only being compelled to do so for subjectively-grounded reasons. In the latter case (and this is Kant's view) the principle of the objective purposiveness of nature generates a necessary illusion, not unlike how the forms of time and space generate the necessary illusion that what is only empirically real appears to be what is absolutely real.

BEAUTY AS A SYMBOL OF MORALITY

[§59: "Concerning beauty as the symbol of morality"; §60: "Appendix – Concerning the methodology of taste"] The Critique of Aesthetic Judgment concludes with some integrative reflections about how beautiful things symbolize moral ideas. The term "symbol" is crucial in this exposition, and Kant is careful to maintain that although the experience of pure beauty has no moral content (the objects "signify nothing" [§4]), it remains strongly suggestive of the essential qualities of moral reflection. Kant always keeps the spheres of beauty and morality from merging into one another, but he also tries to sustain a close relationship between them.

It is essential to preserve a noticeable conceptual distance between beauty and morality within Kant's view, for if judgments of pure beauty necessarily have a moral content, then they would forfeit the non-purpose-related quality that resides at their basis, and would collapse into a species of judgments of perfection. Kant begins the *Critique of the Power of Judgment* by explicitly distinguishing judgments of the morally good from judgments of pure beauty in §4, and he upholds this distinction throughout his aesthetic theory, as can be seen presently in the conclusion to the Critique of Aesthetic Judgment.

In the first remark accompanying §57 (in the second paragraph), Kant stated that "a rational idea can never become a cognition [i.e., it cannot become an object of empirical knowledge], because it contains a concept (of the supersensible) for which no appropriate intuition can ever be given." Insofar as moral ideas are rational ideas, they can never be suitably exhibited in experience and stand, rather, as ideals of human behavior. Only an aspect of a moral idea can be embodied in any specific spatio-temporal situation or object that has a moral content, and insofar as we refer to the concrete exemplification of rational moral ideas in space and time, that exemplification remains incomplete.

Within the artistic context, we have already described one way in which Kant conceives of the concrete, or sensory, exemplification of moral ideas. This is in relation to the artistic genius's production of aesthetic ideas. He describes this in §49:

> One can call such representations of the imagination *ideas*: on the one hand, because they at least strive toward what lies beyond the borders of experience, and thus seek to come close to a presentation of rational concepts (of intellectual ideas), which gives to them the appearance of an objective reality; on the other hand, and indeed mainly, because no concept can be fully adequate to them as inner intuitions. Using his imagination, the poet ventures to present as visible [*sinnlich*] beyond the limits of experience, the rational ideas of invisible beings such as the realm of the blessed, the realm of hell, eternity, creation, etc., and also those for which we find examples in experience, e.g., death, envy, and all sorts of vices, as well as love, fame, and similar things, with a completeness beyond any examples to be found in nature.
>
> (§49, Ak 314 (193–94), G 192–93, P 182–83, M 176–77, B 157–58)

In some situations, then, the artistic genius has some rational idea in mind, and with this idea in mind accordingly produces a sensory object whose presentation is so resonantly expansive in relation to the rational idea's content that it leads us to contemplate what is supersensible in an effort to grasp more fully the idea that is being expressed.[8] Now here in §§59–60, Kant refers to yet another way to coordinate beauty and morality. This is done in reference to "symbols." Kant regards the production of symbols of rational ideas as having the same purpose as aesthetic ideas, viz., of providing an exemplification of the ideas in sensory experience, except that symbolism achieves this purpose in a different way. Instead of providing a content that expands one's imagination in the direction of the idea, a symbol of a rational idea extracts the formal qualities of the rational idea's meaning and exemplifies these formal qualities alone, in the absence of the rational idea's content.

The process of constructing symbols for rational ideas is straightforward and proceeds as follows. We begin with some object or theme whose content is to be symbolized, and then attend exclusively to the formal qualities of that theme. One could say that in the construction of a symbol, we consider the theme disinterestedly and with respect to its pure beauty alone. The mode of consciousness is related to beauty, except that it bears a closer relationship to taste and the judging of objects in terms of their beauty than it does to the production of beautiful things, which is the concern of artistic genius. After adopting this disinterested approach to the theme and highlighting the theme's formal qualities, we then find some object that embodies those formal qualities and which can thereby stand as the symbol of the original theme or object.

Kant offers the example of a monarchical state which, depending upon the sort of state it happens to be in the instance considered, can be symbolized as either an organic body animated by a rational soul, or as a handmill that grinds people down. In the latter case, the arrangement is as follows:

1. The initial object or theme: a monarchical state
2. The principle of reflection on that object or theme: the thought that the state is not operating well, people are not being respected, and the social condition is oppressive
3. Second object or theme: a handmill that grinds things

The above example shows how the abstract principle that governs a particular kind of monarchical state can be identified and isolated for disinterested contemplation, and how an object that embodies that principle can be used as a symbol for that state. In this way, part of the idea's content, and ideally its essential content considered in its formal contours, is embodied in the symbol. The symbol is not merely a mark or sign for the idea. It actually embodies the idea, but it does so only partially with respect to the idea's formal principle. The symbol and the idea it symbolizes are different things, but their respective meanings have the same formal principle in common.

These examples reveal how there is a mechanical and literalistic flavor to the process of forming symbols that differs from the genius-inspired, metaphor-related, mystifying creation of aesthetic ideas. In a symbol, we take some theme A, find features [g, h, i, j] peculiar to it, and then use these features to link A with B, virtually in the form of a syllogism. This is not the same as creating a metaphor such as "the man is an oak" with "strength" as the middle term, since the meaning of even such a well-worn metaphor has far more involved in it than the connection to strength. In contrast, symbolism is far less imaginatively resonant. To say that "the state is a handmill," although the grammatical structure suggests a metaphor, actually tends to fix the activity of one's imagination rather than stimulate it.

Using this conception of a symbol, Kant maintains that "beauty is the symbol of morality," and identifies four principles that their respective meanings have in common:

1. The initial object or theme: morality
2. The principle(s) of reflection on that object:
   a. Morality satisfies immediately
   b. Morality satisfies disinterestedly
   c. Morality is based on freedom
   d. Morality is established in an *a priori* manner and therefore has a universal validity
3. The second object: beauty (which also has the above features)

The symbolization of morality by beauty does not dissolve the sharp differences between them. Moral awareness may satisfy immediately, but this satisfaction is based on the application of definite rules. Moral awareness may involve a disinterested satisfaction, but moral awareness also involves the interest that moral values, actions, and conditions actually exist in the world. Moral awareness is based on freedom, but this is the freedom of the will rather than the free play of the imagination and understanding in view of cognition. Moral awareness is established in an *a priori* manner, but the respective *a priori* principles underlying moral awareness and the experience of pure beauty are different.

In sum, the symbolic coincidence between morality and beauty is restricted to formal similarities, but beauty does embody these similarities. One could say that beauty embodies morality in a way that recognizes only the abstract form of morality. It is comparable to how the pure beauty of an object concerns only the object's purposive form, and does not consider what the purpose of object happens to be. The content of the object drops out of view. In the assertion that beauty is the symbol of morality, Kant is noticing that the basic, philosophically-formal features of pure beauty match the basic, philosophically-formal features of morality. No features of the object of beauty (e.g., its purposive form) are mentioned at all, as a matter of fact. The symbolic relationship between beauty and morality concerns parallels in the qualities of the respective kinds of judgment involved or in the subjective qualities of moral vs. reflective aesthetic awareness of beauty. In saying that beauty is *the* symbol of morality, Kant also seems to be suggesting that only beauty embodies such parallels and that it is consequently a unique symbol for morality at this level of generality.

With respect to the structural parallels between judgments of pure beauty and moral judgments, one parallel in particular is central. This is how a judgment of pure beauty is grounded in a satisfaction that radiates from the internal operations of the mind itself. As we know, Kant maintains that the satisfaction in pure beauty is not a sensory satisfaction, and in this respect one could say that in reference to the objects of such a pure satisfaction, the power of judgment "gives the law to itself." This is analogous to the dynamics of moral judgment, where the moral law also stems exclusively from within oneself. The difference is that the moral law, along with moral feeling, issues from our reason, whereas the feeling of beauty radiates from the operations of our cognitive faculties.

Since the universal validity of judgments of pure beauty depends upon the operations of the cognitive faculties that are assumed to be the same in all people, and since the analogy to the morally good would itself not be possible, if such a universal validity were absent, it could be said – as Kant does – that only insofar as beauty is a symbol of the morally good does it make sense to expect others to agree with one's judgments of pure beauty. The universal validity of judgments of pure beauty does not directly depend upon the analogy to the morally good, but if it were impossible to draw such an analogy, it would imply that judgments of pure beauty did not have the quality of universal validity.

Within the present context, a distinction between symbolism and aesthetic ideas is useful, for the way in which symbolism operates to display moral ideas differs from how aesthetic ideas achieve the same end. In symbolism, we have a literalistic reiteration in the symbol, the very same formal principles that are present in that which the symbol symbolizes, and not much more. The formal principles remain invariant and congruent in both. In contrast, an aesthetic idea need not embody the same formal principles as morality in its imaginative role of expressing this or that particular moral idea. As an expression of beauty itself, an aesthetic idea's purposive form would potentially generate in a perceiver the feeling of disinterested satisfaction, and so on, but the way it expresses the moral idea depends upon how it stimulates the expansion of the imagination.

Symbols of morality – considered in their capacity as symbols – do not expand the imagination in the direction of totalities and reason. Rather, they literalistically embody features shared by morality and beauty that arise from the philosophic analysis of them both. The claim that "beauty is the symbol of morality" and the claim that "beauty is the expression of aesthetic ideas" could lead one to conclude that aesthetic ideas symbolize morality and therefore operate symbolically in their artistic role of expressing moral ideas. This cannot be the case, since symbols do not operate by expanding one's imagination through an inexhaustibility of suggestions due mainly to the presence of metaphor. Unlike the case of metaphor, there is little mystery about how symbols have their effect, since they lack an excess of meaning that expands incomprehensibly upon what they symbolize.

There is a philosophical advantage to developing a relationship between morality and beauty in reference to symbolism, however, as opposed to invoking the terminology and processes associated with of aesthetic ideas and artistic genius. This is because symbolism is a more manageable, determinate, logically-amenable, and philosophically-effective concept from the standpoint of literalistic, systematic philosophy. At the end of the Critique of Aesthetic Judgment, Kant draws his discussion to a close by highlighting how beauty serves as an intermediary between morality and nature. This reveals his interest in illustrating how the theory of beauty can help explain how moral dictates have a reasonable chance of being instantiated in a physical world that, from the standpoint of theoretical reason, seems to run blindly according to the pure mechanism of natural laws.

CROSSING THE "INCALCULABLE GULF" BETWEEN NATURE AND MORALITY

In the introduction to the *Critique of the Power of Judgment*, Kant refers to an unsurveyable chasm (*unübersehbare Kluft*, §II) and great chasm (*große Kluft*, §IX) between the supersensible domain of the concept of freedom and the phenomenal domain of the concept of nature. One of the third *Critique*'s main concerns is to cross this fundamental and intimidating gap. Kant's account of how beauty is the symbol of morality takes a large step in this direction, since the core account of the satisfaction that grounds judgments of pure beauty is given in reference to the harmony of the cognitive faculties, which directly concerns not morality but our empirical knowledge of nature. So with the assertion that beauty is the symbol of morality, Kant solidifies the relationship between beauty and reason (i.e., morality), having already established it between beauty and the understanding (i.e., nature). This explicitly locates beauty at a logically intermediary position between morality and nature. Speaking more generally, it locates the concept of beauty as the intermediary between the concepts of moral goodness and empirical truth, expressive of the classical goodness–beauty–truth triad.

When we apprehend a beautiful object in an ideal way, we experience an immediate satisfaction that involves disinterestedness, freedom, and universality. The aesthetic idea expands our imagination and we are directed towards what is supersensible, much in the way the imagination expands in the experience of the sublime and draws our attention to our supersensible moral nature. In conjunction with this, the qualities of immediacy, disinterestedness, freedom, and universality serve as the basis for a transition to moral awareness insofar as the experience of beauty shares formally the same qualities with moral awareness. In at least two ways at once,[9] then, our attention is directed towards morality in the experience of beauty. Making such symbolic and aesthetic-ideas-related connections between beauty and morality is not necessary, but the coincidence between beauty and morality in their various formal qualities goes some distance in support of the cultivation of moral awareness.

In terms of the broader theory, Kant integrates nature, beauty, and morality in an attempt to cross the gulf between nature and morality in the following excerpt from the Introduction. It echoes the excerpt from §57 quoted above, here reiterated in the second of the following passages:

> The understanding gives a proof through the possibility of its *a priori* laws for nature, that nature is knowable by us only as appearance, and hence it provides an indication of its supersensible substrate, but leaves it completely *undetermined* [*unbestimmt*]. The power of judgment, through its *a priori* principle of judging nature through possible particular laws for it, gives the supersensible substrate (in us as well as outside us) *determinability* [*Bestimmbarkeit*] *through the intellectual faculty*. Reason, however, through its *a priori* practical law gives *determination* [*Bestimmung*] to the same substrate. Therefore the power of judgment makes possible the transition from the realm of the concept of nature to that of the concept of freedom.
>
> (Introduction, IX, Ak 196 (LVI), G 82, P 37, M 38, B 33)[10]

> If it is granted that our deduction is at least on the right path, even if it has not been made clear enough in all of its details, then three ideas are displayed: *first*, that of the supersensible in general without further determination as the substrate of nature; *second*, the very same thing as the principle of the subjective purposiveness of nature for our cognitive faculty; *third*, the very same thing, as the principle of the purposes of freedom and principle of the agreement of freedom with those purposes in the moral sphere.
>
> (§57, Remark II, Ak 346 (245), G 220–21, P 219–20, M 215, B 191)

Kant's logical systematization of nature, beauty, and morality is done in reference to the introduction and gradual specification of the idea of a supersensible substrate. The *Critique of Pure Reason* argues that we can only know objects as they appear to us in space and time and in accord with *a priori* laws of cognition, not as these objects are in themselves independently of our humanly-interpreting presence. The upshot of this is to distinguish between the unknowable supersensible substrate of nature and the spatio-temporal appearance of this substrate in its relationship with us.

In the theory of judgment, Kant argues that we need to suppose *a priori*, that in its empirical laws, nature operates favorably towards our efforts to comprehend nature, since it is possible that despite the regulations of time, space, and the categories of the understanding, nature's empirical laws could be so diverse and confusing that coherent experience would hardly be possible. So as a condition for successfully making judgments about nature and its processes, we need to assume that nature operates favorably with respect to our cognitive effort to comprehend individuals in terms of general concepts.

Another way to phrase this is to say that a condition for cognition in general and its perfection in the optimal *subjective* attunement of the understanding and imagination is the supposition that, *objectively*, there is an intelligence underlying nature that allows for the optimal attunement of the cognitive faculties to be effective in the production of empirical knowledge. This supposition is the principle of the objective purposiveness of nature:

> Now this principle can be no other than: that, since universal natural laws have their ground in our understanding, which prescribes them to nature (although only according to the universal concept of it as nature), so the particular empirical laws, in reference to that which in them is left indeterminate by the universal natural laws, must be considered in terms of the sort of unity they would have if an understanding (although not ours) had given them for the sake of our cognitive faculty, to make a system of experience in accordance with particular laws of nature possible.
>
> (Introduction, IV, Ak 180 (XXVII), G 67, P 19, M 19, B 16)

> ... the principle of the power of judgment in reference to the form of things in nature under empirical laws in general is *the purposiveness of nature* in its manifoldness, i.e., nature is represented through this concept, as if an understanding contained the ground of the unity of the manifold of its empirical laws.
>
> (Introduction, IV, Ak 180–81 (XXVIII), G 68, P 20, M 19–20, B 17)

The principle of the objective purposiveness of nature states that we must assume *a priori* that nature in its empirical regularities operates as if it were designed by an intelligence that has our cognitive interests positively in mind. We need not assume the actual presence of such an intelligence; we need only assume that nature operates *as if* there were such a being. This lends to nature a "determinability" or susceptibility to being intellectually determined on account of a rationally postulated intelligence that needs to be thought of behind nature as a condition for complete scientific comprehension. It is the principle of the objective purposiveness of nature, not beauty *per se*, that introduces the notion of purposiveness that shows itself in the beautiful forms of things. The *a priori* principle of the power of judgment itself and its subjective projection of a supersensible intelligence, then, is what syllogistically mediates the chasm between morality and nature.

Kant's moral theory, as a theory derived from the concept of law itself in its application to human activity, contains formulations of determinate rules for human behavior that derive from reason alone. So the intellectual determinability of nature, or potentiality to be specified in terms of moral concepts, is rendered possible by assuming the principle of the objective purposiveness of nature. This is to say that for scientific purposes, since we cannot avoid regarding nature as if it were governed by an intelligence, it is consistent for us to project a specific intellectual and moral content on the substrate of nature, as speculative as this projection might be. Upon doing so, though, and with the realization that the moral and intellectual contents that we are projecting are more directly expressive of the substrate of humanity that resides within *ourselves*, it becomes clear that the projection of moral contents onto the substrate of nature amounts to an effort to humanize the universe as a whole and to render it more friendly to our moral dictates.

The final remarks in the Critique of Aesthetic Judgment accordingly have a moral and political import, and in light of them we can observe how Kant's example of the monarchy that can be either humanistic or dehumanizing was not arbitrarily chosen. He states in the concluding paragraph that "taste is fundamentally [*im Grunde*] a capacity for judging the sensible presentation of moral ideas (by means of a certain analogy of the reflection on both)" and suggests that our experiences of beauty have a higher purpose than confirming that nature is amenable to scientific judgment, as useful as the latter might be. Since beauty only symbolizes and does not embody moral content, and since artistic expression can be used for trivial purposes, the development of moral consciousness neither logically follows from, nor is it necessitated by, the development of taste.

Kant's final statement is complicated in its meaning, for he states that since taste is fundamentally a capacity for judging how moral ideas are exhibited in sense experience, the development of taste itself depends upon the development of moral ideas and the cultivation of moral feeling. That is, he believes that if we had an undeveloped moral awareness, then this would hinder our appreciation of the world's natural beauty. This reflection makes it unclear whether the appreciation of beauty helps foster a stronger moral awareness, or whether moral awareness helps foster the appreciation of beauty.

It is easy to see how both are true, and also how this relationship between beauty and morality is a central theme in the Critique of Aesthetic Judgment. In §42, Kant asserted more specifically that taking an immediate interest in natural beauty is the mark of a morally good soul, and that this interest indicates a frame of mind supportive of moral feeling. The suggestion in §42 is that moral awareness fosters the appreciation of beauty, rather than the other way around. At the same time, though, the progression from science, to beauty, to morality suggests an ascending path from the realm of mechanical determination to the realm of intellectual self-determination via the intermediary of beauty. In this respect, beauty can lift us out of the field of sensory gratification to appreciate the purely intelligible moral realm.

Despite these reciprocities, Kant states several times in this final section that the propaedeutic, or preparatory conditions, for beauti-

ful art with regard to art's highest level of achievement is the feeling of community and sociality that expresses the perception of
oneself as a human being in general. With this in mind, he adds
that in the effort to develop a good society, it is necessary to exercise one's taste in adjudicating between the demands of the rich
versus the poor, the educated versus the uneducated, and the jaded
versus those of plain sensibilities.

There is no mechanical way to make these adjudications and
Kant believes that the development of taste can, in forging better
judges, therefore help forge a better society. Knowing where one is
morally aiming, however, is the preliminary and unconditional
step, and for this reason it seems as if Kant's stronger disposition is
to start with morality, and then use beauty as a way to bring the
domain of rational ideas down to earth, as opposed to conceiving of
beauty mainly as an aesthetic educator for those who are sub-
merged in the realm of sensory gratification, although it can
undoubtedly serve this purpose well.

BEAUTY AS A SYMBOL OF SCIENTIFIC COMPLETENESS

Given the emphasis upon morality in its relationship to beauty
that we encounter in the second half of the Critique of Aesthetic
Judgment, one can quickly lose sight of how the disinterested satisfaction that grounds judgments of beauty is characterized in reference to the harmony of the *cognitive* faculties of imagination and
understanding. Cognition is paradigmatically about the attainment
of literalistic and scientific knowledge. Its purpose is to know
empirically about nature and its mechanisms.

Admittedly, here in §59, Kant widens the scope of the term
"cognition" to include a "symbolic cognition" that allows him to
refer to a cognition of morality through beauty, but it is also clear
that such a cognition does not provide empirical knowledge. Kant is
clear in his writings that he believes that the existence of God cannot be proven, and he states accordingly that "all of our cognition
of God is merely symbolic."

One can say confidently that the harmony of the cognitive faculties is *prima facie* about the conditions directly necessary for the

acquisition of empirical knowledge. The immediate purpose of the power of judgment is to subsume individuals under general concepts, and empirical knowledge requires that we successfully do this. Such knowledge does not arise when we have, for example, aesthetic ideas (which are intuitions) for which no determinate concepts are adequate, or when we have rational ideas for which no finite set of intuitions is adequate.

This indicates that the satisfaction in an object's pure beauty is directly related to the scientific enterprise and indirectly related to morality. Since nature need not be well integrated in the array of empirical natural laws that prescribe its mechanical relationships, the principle of the objective purposiveness of nature refers to our need to operate as if a governing intelligence behind the scenes were directing nature in an economic and comprehensible manner. Whether the governing intelligence is also a moral intelligence is a further matter. Beauty regarded as the expression of aesthetic ideas or as the presence of systematically-organized form does support this hypothesis, though.

Kant invokes common sayings in his antinomy of taste, and he does the same in reference to the principle of the objective purposiveness of nature. In particular, he mentions sayings that express the principles of parsimony, continuity, and simplicity, e.g., "nature takes the shortest way" and "nature makes no leaps," and "nature's principles are ultimately simple." The *a priori* principle of judgment – the principle of the objective purposiveness of nature for our cognition – is mainly about how we need to conceive of nature for scientific comprehension to be possible.

The purposiveness of an object's abstract design that we apprehend when we appreciate the object's beauty, then, suggests to us primarily a scientific designer behind nature, whose understanding has prescribed the empirical laws of nature. So the intelligibility of the beautiful forms that we apprehend directly suggests that nature is amenable to our effort to comprehend things fully in scientific terms. The presence of beauty aesthetically confirms that our scientific efforts are not fruitless.

It would follow, then, that the more intense an object's pure beauty happens to be, the more it would reinforce the idea that a scientific system is achievable. One could say that the beautiful natural objects are symbols of the scientific ideal and reflect the perfection of empirical cognitions. The abstract forms of a beautiful snowflake or a beautiful tulip, for example, symbolize how scientific theories are integrated in their parts and how these parts constitute an organic whole. The abstract forms also stand as items that stimulate a perfect attunement between our understanding and imagination. In these respects, just as one can say that beauty is the symbol of morality in Kant's specific sense of "symbol," one can say that beauty is the symbol of the scientific ideal.

This once again locates beauty at the interface between morality and science, like the intermediary link in a syllogism. Morality is linked with beauty symbolically in terms of their shared immediacy, universality, disinterestedness, and freedom, and beauty is linked symbolically with the scientific ideal in terms of its formal intelligibility, systematicity, and organic unity. The beautiful object's purposiveness of form points in both directions and associates morality and nature thereby.

Kant does not explicitly develop this further interconnection between science, beauty, and morality, but it is implicit in his final remarks about taste as a means to cultivate a good society. The systematicity of a beautiful object's purposive form directly stands as a symbol for the scientific ideal, but it remains that this systematicity can still be taken to express not simply the actions of a hypothetical intelligence that economizes the empirical laws of nature. The purposive form can also be taken to express lawful governance in general, and in this regard, an item such as a snowflake or tulip can be taken in reference to the form alone, as a symbol for the organization one would hope for in a good society, where people operate rationally and with mutual respect for one another. In the bare notion of systematicity that the beautiful object's form exemplifies, we can think of either the system of moral laws, or the system of natural laws, or as Kant phrased it in the first lines to the conclusion of the *Critique of Practical Reason*, the starry skies above me and the moral law within me.

5

LIVING ORGANISMS, GOD, AND INTELLIGENT DESIGN (§§61–91)

NATURAL PURPOSES (§§61–68)

The second half of *The Critique of the Power of Judgment* provides an analysis of teleological judgments, i.e., judgments that ascribe purposes to things. The subject-matter of this half is accordingly referred to as "teleology," and Kant divides it into three broad segments which we will also follow in organizing the present exposition:

(1) The "analytic" of the teleological power of judgment, which concerns biological entities and, more specifically and fundamentally, the intrinsic purposes that they appear to embody.
(2) The "dialectic" of the teleological power of judgment, which addresses the question of whether the tension between mechanical causality and teleological causality (i.e., causality in reference to prior plans or purposes) is irresolvably contradictory.
(3) A modest-sounding "appendix" that concludes the third *Critique* with a topic vital to integrating Kant's philosophy as a whole, namely, the moral argument for God's existence.

The initial, definition-centered, analytic section concerning teleological judgment develops the core notion of a "natural purpose" (*Naturzweck*) – an idea Kant believes is exemplified in the physical world by living things. This concept of a natural purpose constitutes the thematic basis for the whole of the Critique of Teleological Judgment. The second section on the dialectic of teleological judgment examines an antinomy that teleological judgment appears to produce, and asks how one can compatibly understand that, given our mental constitution, we need to assume *a priori* that everything in nature is thoroughly understandable in mechanical terms, even though in experience we also observe living things that appear to defy mechanical analysis. Kant's resolution of this tension will reside in distinguishing different ways that the world appears to us relative to the different mental faculties we have. For the faculty of understanding, all material things admit of a mechanical analysis; for the faculty of judgment, some admit of a teleological analysis.

As an upshot of resolving the above antinomy of teleological judgment, Kant asks from the standpoint of the faculty of judgment whether nature as a whole has an ultimate purpose. This grand theme arises through reflections upon our moral interests, and Kant is concerned within the context of his discussion of natural purposes, whether nature as a whole is receptive and supportive of our moral obligation to act in accord with what duty requires. If nature is to be conceived of as being supportive of our moral interests, then nature itself would have a moral purpose. This introduces the question of how such a moral purpose of nature could be possible, and Kant answers this by referring to a morally-constituted God. The *Critique of the Power of Judgment* concludes on this theological note with some important reflections on the strength of the moral proof for God's existence.

Let us then begin articulating the above series of themes by considering Kant's initial discussion of natural purposes, upon which he focusses this second half of the third *Critique*. Obtaining a clear conception of a natural purpose is essential for understanding the third *Critique* as a whole, for this conception illuminates how both natural beauty and living things stand similarly for Kant as empirical indicators of God's existence. Since they are merely empirical indicators, natural beauty and living things are limited in their evidential role, however, and they can do nothing more than confirm what reflection on morality independently leads us to postulate on stronger, unconditional grounds.

[§61: "Concerning the objective purposiveness of nature"] To provide a transition from the first to the second halves of the third *Critique*, viz., from the Critique of Aesthetic Judgment to the Critique of Teleological Judgment, Kant begins by excellently summarizing the subjective status of the principle of the objective purposiveness of nature in reference to the experience of beauty. To recall, a judgment of pure beauty does not attribute any purpose to a beautiful object, but only reflects upon the beautiful object's form in view of its compelling suitability to be understood in reference to some purpose. The object's beauty is centered around this suitability *per se*, and is not about any purpose that the object might have. In contrast, a teleological judgment more determinately ascribes a purpose to an object, as would be the case when we say that a tree's roots have the purpose of absorbing nourishment from the soil, or when we say that a human body has the purpose of bringing moral content into the world.

In the following excerpt, Kant situates beautiful natural objects within the wider context of our examination of nature in the search for empirical laws, and the excerpt shows how the presence of beautiful natural objects suggests that our scientific quest is well received by nature itself, insofar as the presence of such objects leads us to imagine an intelligence that governs nature:

> According to transcendental principles, one has good reason to assume a subjective purposiveness of nature in its particular laws with respect to their comprehensibility by the human power of judgment, along with the possibility of the connection of particular experiences in a system; where among its many products, we can expect that some to be possible which – just as if they were put especially before our power of judgment – contain a form specifically appropriate for it, which through their manifoldness and unity ... serve to support and strengthen our mental powers, and which are given the name *beautiful* forms.
>
> (§61, Ak 359 (267), G 233, P 235, M 3 [Pt II], B 205)

Beautiful natural forms fit well with the design of our faculty of judgment, and present themselves as tantalizing suggestions that a non-human intelligence intentionally informs nature's mechanical workings. Although in our scientific endeavors we cannot but assume the principle of the objective purposiveness of nature and regard nature as if it were intelligently-directed, the presence of beautiful forms reinforces this science-governing assumption that nature is intelligently directed. The more beautiful nature happens to be, the more the supposition of an underlying intelligence is confirmed, even though if nature were maximally beautiful, this would not prove the existence of a designer. That beautiful forms exist at all, though, is a major point in our scientific favor and a significant point in relation to religious interests. Beautiful forms themselves do not provide scientific knowledge, but their rationality of form is exactly the sort of thing we are generally looking for when trying to formulate empirical laws in scientific inquiry.

In connection with our experience of beauty, the projection that a non-human intelligence underlies nature is grounded in our rational interest in increasing as far as we can, our empirical knowledge of how nature operates. The principle of the objective purposiveness of nature that supports these projections is simply an assumption we need to make about nature's relationship to us, namely, that nature is in itself supportive of our scientific efforts. For all we know, empirical nature might not follow suit with human intellectual needs, even though we rationally need to assume that it will.

When reflecting upon nature in a more directly scientific fashion, independently of the aesthetic support beautiful objects provide, one could, for instance, consider the interrelationships of means to ends that the things in nature bear to each other, independently of our own interests. Such would be the standpoint of the biologist, for instance, who, although perhaps impressed by a swan's beauty, would also marvel at the construction of the swan's neck, bones, and feathers in its effective relationship to its environment.

Mechanical relationships are certainly contained in such reflections, but there is an overriding and integrative apprehension of the respective purposes of each biological part, and these latter considerations involve teleological judgments. It is only a short step from initially projecting purposes onto biological organisms relative to our own cognitive interests, to suspecting that these projected purposes are intrinsic to the biological organisms themselves. Upon suspecting that the purposes are indeed intrinsic to the organisms, a question that poses itself is how these purposes objectively came to be there. One hypothesis – coincident with the principle of the objective purposiveness of nature – is that some non-human intelligence is responsible for locating them there. As we shall see, Kant advocates this view after sequentially eliminating every other competing explanation.

When hypothesizing that such highly organized and effectively-engineered biological structures are unlikely to have arisen by accident, and upon taking the giant step of projecting behind nature the presence of an intelligence responsible for the biological designs, the biologist would then be thinking in terms of what Kant refers to generally as nature's objective purposiveness, as opposed to a more human-relative subjective purposiveness that underlies the purposes we project from our cognitive interests alone.

The Critique of Teleological Judgment explores this idea of objective purposiveness and it reflects upon how things in nature serve each other, how they are internally constructed, and how, in this latter respect, their presence leads us to consider them as having been, either directly or remotely, intelligently caused rather than mechanically caused. As noted above, this second half of the third *Critique* incorporates teleological considerations into the wider and more basic Kantian theme of how moral behavior is realizable in the mechanical natural world, particularly in reference to what we need to assume about nature and the intelligence supposedly underlying it, to render possible the best realization of an ideal moral world. One of the systematic purposes of the third *Critique* is to situate beauty and living organisms within the larger context of articulating the philosophical conditions for realizing the highest good, and Kant formulates his discussions of aesthetic judgment and teleological judgment with this supreme moral end in mind.

Kant presents his analysis of teleological judgment in highly technical and abstract terms, but we nonetheless remain in familiar territory, since, just as everyone has experienced beautiful things, everyone has had at one time or another wondered about the ultimate origins of living organisms, and hence of our own living bodies, in view of their amazing structure and interrelationships. Such reflections motivate, for example, the teleological argument for God's existence (i.e., the argument from design) which forms an undercurrent to, and motivation for, Kant's discussions in this second half of the book.

It is a common experience to reflect that living organisms defy mechanical explanation, or to marvel at how the planets and galaxies are so well attuned to each other in their movements, and be tempted to conclude – even if one resists the conclusion after some further philosophical inquiry – that behind nature a non-human intelligence is responsible for how the empirical details of nature are organized. We seem not to be thinking mainly of our own projections and conceptual creations in such reflections, but find ourselves attending to nature's empirical workings independently of how we must conceive of nature generically according to the forms of space and time, and independently of our interests in constructing scientific theories, even though an underlying intelligibility that governs nature would serve the latter purpose well. Our reflections are directed upon nature as it is according to its own empirical and contingent workings, and upon how these appear to exhibit an intelligence whose power goes far beyond what we contribute to the situation with our human presence.

[§62: "Concerning the objective purposiveness which is merely formal, in contrast to that which is material"] In his inquiry into the structure of natural purposes and of the things in nature that exemplify them, Kant begins by distinguishing between various sorts of means – ends relationships that we can observe in both nature and ourselves. His hope is to identify a species of means – ends relationships whose teleological contents are not easily explainable in reference merely to our own internal constitution and conceptual projections. The resulting taxonomy, which we will develop below, is as follows:

I.   Subjective Purposiveness
       (which was considered in the Critique of Aesthetic Judgment)

   II. Objective Purposiveness
       (which is now being considered in the Critique of Teleological
       Judgment)
     A. Formal Objective Purposiveness
       (which derives from space and time within us)
     B. Material Objective Purposiveness
       (which is observable in empirical nature outside of us)
       1. Relative, or External, Material Objective Purposiveness
          a. Accidental means–ends relationships among natu-
             ral objects (e.g., how rivers help plant growth)
          b. Human designs (e.g., works of art)
       2. Absolute, or Inner, Material Objective Purposiveness
          a. Natural purposes (e.g., living organisms as natural
             purposes)

The last type of purposiveness in the above outline (viz., inner material objective purposiveness) that characterizes natural purposes and the living things that exemplify them is the type of purposiveness towards which Kant's investigation gravitates, and its analysis leads Kant to postulate a non-human intelligence behind nature. As mentioned, his wider interest is in understanding the conditions for postulating a non-human, supersensible intelligence in connection with realizing moral purposes in the world, and among the several types of objective purposiveness, he maintains through a process of elimination, that only natural purposes indicate the presence of this non-human intelligence, which he eventually equates with God (conceived of as a being that is all-knowing, all-powerful, and all-good).

Formal Objective Purposiveness

To develop the above taxonomy and to arrive at the key idea of a natural purpose, Kant first considers the many mathematical purposes to which geometrical figures can be put. He incidentally believes that a recognition of these purposes illuminates the commonly-held view that certain well-composed geometrical figures such as circles are beautiful. Kant traces the admiration for such figures to a source other than beauty, however, suggesting that we tend to call circles and other such figures beautiful, owing to a pragmatic appreciation of their utility. These figures can be used effectively in many circumstances to solve problems of both a purely conceptual (e.g., in mathematics) and empirical (e.g., in engineering) sort, and he argues that this suitability to be used for all kinds of purposes is the main source of their attractiveness. For Kant, this expresses the concept of perfection in a practical sense, and it has nothing directly to do with the figures' pure beauty, which is independent of the concept of perfection.

Independently of noting how there is an attractiveness to geometrical figures that is explainable in terms that are independent of whatever pure beauty they might have, Kant's larger purpose in accounting for this attractiveness is to initiate his taxonomy of types of objective purposiveness. The first of these types is the formal objective purposiveness that he defines here in reference to the usefulness of geometric forms. This formal purposiveness will contrast generally with several varieties of material objective purposiveness. The sense of the term "form" in this geometrical context is multiple.

Formal objective purposiveness refers to a quality of geometrical forms in reference to their possible uses. Most importantly, however, these forms are themselves specifications of the *a priori* form of space. Moreover, formal purposiveness is not related merely to geometrical forms on an individual, case-by-case, basis, but concerns more generally and immediately the *a priori* form of space, its subjective status in Kant's theory of knowledge, and the implications that can be drawn from this status. One of the implications of recognizing the subjectivity of space is that the apprehension of a geometrical figure's formal purposiveness does not strongly compel us to postulate purposes that reside outside of ourselves in, or as, the substrate of nature. This is because as far as we can know (according to Kant), space is not a quality of things in themselves, but is a feature of our own minds. Consequently, the formal purposiveness of geometrical figures mainly concerns ourselves and our mental constitution.

Kant is intellectually impressed by the fact that geometrical figures such as circles, quite apart from their conceptual definition, present themselves as straightforward, simple, visual solutions to an array of complicated mathematical problems that would otherwise seem intractable. The same is true for other figures such as the ellipse and the parabola. That these figures represent solutions to such complicated problems is startling and it leads one to speculate why this is so. Now there is no obvious answer to this, and Kant believes that the mystery stimulates our admiration of such figures and our consequent references to them as beautiful (although, as we know, given his aesthetic theory, this amounts to a misuse of the term "beautiful"). His key point is that the mystery of these figures' suitability (or purposiveness) to resolve complex problems invokes thoughts of an unfathomable integration within the complexity of spatial and mathematical relationships within ourselves. It does not immediately direct us outward to reflect upon what underlies nature.

Kant supplements his account of why we value basic geometrical figures with some reflections on Plato's admiration for geometrical and mathematical forms. He believes that Plato was impressed by circles and numbers on account of their dual quality of being purely conceptual entities, while yet having the practical capacity to reveal the world's empirical structure. According to Kant, this dual quality suggested to Plato that geometrical and mathematical forms are embedded in the fabric of things independently of us, and that we can also apprehend them more purely in their timeless, mind-independent reality by means of pure contemplation.

To temper and restrain this Platonic metaphysical vision about how things are in themselves, Kant recalls his own account of the synthetic *a priori* nature of space and time which concludes that space (and hence geometry) and time (and hence mathematics) are only forms within ourselves. This is exactly why their complicated configurations are knowable independently of all experience. On Kant's view, space and time have the crucial role of informing our experience with their geometrical and mathematical structures while at the same time lending a publicity and intersubjective agreement to our experience.

The apprehension of this publicity and empirical reality that comes along with the forms of space and time generates the mistaken belief that the purposiveness of figures such as the circle arises from outside of ourselves in whatever lies behind nature itself. If Kant's arguments are sound, then the circles and their geometrical relationships derive exclusively from within ourselves, so the mysterious attractiveness of the circle's capacity to resolve complex geometrical problems resides within ourselves as well.

Kant consequently looks elsewhere for a kind of objective purposiveness that can genuinely ground a supposition that a nonhuman intelligence with determinate purposes resides behind nature. As a result of his analysis of geometrical figures' attractive utility, we now have before us a distinction between *formal* objective purposiveness – an objective purposiveness associated with geometrical figures that, upon analysis, does not lead us to postulate an intelligent force in the substrate of nature – and a contrasting sort of objective purposiveness, namely, *material* objective purposiveness, whose qualities Kant now explores. He will define these latter qualities not in reference to synthetic *a priori* forms that reside squarely within the human being, but in reference to empirical objects and situations such as plants and animals, along with their environmental interrelationships.

Material Objective Purposiveness: External and Internal

[§63: "Concerning the relative purposiveness of nature in contrast to the inner (purposiveness of nature)"] Since the usefulness of abstract geometrical forms to resolve mathematical problems is in principle explainable in reference to the properties of space and time themselves, and does not require judgments that indicate an intelligence underlying nature, Kant accordingly directs his attention to the physical world itself and considers whether purposive interrelationships among natural things indicate a supersensible intelligence. He begins with a general characterization of material objective purposiveness, as opposed to the formal objective purposiveness that we have seen in geometrical forms. A judgment of material objective purposiveness arises when we perceive some natural object or situation and maintain that it could not be possible unless one of its necessary conditions is itself intellectual. This recalls Kant's definition of "purpose" in §10:

> Thus where not merely the cognition of an object but the object itself (the form or existence of the object) as an effect is thought of as possible only through [*nur als durch*] a concept of the object, there one thinks of a purpose.
>
> (§10, Ak 220 (32), G 105, P 65, M 61, B 55)

In the present context, Kant initially applies this conception of purpose to how material objects display means–ends relationships among themselves, and asks how we are to judge situations where, for example, a river deposits sand that leads to the growth of a pine tree forest on its delta. Judging the situation in a teleological fashion supposes that the river deposited the sand *for the sake of* the pine trees (i.e., with the pine trees in mind). Kant observes that this supposition generates a regress where purposes begin to fan out antecedently in all directions, and where it becomes necessary to maintain that, for example, the rain fell for the sake of the river, the mountains were present for the sake of the rain, the geological dynamics beneath the earth's surface were there for the sake of the mountain, *ad infinitum*.

None of these innumerable purposes seem to be objectively present and interconnected in the fabric of things, however, since they are not necessarily connected with each other. It is easy to imagine the river existing without the pine trees having appeared, and so the river's existence cannot be for the sake of the pine trees. Such means–ends relationships can consequently be characterized as only "relative" purposes, for they have simply to do with one thing being accidentally or conditionally advantageous for another thing, as opposed to one thing existing intentionally for the sake of another thing. This indicates to Kant that material objective purposiveness of merely a relative sort does not justify the assertion of a teleological judgment that compels us to postulate a supersensible intelligence that underlies nature.

[§64: "Concerning the distinctive character of things as natural purposes"] To arrive at a type of material objective purposiveness that *would* require an intelligence underlying nature to explain a given object's presence, Kant asks what structure a physical object would need to have, if that object were to compel a teleological judgment concerning its origin. This question introduces the characterization of structures that cannot be explained solely in reference to mechanical natural laws.

In effect, Kant is searching for evidence of an alternative kind of causality in nature that is compatible with, but is not obviously reducible to, mechanical causality. To do this, he first aims to become clear about how this different kind of causality would be theoretically structured, and second, what the observable structure of material objects that exemplified this structure would look like. He accordingly develops an ideal conception of what he refers to as a natural end or natural purpose (*Naturzweck*) and then looks for its instantiations in material objects. I will describe this theoretical structure in a moment.

Kant observes incidentally that *living things* exemplify this structure well enough to use as examples to introduce his conception of a natural purpose. So before presenting his theoretical characterization of a natural purpose, he illustrates the idea by using a tree as an example of an object that, to him, exemplifies a type of causality – viz., final causality (*Causalität der Endursachen*), which he also refers to as teleological causality (*teleologische Causalität*) – that is structurally different from mechanical causality. He will maintain the tree's embodiment of this teleological causality is what expresses the tree's life.

The tree in this example stands as a representative for all living things and of all material things that would instantiate the idea of a natural purpose, and Kant's wider claim concerning the world around us is that all living things exemplify a sort of causality that for us cannot be reduced to mechanical explanation. His abstract characterization of this sort of causality is philosophically eye-popping, for he asserts that a natural purpose – an object that for us defies explanation in exclusively mechanical terms – is "cause and effect of itself (although in a twofold sense)."

This is paradoxical since it is a challenge to conceive of how a thing can be both the cause and the effect of itself. On the face of things, if something is the cause and the effect of itself, then it is self-caused, and, hence, needs to be before it can be. This is a contradiction. It seems that self-causation makes no sense, and this makes the presence of living things a doubly puzzling affair, firstly because their very apprehension suggests that their internal reality is non-mechanical, and secondly because Kant's characterization of them involves the paradoxical idea of self-causation.

Kant resolves this conceptual difficulty by (1) amalgamating individualistic and generic levels of description into a single account, by (2) referring to a material object's presence over time, and by (3) referring to the interrelationship of a material object's parts at any given moment of time. A tree, for instance, is "cause and effect" of itself in a threefold sense. First, at the generic level, one individual tree produces another individual tree of the same species, and so the first tree reproduces itself in the generic sense, through an activity that allows its type, or kind, to continue. This is captured in how two people can be said to help reproduce the human species when they produce children, and thereby reproduce themselves as human beings. In this case, the species-type is itself regarded as a self-sustaining being. This is reminiscent of the Stoic λόγος σπερματικος (logos spermatikos), viz., the divine creative genius that gives life to everything through its infusion into inanimate matter, and which gives each things its specific character.[1]

Second, at the individual level, a tree reproduces itself over time in the sense of assimilating food and keeping itself alive. The tree that existed yesterday produced the tree that exists today. Since it is one and the same physical body that is being sustained over time and referred to in this process, the tree of today is the cause of itself, for it is the same tree (as opposed to the tree growing next to it) today, as it was yesterday.

Third, at the individual level, a tree has a set of interdependent parts, so the production and sustenance of one part by another part is understandable as the tree acting as cause and effect of itself. For instance, the activity of a tree's roots helps keep the leaves alive and the activity of the leaves helps keep the roots alive. Although some parts of the tree are not alive (e.g., the bark, or in a mammal, the hair), in general the tree's parts operate in an organic unity and are inextricable aspects of the tree as a whole. No particular living thing perfectly exemplifies the ideal of total organic unity, but living things exemplify it well enough to defy mechanical analysis.[2]

Kant's definition of a natural purpose aims to show how living things embody a self-sufficiency, self-sustenance, and self-determination that is analogous to (one could also say "symbolic of") the free, autonomous human personality. In light of this analogy, and in conjunction with his belief that it is impossible for us to conceive of how a living thing's reproductive, self-sustaining, and organically-unified qualities could be reduced to mechanical causes (although they might be in principle, from a higher, non-human perspective), Kant argues that we are inevitably led to postulate an intelligent cause that underlies living things, owing to how well they exemplify the idea of a natural purpose.

[§65: "Things as natural purposes are organized beings"] Kant articulates his idea of a natural purpose by defining a broader distinction between two different and exhaustive kinds of causality – mechanical causality (i.e. efficient causality) and teleological causality (i.e., final causality), where natural purposes will be a species of the latter. Kant refers to mechanical causality as defining a descending matrix of real causes, such that A is the effect of B, and B, in turn, has causes that cannot be A. He refers to teleological causality as defining a matrix of both descending and ascending ideal causes, such that A is the effect of B, but A is also among the causes of B. Mechanical causality, as defined here, is intended to be consistent with the familiar concept of causality that obtains among inanimate objects, as when one billiard ball hits another billiard ball and causes it to move on. As noted, teleological causality has two species, artifactual and natural. I will describe this distinction at greater length in the next section below.

Teleological causality is obviously more peculiarly structured than mechanical causality, and Kant helps clarify the idea through the example of a house whose rental generates income, but which was itself built with the image of generating rental income in mind. The potential income is the house's motivating cause and the actual income is the house's material effect. The income itself (potential and actual) thus stands as both the cause and effect of the house, and the actual house stands as the both the cause and the effect of the income (actual and potential). Circularities and mutual dependencies permeate the situation.

As the example of the house illustrates, teleological causality is evident in cases where some prior plan is intentionally realized. The plan, in a sense, causes its own realization. A person is motivated by the prospect of receiving rental income, for instance, builds a house to rent, later collects the rents from the house, and thereby realizes the plan. Or similarly, a person imagines the expression of some idea and creates an art work that expresses the idea, again thus realizing the plan.

In each of these cases, the motivating plan exists separately from, and outside of, the actualization of the idea, as would also be the case in the construction of a watch – an example which figures centrally in often-cited formulations of the teleological argument for God's existence.[3] Owing to this external relationship between the plan and its realization, we have here instances of what can be called an artifactual kind of teleological causality. Some designs for watches (i.e., artifacts) remain on the drawing board and are never realized. Neither was the plan to build a house in the above example in the nature of the house itself.

Human Purposes, Natural Purposes, and Divine Purposes

Kant observes that human artifacts or works of human art, such as watches, although they are the products of intentional activity that realize a prior plan and exemplify teleological causality in general, cannot be called natural purposes for two reasons. The first is that an artifact's plan is conceived of independently of the artifact and can exist without the product. This is true for all intentionally-designed human artifacts such as watches, houses, and the like. The second is that the parts of an artifact do not produce and sustain each other, whereas the parts of a natural purpose do.

With respect to the first reason, the independence of plan and product that characterizes human art would not, by the way, be true of divine art, although one might initially think so. It is easy to imagine (mistakenly) that plan and product would be independent of each other in all cases of natural beauty considered as divine art, for example. This, to recall, is where the indeterminate rule expressed in the object's purposive form, or aesthetic idea, is conceived of as residing behind the phenomenal scenes and hence, as distinct from the object's phenomenal presence.

However, Kant maintains that if God conceives of something, then it must be actualized thereby, so there can be no separation of

God's plans from the things that instantiate those plans. The divine thought of the plan, and the creation of the thing that instantiates the plan, are one and the same. So in every case of natural beauty, the object's respective indeterminate rule, presumably divinely inspired, could not be independent of the beautiful object's purposive form.

These considerations define three items expressive of teleological causality that need to be kept theoretically distinct, namely, natural purposes, human artifactual purposes (i.e., works of human art), and God's plans and their instantiations (i.e., divine art), which would include objects of natural beauty considered as divine art. It remains to be seen how Kant formulates the relationship between natural purposes and divine art. The stronger the relationship turns out to be, though, the closer living organisms will be to objects of natural beauty, since they would both turn out to be expressions of divine art.

We can pursue this crucial question of the relationship between natural purposes and divine art by noting, first of all, that if a natural object is regarded as a natural purpose, then its motivating plan cannot be conceived of as being independent of that natural object. The plan and the natural object must be necessarily connected. With respect to this consideration alone, this condition would be satisfied, for example, if God were to conceive of the natural object's purpose.

It is not clear, though, that such a necessary relationship between plans and products itself entails that the plan would therefore be "inner," internal or intrinsic to the product, since the idea of divine art appears itself to be a counterexample. In divine art, God conceives of the plan, say, for a flower, and the plan is immediately realized with the flower's simultaneous realization. The realization of God's plan in the actual flower, however, is a situation where it does not seem that the flower's plan is internal or intrinsic to the flower in any self-sufficient sense. The flower's plan is God's plan and is not the flower's own plan, as would otherwise be the case if the flower were in itself a completely self-determining intelligence.

This is where some conflict and complication enters into the relationship between divine art and natural purposes, for contrary to the above reasoning, Kant maintains that the flower is a natural purpose and that we need to conceive of the flower's purpose as originating in God. He can find no other plausible alternative for the origin of the flower's purpose. The flower may be alive, but it does not have any self-consciousness that would account for its life and motivating plan as self-sufficiently originating within the flower itself.

Kant is clearly impressed by how the structure of living things embodies the structure of teleological causation. We have also seen how, relative to the structure of mechanical causation, the structure of teleological causation is more peculiar. We do, though, have easily-understandable paradigm cases of teleological causality, as in the house and rental income example above. Problems arise when models on the order of the house and rental income example are applied to living things such as flowers, since flowers do not seem to have any concept-producing intelligence of their own.

If we turn now to the second reason that human artifacts are distinguished from natural purposes mentioned above, we can recall that natural objects judged as natural purposes – viz., natural objects that exhibit a life of their own – display internal relationships among their parts that, for us, are not comprehensible by what mechanical causality can identify within its own terms. Even with respect to the general distinction between mechanical and teleological causality and in tune with the artifactual example of a watch, a living thing's parts are only understandable in relation to the whole organism, just as the various parts of a watch are understandable only in relation to the watch's plan or design.

This distinguishes living things and human artifacts from rocks and rivers in reference to the former pair's teleological causality, but it does not distinguish human artifacts from living things. Kant adds accordingly that living things, considered as natural purposes, differ from human artifacts in that the parts of a living thing are reciprocally related insofar as they produce and sustain each other. When a part of a watch breaks, the other parts of the watch do not act in concert to repair or replace the missing part. Living things, however, do this. If we are to apply the model of teleological causality to a living thing and aim to draw a further distinction between human artifacts and natural purposes, then we need to add that unlike human artifacts, the plan is inner, internal or intrinsic to the living thing, since that plan motivates, produces, and reproduces the living thing through the action of the living thing itself.

Living things as natural purposes thus differ from both beautiful works of human art and beautiful works of divine art (i.e., objects of natural beauty, such as non-living snowflakes), even though all are conceived in terms of teleological causality. The motivating plan or concept is intrinsic to the object that is judged to be a natural purpose, and this renders the object more directly analogous to a being that exhibits a self-directedness, self-organization, self-determination, self-sufficiency, and autonomy. Natural purposes, or living things, while having an affinity with objects of natural beauty, also embody analogously the sort of autonomy that we encounter in the moral sphere. They display a freedom from mere mechanical causes. Whether natural purposes can consistently be conceived alternatively as products of divine art still remains an open question, although some tensions in the equation have now been suggested.

In any case, none of these considerations entail that mechanical and teleological causes are irreconcilably inconsistent with each other, since regarding any natural object as a natural purpose can help us comprehend the object in mechanical terms. Insofar as teleological causation can help in this scientific effort, it cannot be unrelated and inconsistent with scientific causality. It is simply that for us, the mechanical analysis can go only so far before we encounter incomprehensible aspects of the natural purpose. Kant is very clear about his belief that mechanical and teleological causality are compatible:

> For a body, in itself and according to its inner possibility, to be judged therefore as a natural purpose, it is required that the parts produce each other with respect to their form as well as their interconnection, and thereby a whole from their own causality, whose concept could . . . conversely be the cause of the body according to a principle. Consequently, the connection of *efficient causes* [*wirkenden Ursachen*] could be judged at the same time as an *effect through teleological causes* [*Wirkung durch Endursachen*].
>
> (§65, Ak 373 (291), G 245, P 252–53, M 21 [Pt II], B 219–20)

If we translate this passage into the Aristotelian terms that inspire it, Kant states that the purpose of a flower, for instance, is the principle within the flower responsible for the flower's life. The flower's purpose organizes the flower as a whole and it governs the flower's growth, reproduction, and self-maintenance. This inner purpose is the flower's "form" that defines the flower's potentiality, and that is actualized in the flower's growth to maturity and consequent self-maintenance in that mature condition. This form is also the "cause" of the flower and it is internal to the flower. One could also say this form, or purpose, is the essence of the flower. Perhaps strange to say, the embodied definition of the flower is what expresses its life.

The above formulation helps to bring together the themes of the first and second half of the third *Critique* by exposing some structural similarities between the idea of a natural purpose and Kant's theory of aesthetic ideas in relation to both natural beauty and human beauty. The theory of aesthetic ideas leads us to postulate a single indeterminate rule underlying the beautiful object in question – it could be either a beautiful work of art or a beautiful natural object – that the beautiful object's purposive form, or aesthetic idea, expresses.

In the case of natural beauty, this indeterminate rule is the focal point for our projections of a supersensible intelligence behind nature and is the aesthetic analogue for the object's purpose. One could say that the indeterminate rule constitutes the overriding form or style of the aesthetic idea's purposive form. As we have seen, conceiving of aesthetic ideas in this manner allows the theory of genius and the theory of natural beauty – both of which are expressed in terms of the presentation of aesthetic ideas – to match in their structural contours. Just as the artistic genius (whose talents are natural energies) produces aesthetic ideas, nature, conceived of in its empirical qualities as the expression of a divine artist, produces aesthetic ideas in the stylistic formation of beautiful things.

The projected indeterminate rule that underlies any beautiful natural object is not, however, the same as the rule, purpose, or form that is intrinsic to that object as a natural purpose. Some beautiful natural objects, such as snowflakes, are not alive at all and this is sufficient to distinguish the two types of forms. Neither is the particular free beauty of any given snowflake, or flower, understandable in reference to the scientific definitions of snowflakes or flowers. When we appreciate the pure beauty of a flower, we do not consider the flower as a natural purpose, and do not thereby consider the flower's purpose as would a botanist, even though the principle that underlies the flower's life and the principle that underlies the flower's beauty are both examples of teleological causes traceable to the same divine source. The commonality among these examples is that the divine intelligence behind nature is assumed to produce the determinate empirical natural laws, the determinate natural purposes and the indeterminate aesthetic styles that are expressed in beautiful natural objects. Again, though, it remains to be seen whether it makes clear sense for Kant to maintain that natural purposes are comprehensible as the expressions of divine art.

The above distinctions and parallelisms render it all the more significant that, in the case of human beauty, the natural purpose of the living human body and the artifactual and rational teleological causality within it can be brought into coincidence. According to Kant, the essence of the human being is rationality as implying a moral content, and this rationality can ideally govern not only the beautiful human bodily form (as exhibited in classical Greek sculpture and as we have seen in §17) and human behavior (as in moral action). It can also govern the living quality of the human body insofar as its parts reciprocally produce and reproduce each other. This triple coincidence comes to the surface, at least, if we identify the form of a living thing with that living thing's essence, for with this follows the coincidence of human rationality with the motivating principle of the living body.

This coincidence between human rationality and the motivating plan of the living human body stands importantly as a third example of nature's compatibility with moral demands. The first of these arises in the discussion of the ideal of beauty (§17), where an idealized and standardized human form (the diagrammatic aesthetic normal idea) is fused with moral content (a rational idea). The second is in the artistic genius (§§46–50), where the genius's creative power is defined as an expression of natural forces but where, in addition, the genius's rational, human quality leads to the natural expression of moral content through the production of aesthetic ideas.

In this third coincidence of human rationality and bodily life, the autonomy of the reflective moral agent matches, at least potentially, the autonomy of the human body in its self-organizing, self-sufficient, and self-determining living quality. The teleological cause of the moral agent and the teleological cause of the living human body are in principle the same, in other words, although they are usually in tension with one another. It would therefore be nature's mechanical causality operating of itself in the human body (as a raw material object) that interferes primarily with the realization of moral demands, rather than the pressures of the human organism itself (as a living being) considered teleologically as a natural purpose.

Nature Itself as a Single, Living Organism

[§66: "Concerning the principle for judging the inner purposiveness in organized beings"] Kant considers the result of immeasurably extending the idea of a natural purpose beyond its application to individual material objects to the point where it encompasses the entirety of nature. To express this, he recalls an assumption that governs the judgment of things as natural purposes: in judging an object as a natural purpose, it must be assumed that each part of the object is reciprocally an end and means as well. The organic unity is strong and it is assumed that among the object's parts there is nothing superfluous, accidental, and non-functional. Insofar as anything is considered to be a natural purpose, one assumes that the item has no dead spots and that it is fully integrated with respect to its purpose.

This assumption about the reciprocity of part and whole characterizes merely an *a priori* principle of judgment, and it does not entail that the objects one observes will display the principle perfectly. It is an idealization, as is the very idea of a natural purpose that it specifies. Upon extending this idea to cover all of nature, we arrive at an idealized conception of nature as a vast, living, self-sufficient organism where everything is interconnected and where nothing happens in vain.

[§67: "Concerning the principle of the teleological judging of nature in general as a system of purposes"] Less dramatically and more traditionally, and, as has been suggested, with nonetheless some questionability, the extension of the concept of a natural purpose to cover all of nature can also suggest the idea of nature as a divine work of art – one where nature's plan is determined from behind or beyond nature by a supersensible intelligence. Kant himself believes that when we extend the principle of judging things as purposes to encompass the whole of nature, our intellectual focus is ultimately led beyond the sensible world. His arguments are less than transparent since, on the face of things, the concept of a natural purpose requires that the natural purpose's motivating plan be conceived of as *internal* to the object, as opposed to being derived from outside of the object. If this purpose is alternatively derived from outside of the object, then it would be a case of teleological causality of an artifactual sort, rather than one characteristic of natural purposes.

It is true that we only conceive of, and do not directly perceive the purpose of any object considered as a natural purpose, since this purpose is a concept. This is not, however, what Kant means when he maintains that we are led beyond the sensible world to the realm of the supersensible when reflecting upon nature itself as a natural purpose. The idea of the supersensible refers particularly to a being, or to a realm of being, that is independent of the human mind.

We can clarify the emerging problem by distinguishing between (1) nature conceived of as a whole, as a natural purpose itself, in which case its purpose would be internal to it, and (2) nature conceived of as a whole in terms of teleological causes in general. The latter, more generic, conception is consistent with nature itself not being a natural purpose, but where its purpose stems from a being outside of nature, such as God, whose existence is independent of nature.

Kant refers to nature as a whole, when considered as a natural purpose, as a "system of purposes" (*System der Zwecke*). Questions arise when we consider the possible source of each natural purpose that constitutes the total system of nature as an organically-unified set of natural purposes. If a natural purpose requires that each of its parts produces the whole and vice-versa, then each individual natural purpose in the system of nature must count as a part of the full system of natural purposes. Each of these parts would produce the whole and the whole would determine the production of the parts, as is the case with any living organism, and as follows from the definition of natural purpose. The entire arrangement would therefore be self-contained and self-sustaining. This would make it contradictory to introduce an independent supersensible intelligence that governs both the whole and the individual natural purposes. The impossibility arises because the whole and the parts within a natural purpose define a self-enclosed whole; one produces the other and they stand in a relationship of reciprocal dependence.

Another way to express the difficulty with Kant's suggestion that judging nature itself as a natural purpose leads us to postulate a supersensible intelligence is to ask why we are fascinated with and intellectually challenged by a natural object such as a flower. Mechanical explanation can go only so far to explain why the object is intriguing. Considering the flower as an artifact, whether divine or human, tends to reduce the flower's life to a life that is not its own, but rather the life of something else. At the same time, however, ascribing an intelligence to the flower itself to explain its living quality is unsatisfactory, since the flower does not display the sort of complex intelligence that would seem to be required to organize such a being. So there is a triple bind: neither mechanical causality, nor God, nor the flower itself can satisfactorily explain the flower's presence as a living being. Kant regards the flower as a work of divine art, but this robs the flower of the self-sufficient quality we admire in it as a living being.

Throughout his discussions, it important to emphasize that Kant is careful to say that the principle of the objective purposiveness of nature, whose application leads to the queries and conclusions mentioned above, is only regulative. We are directed to consider nature *as if* there were a supersensible intelligence behind it, although we can never know that there is such an intelligence. This softens the contradiction between judging an object as a natural purpose (that has an "inner natural perfection" (§65)) while invoking God – a being that exists independently of that object – to explain the presence of that natural purpose. The contradiction is softened because the projections of intelligibility that we make in our judgments of things as natural purposes cannot be proven to be either true or false. Kant states:

> It is obvious that this is not a principle for the determining, but only for the reflecting power of judgment, which is regulative and not constitutive. We receive through this principle only a guide for considering natural things according to a new lawful order in relation to a determining ground that is already given, and for extending natural science according to a different principle, viz., that of teleological causation, however without damaging the principle of mechanical causality.
>
> (§67, Ak 379 (301), G 250–51, P 259, M 28 [Pt II], B 226)

Kant underscores the compatibility of teleological causation with mechanical causation and he advances no claims to scientific knowledge in connection with the principle of teleological causation. At the same time, though, we should recall that he identified the principle of teleological causation as necessitated by the additional presence of teleological causality in certain natural objects, namely, living things. Teleological causation is not reducible to mechanical causation, but neither is it a mere illusion that we can set aside.

Kant argued earlier that external objective purposiveness – the purposiveness displayed in how rivers leave soil deposits that assists the growth of plants – provides no evidence for the presence of natural purposes. What has happened in Kant's exposition is that after having rejected external purposiveness as evidence for the presence of natural purposes, and after having found evidence of natural purposes elsewhere in the structure of living things, he extended the principle of conceiving things in terms of natural purposes to cover nature as a whole, which has now resulted in an idealized conception of nature as a single organism. This poses the question of where nature's purpose could originate under such a conception.

However this question is answered, either in reference to a divine intelligence or in reference to nature itself, under this extrapolated teleological conception of nature, the soil is considered to be a part of the organism of nature as are the plants it helps sustain. So upon expanding the concept of a natural purpose to encompass all of nature as a system of natural purposes, what first appeared to be external objective purposiveness becomes reinterpreted as internal objective purposiveness, since we now assume from the start that nature is an immense organism. Unlike his German Idealist successors (e.g., Hegel), Kant does not believe that this idea of nature as a living whole expresses a provable truth about nature, but he does believe that such an idea is necessary to guide our scientific quest to uncover relationships of mechanical causality in nature. Strange to say, complete scientific knowledge – the perfection of cognition – requires that we conceive of nature itself as a living organism.

[§68: "Concerning the principle of teleology as an inner principle of natural science"] Despite the need to assume for the sake of conducting scientific inquiry, that nature has a purpose and contains within itself many sub-purposes, this full-blown teleological conception of nature does not constitute scientific knowledge. In the course of expressing this point, Kant maintains that natural purposes are conceivable as being either intentional or unintentional. This is useful for understanding his references to God and to a divine intelligence behind nature in connection with the teleological conception of nature as a system of natural purposes. The teleological understanding of nature gravitates inevitably towards a reference to God, if natural purposes are conceived of as intentional, as opposed to unintentional, since the idea of an unintentional purpose (i.e., as if concepts that define plans, goals, and patterns of development could exist of their own accord) is difficult to understand. Kant himself maintains (in §72) that the concept of an unintentional purpose is contradictory.

This distinction between intentional and unintentional purposes does not alleviate the problem of interpreting nature as a divine artifact and thereby removing its self-sufficient life, since the very concept of natural purpose still requires that the purpose is somehow conceived of as being *intrinsic* to the natural purpose. Kant is clear about this, although he continues to refine the idea in later discussions:

... a thing, which is a natural product, but which is to be cognized simultaneously, however, as possible only as a natural purpose, must be reciprocally related to itself as both cause and effect ...

(§65, Ak 372 (289), G 244, P 251, M 19–20 [Pt II], B 218)

An organized product of nature is that in which everything is a purpose and reciprocally also a means [to that purpose].

(§66, Ak 376 (296), G 247–48, P 255, M 24 [Pt II], B 222)

... *inner natural perfection* [is] possessed by those things that are possible only as *natural purposes* ...

(§65, Ak 375 (294), G 247, P 254, M 23 [Pt II], B 222)

The only example of an intentional and inner purpose of nature might be the human body – and even this is an imperfect example – whose direction is in part governed by intentional behavior. Since in this case the human intentionality is (for Kant) ultimately grounded in the supersensible realm, it remains a mystery how the connection is made between the mind and the body, aside from stipulating that they have the same rational essence. In the case of the system of nature as a system of purposes, there is no conception of nature as being God's body within this Kantian formulation, so it remains difficult to understand how Kant can consistently refer to God as a supersensible intelligence that defines nature's purpose, if nature is to be conceived of self-sufficiently as a natural purpose and living organism, since the latter characterization precludes its being conceived of as a divine work of art.

THE COMPATIBILITY OF SCIENCE AND MORALITY (§§69–78)

The Antinomy of Teleological Judgment

[**§69: "What an antinomy of the power of judgment is"; §70: "Representation of this antinomy"; §71: "Preparation for the solution of the above antinomy"**] Just as Kant identified an antinomy of taste in connection with judgments of pure beauty, he now considers whether within the field of our teleological reflections on nature and its workings, there are any foundational conflicts in the principles we use. This inquiry constitutes the "dialectic of the teleological power of judgment," where the term "dialectic" suggests logical illusion or deception. Kant believes that there are indeed some serious tensions underlying our judgments of natural objects as natural purposes, but that they can be resolved if we recall the essentially regulative, rather than constitutive, status of the principles that issue from faculty of judgment. Constitutive principles yield knowledge of what is actually the case; regulative principles only require us to consider a situation "as if" such-and-such were the case.

As we have seen, Kant maintains that with respect to the formulation of empirical laws, we need to suppose that nature operates economically, since the sheer number of possible empirical laws defies comprehension. This quest for economy entails conceiving of nature as if it were operating in accord with the principle of the objective purposiveness of nature. The principle is necessary as a guide for scientific reasoning and only dictates how we need to assume nature will operate if scientific theorizing is to be successful, not how nature must be.

In the analytic section of the Critique of Teleological Judgment (§§61–68 above), Kant defined the idea of a natural purpose, and he outlined its application in reference to a mode of judging or interpreting an object. Specifically, the idea applies when we judge the object as exhibiting a causality that is distinct from mechanical causality whereby the purpose of the object is apprehended as being internal to it. Although Kant believes that judging an object as a natural purpose is in principle (i.e., from a God's-eye view) compatible with judging it in terms of mechanical causality, to judge an object as a natural purpose implies for us that the object's presence cannot be fully explained in terms of mechanical causality, since teleological causality, of which natural purposes are a species, is generically different from mechanical causality. The natural objects that invite judgments of them as natural purposes are living things, and insofar as we cannot resist judging these objects as such, we recognize that both mechanical causality and teleological causality of an intrinsic sort are present in nature.

Kant offers an abstract and idealized analysis of the concept of a natural purpose, but it is fair to say that his observation of living things inspires the idea. This introduces some unclarity about how we are ultimately to appreciate his careful formulation of natural purposes in terms of how we can choose to judge things. On the one hand, if living things are in themselves natural purposes, then mechanical causality will never be sufficient for us to explain all of the objects that occur in nature. On the other hand, if living things might not be natural purposes, then they could be mere mechanisms, and the principle of judging objects in reference to natural purposes could never reflect how the living things in nature are actually constituted. It would only be a regulative principle with no further potential to say anything true about the objects themselves.

Under ordinary circumstances, it nonetheless remains close to impossible to observe a living organism and not see it as being alive, but as instead being merely the ontological equal of an inanimate chair or table. So judging certain objects as natural purposes is not a matter of simply reinterpreting some object's presentation to see it exclusively and easily from another angle. Detaching the object's purpose from one's consideration is difficult to achieve.

The situation here is reminiscent of Kant's conception of adherent beauty, where certain objects' (e.g., horses, churches, people) respective purposes are difficult to detach from our apprehension of them. Just as it is close to impossible under ordinary circumstances to conceive of a human body *qua* person as an inanimate object, and just as it is difficult to contemplate aesthetically a church or a horse, without considering its purpose, Kant believes that it is close to impossible to conceive of a living body, whether it be that of an animal or person, as being an inanimate object.

This tension between interpreting living organisms as natural ends and interpreting them as sheer mechanisms is expressed and clarified in the antinomy of teleological judgment. Kant's solution to the antinomy underscores how our compulsion to judge living things as natural purposes does not imply that these objects are in themselves natural purposes. This leaves us free, at least in principle, to regard them as merely mechanical products of nature, despite the compelling qualities of the objects that suggest that they are in fact natural purposes.

Kant offers two formulations of the antinomy. The first presents a direct conflict between principles that operate within the context of judging things as natural purposes; the second offers a more resolvable tension. The first, impossible-to-resolve formulation is as follows:

Strong Initial Proposition (*Satz*): All generation of material things is possible according to merely mechanical laws

Strong Opposing Proposition (*Gegensatz*): Some generation of such things is not possible according to merely mechanical laws
(§70, Ak 387 (314), G 259, P 267, M 37 [Pt II], B 234)

There is a logical contradiction between the above two propositions, and Kant states there is no resolution of this antinomy *per se* whereby the two claims can be rendered compatible. Either the initial proposition (i.e., thesis) or the opposing proposition (i.e., antithesis) is false. This initial formulation, however, disregards how the subject at hand more precisely concerns opposing principles of judgment, and how the primary question is whether we need to, or whether we can, regard given natural objects from this or that perspective. The second formulation that takes this subjective factor into account is as follows:

Qualified Initial Proposition (*Satz*): All generation of material things and their forms must be judged as possible according to merely mechanical laws.

Qualified Opposing Proposition (*Gegensatz*): Some products of material nature cannot be judged as possible according to merely mechanical laws (their judgment requires a completely different law of causality, namely that of teleological causes).
(§70, Ak 387 (314), G 258–59, P 267, M 37 [Pt II], B 234)

This second formulation refers not to how material things are independently of how we need to judge them, but refers more subjectively to how we need to *conceive* of certain material things. Here, Kant relies upon the distinction between how we must conceive of something and how the thing is in itself. It reflects his distinction between purpose and purposiveness mentioned earlier in §10 (boldface emphases here added):

[**Purpose**] Thus where not merely the cognition of an object but the **object itself** (its form or its existence) as an effect is thought of [*gedacht*] as possible only through [*nur als durch*] a concept of the latter, there one thinks of a purpose. (§10, Ak 220 (32), G 105, P 65, M 61, B 55)

[**Purposiveness**] An object or state of mind or even an action is called purposive – even if its possibility does not necessarily presuppose the representation of a purpose – merely because its possibility **for us** can only be explained and conceived insofar as we assume as its ground a causality according to purposes, i.e., a will that has arranged them so in accordance with the representation of a certain rule.

(§10, Ak 220 (33), G 105, P 65, M 61–62, B 55)

We are presently contrasting not "purpose" and "purposiveness," but that of being able to judge objects as having a purpose as opposed to judging objects as being produced by mechanical causes alone. Kant resolves the latter conflict by stating that if we are to produce scientific knowledge, then we must acknowledge the Qualified Initial Proposition, and therefore recognize only the "descending" series of causes referred to in §65. This affirmation is not necessary, however, if we are not interested in producing scientific knowledge, but are interested in judging objects according to a principle that guides scientific knowledge, although that principle does not itself produce scientific knowledge.[4] The relationship between the latter activity and the above definition of purposiveness is close and informative nonetheless, since it supports the idea that even if, given our mental constitution, we are compelled to judge things in a certain way and ascribe certain qualities to them, this does not imply that the things actually have those qualities in themselves. We might find it irresistible to judge certain objects as natural purposes under certain circumstances, but this does not imply that they are in fact natural purposes.

Once again, though, this is only to say that as far as we know, nothing in the nature of things prevents us from attempting to interpret all material objects in purely mechanical items, despite the psychological tension involved in treating living things, and especially human beings, in this manner. If we judge some objects as natural purposes, we are not in logical contradiction with the quest for scientific knowledge.

Four Philosophical Explanations for the Presence of Life

It will now help to clarify how we are to interpret the strong pre-disposition, if not sheer naturalness, of regarding some natural objects as natural purposes. This tendency is obviously most pro-nounced when we judge objects that are living human bodies. To consider these material objects as mechanisms without also judg-ing them as people, perhaps occurs in extraordinary (e.g., the dur-ing surgery) or pathological (e.g., psychopathic) circumstances, but normally, it is virtually impossible not to see living human bodies as expressive of self-conscious, free, and rational people.

An obvious case is how it is impossible to see consistently one's own body as not expressing one's own material and living presence. Animals as well are difficult to judge as pure mechanisms (although some philosophical theories such as Descartes' have maintained that animals are nothing more than mechanisms). So although Kant has in principle resolved the tension between mechanistic causality and teleological causality with respect to living organisms, the ten-dency to regard some material objects as actual natural purposes is strong, and this makes the tension between scientific mechanism and teleological judgment that much more pronounced.

[§72: "Concerning the various systems dealing with the sys-tematicity of nature"] Assuming that there are natural purposes, at least with respect to acknowledging how we each appear to our-selves and extrapolating from this first-person fact, then there are several philosophical ways to account for one's presence, the pres-ence of other people, and the presence of life in general. Kant out-lines four general philosophical possibilities that he believes exhaust all the ways to explain the presence of life. Each postulates a universe that respectively explains the presence of natural pur-poses (here referred to as instances of "inner teleological causality" to distinguish them from instances of "external teleological causal-ity" that is exhibited in human planning) in reference to:

(1) **Lifeless matter** (i.e., materialism); this transforms or reduces inner teleological causality to mechanical causality
(2) **Lifeless God** of a non-physical sort; this transforms or reduces inner teleological causality to the activity of a non-intelligent

being, where inner teleological causality is, as in (1), similarly conceived of as not being in the ultimate fabric of things

(3) **Living matter** (i.e., hylozoism – "matter-life"-ism); this acknowledges inner teleological causality as stemming from the physical world itself, conceived of as an immense living organism

(4) **Living God** of a non-physical sort (i.e., theism); this acknowledges inner teleological causality as stemming from outside the physical world in an intelligent being

The contents of the theoretical options are straightforwardly understandable except for the second, with which Kant associates no established philosophical name. Kant refers to Spinoza's philosophy in this context, presumably because Spinoza abstractly and impersonally defined "God" as "substance." Another, perhaps better, example in the history of philosophy subsequent to Kant, would be Arthur Schopenhauer's assertion that the universe is fundamentally a blind, aimless "will" that lacks both intelligence and purpose. As examples of materialism, Kant refers to Epicurus (341–270 BCE) and Democritus (c. 460–370 BCE). He identifies no particular philosopher with hylozoism in this section, but he has in mind the views of his contemporary, Johann Gottfried von Herder (1744–1803), as an example.

However we illustrate these options, (1) and (2) do not *positively* explain the presence of inner teleological causes (i.e., natural purposes) in reference to the ultimate ground of the universe. Since they are based on lifeless foundations, they instead transform or reduce natural purposes to some other sort of impersonal, non-living activity. In contrast, options (3) and (4) assert that natural purposes cannot be explained away as an artifact of the human perspective, that their essential principle differs from mechanical causality, and that their source is in some living (in the broad sense, where God can be said to be living), human-independent grounds.

[§73: "None of the above systems achieves what it aspires to do"] Since the above list is set forth as exhaustive, one might expect Kant to advocate one of the four choices. There is an important sense, though, in which he stands aside from them all. Kant argued in the *Critique of Pure Reason* that speculative philosophy cannot succeed in providing metaphysical knowledge, and he argues accordingly in the present context to show that each of the above options is inconclusive. Kant rejects materialism (option 1) because the reduction of inner teleological causes to mechanistic causes remains mysterious. (Consider, for instance, how philosophically difficult it is to explain the presence of human consciousness in exclusive reference to scientific facts about the brain.) Although materialism assumes that all causation is mechanical, no proofs are advanced that successfully reduce inner teleological causation to mechanical causation. Kant shows little patience for materialism as a matter of fact, and he dismisses it quickly as inconclusive in its effort to dissolve inner teleological causality into mechanical causality rather than explain it in positive terms.

He has a similarly dubious attitude towards world-views that postulate a supersensible, but nonetheless lifeless and unintelligent reality. These views postulate a substrate to the natural purposes, but since this substrate is characterized as being either indeterminate or lifeless, the substrate remains unable to explain the presence of natural purposes with respect to their particular structure of teleological causality. Since such views can only assert a relationship between the substrate and the natural purposes that is not intentional, the philosophical result is as if one were to try to reduce all teleological causality to mechanical causality.

With respect to solutions that positively explain the presence of natural purposes in reference to a living being of some sort, Kant initially argues that option (3) – the hylozoic postulation that the ground of natural purposes resides *in nature itself* – is problematic for two reasons. If matter is assumed to be lifeless and inert, then the concept of "matter that is alive" (i.e., as is reflected in the term, "hylozoism") is a contradiction. Second, it is impossible to prove *a priori* that matter is essentially living, since empirical efforts to establish this position are circular. We cannot begin by observing individual living organisms, then postulate generally that all matter is therefore alive, and conclude by explaining living organisms in reference to the postulated living matter. This is because the very conception of living matter is derived from the observation of the living organisms to begin with. Such a vision of things might be practically useful as a guide for revealing mechanical, scientific connections among things (see §67 above), but there is a difference between maintaining that the view has pragmatic advantages, as opposed to asserting it as a metaphysical truth.

Owing to the circularity of reasoning involved in trying to prove that matter itself is alive, Kant concludes that hylozoism – the only genuine and positive competitor to theism that he can imagine – is inconclusive. To appreciate this, we can note how the logic underlying the proof of hylozoism resembles the following, where "human self-consciousness" takes the place of "life" in the argument: one observes that human beings are self-conscious, and postulates that the universe as a whole must therefore be self-conscious in some rudimentary way to account for the presence of self-conscious human beings as the developed outcomes of the self-conscious universe. The circularity resides in the derivation of a self-conscious universe from the self-conscious human beings that the self-conscious universe is then used to explain.

With respect to the fourth, theistic option above, Kant also argues that theism is inconclusive as a positive speculative philosophy. The reason is that theism cannot prove that materialism is contradictory. Kant acknowledges that materialism is mysterious and that we cannot conceive of how teleological causes can be reduced to mechanical causes without remainder, but he also admits that such a reduction remains a logical possibility. As we will see, Kant nonetheless advocates theism as far as he can, starting from the fact that the principle of the objective purposiveness of nature ultimately leads to theism. He supplements this with an independent postulation of God's existence on moral grounds. Kant takes this route in part because he is convinced that advocating hylozoism is out of the question, given that it has no *a priori* philosophical foundation.

[§74: "The inexplicability of a natural purpose, is the cause of the impossibility of treating dogmatically the concept of a technic of nature"] To reveal further why each philosophical system that aims to explain the presence of natural purposes does not succeed, Kant explicitly recalls his analysis of the necessary constituents of human experience in the *Critique of Pure Reason*. This analysis sets forth a number of concepts and intuitive forms that are necessary for human experience and concludes (among other results) that all human experience must be organized according to the concept of causality, as expressed in the phrase, "every event has a cause." This implies that the more specific teleological style of causality is a non-necessary feature of human experience with respect to what we can determinately know *a priori* about it.

The question at hand is how one can account specifically for the origin of natural purposes, rather than the question of accounting more broadly for teleological causation in general. We know from the presence of human creative activities that teleological causes have an objective reality in our experience. What is less certain is whether the model of the action of human beings in light of their prior determinate plans can be located objectively within the field of nature to explain the presence of living things in general. Living things display a structure that bears a close similarity to that of human activity according to plans (e.g., they have structures that involve a self-determining and self-sustaining reciprocity between the whole and parts) and the question concerns how this structure of living things should be best understood.

Kant maintains that the idea of a teleological causality in nature cannot be validated by any experience, because this sort of causality (allegedly) refers us to a supersensible realm and the recognition of an "original ground of nature." Owing to its connection to the supersensible realm, the concept of a natural purpose is essentially speculative, in other words, so it cannot be said that we can prove or empirically know that natural objects, despite their living structure, are governed by a causality that is essentially different from mechanical causality.

§74 concludes with a thought-provoking remark, after having established that we cannot prove either that objects that appear to be natural purposes are not grounded exclusively in a non-mechanistic, teleological causality (in which case the natural purpose would be an illusion), or are grounded exclusively in the activity of a supersensible intelligence (in which case the natural purpose would be real). Kant writes:

> But even supposing that it could be [confirmed that natural purposes exist], how can I include things among the products of nature, things that are certainly regarded as products of divine art, since nature's

very inability to produce such things according to its own laws is what requires one to call upon a causality that is distinct from nature?

(§74, Ak 397 (332–33), G 268, P 279, M 50 [Pt II], B 245)

The curiosity within this observation is in the conclusion that natural purposes, even if real, cannot for us be counted as natural products. The initial definition of a natural purpose explicitly implies that a natural purpose cannot be conceived of as the product of human art, and this is correct. Natural purposes are not like watches, whose purpose comes from a plan and from an intelligence that resides outside of the watch. Rather, natural purposes have a reciprocal relationship between their parts and the whole where, moreover, the purpose of the whole defines the essence of the whole. There is thus an *inner* relationship between a thing's purpose and its parts that precludes the possibility of considering any natural purpose as a work of human art.

If we claim alternatively that natural purposes are the expressions of divine art, however, then this conflicts with the self-sufficiency of natural purposes, since the purposes would depend upon God's thought, just as the plans of a watch depend on the watchmaker's thought. In other words, given that a natural purpose's motivating plan must be regarded as intrinsic to it, it would seem that it cannot be the product of divine art.

Although Kant intends them to be compatible, if not one and the same, these reflections highlight a tension, if not a contradiction, between (1) the teleological conception of nature that is required to guarantee the possibility of effectively formulating empirical laws of nature and (2) the teleological conception of nature that is required to explain the presence of natural purposes. This is because (1) implies that teleological causality and mechanical causality are compatible, and (2) implies that teleological causality and mechanical causality are incompatible. It is not that teleological causality and mechanical causality seem incompatible for us, because that particular tension is resolved by admitting that the two forms of causality could be compatible from a higher perspective.[5] The problem is that postulating God as the ground of natural purposes contradicts how a natural purpose displays self-sufficiency and self-sustenance in its life processes. Kant wishes to postulate that God created life, but he characterizes life as a process that has its own autonomy.

The general conception of art, either human or divine, does not create any tension between divine art and life, since the plans associated with divine art cannot be separated from the instantiations of them (since, according to Kant, whatever God thinks becomes actual in the very thinking of it). The difficulty arises in the requirement that the conceptual basis of a natural purpose is *intrinsic* to the object as a result of the organic relationship between whole and part. As noted above, it would be contrary to this to say, then, that a flower is a product of divine art, since the flower's living quality would not then be one that arises exclusively from the flower's own organically interrelated structure, but would be the result of God's supersensible activity.

Kant maintains nonetheless that reflections upon objects that are judged to be natural purposes leads us to the conception of a supersensible intelligence that stands behind nature, and that we are led to postulate the presence of this supersensible intelligence, not because we can prove that one exists, but because it is virtually impossible for us to conceive of how natural purposes could be reducible to mechanical causality, given their peculiar reciprocal and self-sustaining causal structure.

Despite the need to understand the motivating plan of a natural purpose as being intrinsic to it, Kant does not extensively explore the hylozoistic possibility that natural purposes could derive from a living matter. This is for two reasons, apparently. First, Kant tends to assume in accord with the prevailing spirit of his times that matter is lifeless by definition. Second, he accepts that from a scientific standpoint, all that we can empirically know about matter is in reference to its mechanical determination, and if the scientific standpoint is to have precedence (as it must within his theory of empirical knowledge), then we need to acknowledge that, as far as we can know, matter is lifeless.

Given how science forces us to regard matter as inanimate for the sake of attaining empirical knowledge, upon encountering life, Kant maintains that we are led immediately to postulate a supersensible God, rather than a living, animated matter as the source of natural purposes. Otherwise there would be a conflict in the very conception of matter as being inanimate in the perspective of theoretical, scientific understanding, while being animate in the view of the faculty of judgment. Kant's resolution of the problem is to reject hylozoism and advocate the theistic solution, despite the tension it generates in relation to the definition of a natural purpose, where the teleological causality involved is an inner teleology.

The dilemma that permeates the second half of the third *Critique* can be expressed in general terms. If the physical universe exists contingently, then its unconditional ground needs to be located outside it. If a natural purpose is a self-sufficient being, then its unconditional ground needs to be located inside of the physical universe. Consequently, if the physical universe's existence is contingent, then the unconditional ground of natural purposes needs to be located outside of the natural purposes, and this contradicts the definition of a natural purpose. On the other hand, if the unconditional ground for the natural purpose is located inside of the physical universe, then the physical universe's existence must be regarded as necessary. Kant denies that the physical universe's existence is necessary, so he has no choice but to contradict his conception of natural purpose by introducing a supersensible intelligence to explain how life originates. In the end, the contradiction between God and natural purposes hinges on the assumed contingency of the physical universe.

Teleology: Required for Science and Purposive Towards God

[§75: "The concept of an objective purposiveness of nature is a critical rational principle for the reflecting power of judgment"; §76: "Remark"] In the *Critique of Pure Reason*, Kant argues that the very structure of our minds requires us to experience a spatio-temporal world of objects that, if we are to produce empirical knowledge of them, need to be interpreted as standing in mechanically causal relationships to one another. Since our minds produce this rigid structure of experience for the purposes of empirical knowledge, he concludes that we cannot know that the world in itself, independently of the structure of our experience, is composed of individual spatio-temporal things that stand in mechanically causal relationships to one another. Sometimes Kant even goes so far as to say that the world in itself cannot be spatio-temporal at all, and without the presence of human beings, space and time would have no meaning.

In the *Critique of the Power of Judgment*, Kant argues in the same fashion. Whereas in the first *Critique* he focuses on how the faculty of understanding determines how we must construct our experience to acquire empirical knowledge, in the *Critique of the Power of Judgment* he focuses upon how our faculty of judgment – to ensure that scientific theories can be formulable at all – determines how, for scientific purposes themselves, we must interpret our experience according to assumptions that go beyond what can be scientifically proven. Specifically, the effort to formulate nature's empirical laws requires that we suppose that nature's law-like operations exhibit an economy compatible with the limits of human comprehension. The principle of the objective purposiveness of nature expresses this supposition and it leads us to judge nature, quite unprovably, as if it were the product of divine art that produces an intellectually favorable economy of empirical laws.

When we judge nature accordingly, we postulate purposes that underlie the operations of natural things that guide our scientific reflection upon them. Such purposes may or may not be there, but regarding nature *as if* it were the expression of purposes methodologically simplifies and efficiently conditions our attempts to formulate empirical natural laws. The leading assumption is that the mechanically causal workings of nature that empirical natural laws describe are compatible with regarding all material objects, living and non-living, as if they are the products of divine art. Without this compatibility between divine art and mechanical natural processes, it would be pointless to expect any guidance for science by regarding nature teleologically.

The principle of the objective purposiveness of nature, then, leads us to regard natural objects as intentional products. This is to introduce a principle that explains the presence of objects (e.g., living things) that compel judgments of them as natural purposes, for these objects are especially amenable to interpretation in terms of underlying intentions and purposes. Within such a context, one of the more intriguing parallels between the lines of argument in the

Critique of Pure Reason and the *Critique of the Power of Judgment* arises, since in the latter Kant speaks similarly of the necessity that attends how we need to think about nature, as opposed to how nature happens to be in itself.

The principle of the objective purposiveness of nature characterizes neither things in themselves nor the structural features of scientific knowledge; it simply fulfills the demands of our rational quest for systematic comprehension. It is a subjective principle of our faculty of judgment, although we cannot set it aside if we are to assume that nature is scientifically comprehensible. It does not concern how we must rigidly and logically structure our experience, but how we must interpret it. As such, the principle of the objective purposiveness of nature does not specify the necessary conditions for the constitution of empirical knowledge, but prescribes a way to interpret nature that may or may not reflect how nature is in itself. To formulate empirical laws of nature in an effective manner, we need to regard nature *as if* it were grounded in an underlying intelligence, but the actual presence of such an intelligence remains for us an everlastingly open question.

The *Critique of Pure Reason* defines a situation where we necessarily construct our experience in a certain manner (viz., logically) for a certain purpose (viz., empirical knowledge) and, as a result of this construction, find ourselves precluded from proving how things are in themselves. The *Critique of the Power of Judgment* defines a situation where we necessarily interpret our experience of inanimate things for scientific purposes, and (allegedly) as a result of this interpretation, although we cannot prove that such a being exists, we also cannot but ascribe to nature an unconditional ground in a supersensible, underlying intelligence.

The same hypothesis of a divine intelligence emerges from our judgment of certain material objects as natural purposes. As human beings engaged in the effort to comprehend living things that are judged to instantiate natural purposes, Kant maintains that have no choice but to regard them as if they were a divine and intelligent creation. He states this twice:

> It is impossible to conceive or make the purposiveness that must reside at the basis of even our cognition of the inner possibility of

> many natural things comprehensible, otherwise than by representing those things and the world in general as the product of an intelligible cause (a God[6]) [*einer verständigen Ursache (eines Gottes)*].
>
> (§75, Ak 400 (337), G 270, P 282, M 53 [Pt II], B 247)

> ... we can absolutely locate the possibility of those natural purposes in nothing other than an intelligent being. This alone is suitable to the maxim of our reflecting judgment, and is also a ground that, although subjective, is attached inseparably to the human race.
>
> (§75, Ak 400–401 (338–39), G 271, P 283, M 54 [Pt II], B 248)

Kant equates the intelligent being in the second excerpt with the God referred to in the first, concluding that the teleological interpretation of the world cannot find a complete answer for its inquiries, except in a theology. It is important to note how Kant is now working exclusively with the theistic option for accounting for natural purposes. He rejected hylozoism as the only positively competing possibility for accounting for natural purposes and is now exploring the theistic alternative as the only remaining option. We have noted some problems in this choice of theism over hylozoism, given that Kant was careful to say that natural purposes are not like watches, where the rational cause is distinguished from the matter (§65), for we have seen that natural purposes have their motivating plan *within* them and are not works of art:

> But if a thing as a natural product is nonetheless to contain in itself and its inner possibility a relationship to purposes, i.e., to be possible only as a natural purpose **and without the causality of a concepts of a rational being outside of it**, so is it *secondly* required: that the parts of that thing be connected to the unity of a whole, such that they are with respect to each other reciprocally cause and effect of their form.
>
> (§65, Ak 373 (290–91), G 245, P 252, M 21 [Pt II], B 219–20; boldface added)

This excerpt from §65 reinforces the point made earlier that a natural purpose has an intelligence-expressing principle that is internal to the object itself, and that it does not involve the causality of the concepts of a rational being outside of it. As we have seen, the latter would transform the natural purpose into a work of art and would contradict its living, self-sufficient nature. This is why Kant's reference to the principle of the objective purposiveness of nature as a way to explain the ground of natural purposes remains questionable, if this principle requires that we postulate God, since this has the effect of regarding natural purposes inconsistently as works of divine art.

There is also a paradox in Kant's account of natural purposes, independently of the above issue. If the principle of the objective purposiveness of nature is necessary to comprehend the set of empirical natural laws, then the postulation of a supersensible intelligence must be compatible with mechanical causality, if regarding nature as if it were intelligently-designed is to guide scientific inquiry. The presence of natural purposes, though, creates a tension with purely mechanistic explanation and leads us to recognize a second sort of causality in addition to mechanical causality, namely, teleological causality. Moreover, Kant appeals to the presence of a supersensible intelligence as a way to account for the presence of natural purposes.

The paradox is that the supersensible intelligence introduced through the principle of the objective purposiveness of nature has conflicting functions. On the one hand, the intentions of this intelligence lend a rationality and coherence to the natural laws and are compatible with mechanical causality. On the other hand, the intentions of this intelligence account for the presence of natural purposes (e.g., living things) and, for us, natural purposes defy analysis in exclusively mechanical terms. It is thus unclear whether supersensibly originated intentions help or hinder our quest for scientific knowledge. The very same intention that is supposed to render the physical world more coherent, produces living things that are to us, scientifically incoherent.

Teleology from a God's-eye Viewpoint

Kant underscores the subjectivity or human-relative quality of our need to regard nature as a divine work of art by adopting, somewhat uncharacteristically, a God's-eye view of the situation. He begins by asserting that for a divine intelligence, there is no distinction between what is possible and what is actual, since God's thinking of something immediately actualizes it. So for God, everything is simply actual, and there is neither necessity nor possibility.

This renders the very distinction between possibility and necessity a merely subjective and human-relative one. When we speak doubtfully of God as being a "mere possibility" we speak exclusively from the human perspective, since from the divine perspective such a formulation would make no sense. For this reason, Kant maintains that the principle of the objective purposiveness of nature – the principle through which we regard nature as if it were the product of a divine intelligence and refer to God as a possibility – does not reflect how nature could be in itself or how the divine intelligence that we postulate as the intelligible ground of nature could be in itself.

[§77: "Concerning the distinctive character of the human understanding, though which the concept of a natural purpose is for us possible"] To illuminate the concept of a natural purpose as it is constructed from the human perspective, Kant continues with his reflections of how things would be from a God's-eye standpoint. With respect to the latter, he maintains that God would conceive of a natural purpose in a deductive way such that the whole is conceived first and where the parts of the organic whole follow thereupon with (from our point of view) a necessity, and with a necessity that is exhibited amongst the parts themselves.

In contrast to this, human beings apprehend a natural object as a natural purpose in a more piecemeal fashion, observing the organic interrelationships of its parts, constructing a whole whose contours the interacting parts define, and then projecting a single purpose, concept or intention that is considered to be the teleological ground of the perceived organic unity. Kant concludes that since we represent the natural purpose in a different way from how he imagines it is constructed by the divine intelligence, our conception of natural purpose does not reflect how the natural purpose is in itself, but only represents our human conception of a natural purpose.

Such an exercise in alternative perspective-taking intends to emphasize how mechanical causality and teleological causality as exhibited in natural purposes are compatible. Kant adds that since the very apprehension of some natural objects as natural purposes that are distinct from inanimate objects is a function of our mode of judgment, it remains possible that a higher-level superhuman, but nonetheless finite, intelligence might be able to apprehend how the generation of natural purposes is reducible to mechanical causes.

At this point Kant's discussions continue to depend on the assumption that hylozoism is not a viable metaphysical alternative and that natural purposes must be explained in reference to a supersensible intelligence. His effort to adopt the God's-eye view and to speculate how God would construct a natural purpose helps show in some greater detail to how the theistic explanation would work. At the same time, one can ask what the relationship between God's thoughts and God's being happens to be, for if the natural purposes that God's actualizes are not distinct from God, this would move us in the direction of hylozoism or pantheism, since the natural purposes in nature would be the manifestation of God's very own thoughts (i.e., God's substance) and the sharp distinction between nature and God would start to dissolve. So despite his efforts to develop the theistic alternative, Kant's reasoning suggests that a more consistent analysis would locate the teleological ground of natural purposes within nature itself, conceived somehow as the embodiment and presence of a divine intelligence.

The Perpetual Mystery of Living Organisms

[§78: "Concerning the unification, in the technic of nature, of the principle of the universal mechanism of matter with the teleological principle"] In this concluding section Kant addresses some of the concerns mentioned above that reveal a tension between mechanical and teleological causality, insofar as teleological causality is related to natural purposes. He tries to reconcile mechanical and teleological causality by distinguishing between constitutive principles that yield empirical knowledge and regulative principles that do not, but that nonetheless guide the acquisition of empirical knowledge by focussing the constitutive principles productively.

Analysis in terms of mechanical causality provides empirical knowledge, but as noted above, we need to presuppose as a guide to scientific inquiry, the principle of the objective purposiveness of nature – the regulative assumption that nature is governed by a divine intelligence that intends an economy of empirical natural laws. The principles that derive from the faculties of understanding and judgment, respectively, have different statuses with respect to whether or not they provide empirical knowledge. With respect to principles that extend from the faculty of judgment, Kant explicitly states that supposing that God exists adds nothing to our body of scientific knowledge – the idea of God is not a scientific concept – implying that scientific knowledge is indispensable to discovering how nature operates.

Despite their difference in philosophical status and their consequent lack of head-to-head conflict, Kant explores further considerations that support the view that mechanical causality and teleological causality are compatible. The first of these is the observation that mechanical causal relationships between objects can help to realize goals. It appears, for instance, that mechanical relationships between a living organism's bodily parts help to keep the body alive and thus serve the purpose of the body. It remains important not to confuse mechanical explanation with teleological explanation in such examples, but there is a coincidence between the two types of causality insofar as an achieved goal understandable in teleological terms can be regarded in a scientific light as having resulted from mechanical causes. The electrical impulses in a person's muscular movements help a person realize his or her intention to speak, walk, and so on. Bodily mechanics helps us achieve what we want.

Highlighting how understanding a natural object as a mere mechanical product and as a product of divine intention involves introducing two different perspectives, and concluding thereby how the two types of causality are not, for us, reducible to one another, Kant offers the following example and implicit argument:

> When if, for example, I regard a maggot as if it were a product of the mere mechanism of nature (of a new configuration that nature produces for itself, when its elements are set free through decomposi-

tion), I cannot then derive the same product from the same material, as a causality acting in accordance with purposes.

(§78, Ak 411 (356–57), G 280, P 296, M 69 [Pt II], B 260)

Kant maintains that we cannot ascribe mechanical causes and teleological causes to an object in the same respect. Or, similarly, we cannot regard an object exclusively as an intrinsically lifeless lump of matter and expect to derive both mechanistic and teleological causes from it. A switch in perspective is required to regard the object as a natural purpose, and within our human capacities there is no conceptually smooth transition between the two perspectives, such that we could reduce one sort of causality to the other.

Since mechanical and teleological causality are assumed to be compatible – otherwise, as noted, the principle of the objective purposiveness of nature could not guide scientific inquiry – Kant infers that the ground of this compatibility must reside outside of both sorts of causality in some neutral ground upon which both can be based. This needs to be a ground that is beyond, or outside of nature, since he assumes that within nature itself the only kind of causality that operates is mechanical as far as empirical knowledge is concerned.

Interpreting any natural object as a natural purpose does not therefore yield knowledge, and when we perceive living things as being the expressions of a purpose, we ascribe a non-natural quality to the object, if hylozoism is to be set aside. The assumption of natural purposes as, for instance, exhibited by living organisms, insofar as these stand as a mystery that defies reduction to mechanical analysis, must consequently be judged as a non-natural (i.e., non-scientific; non-mechanical) attribution, and it leads us to project motivating plans onto these natural objects beyond what science can prove. In the preceding §77, Kant is clear about this:

. . . absolutely no human reason (also no finite one that is similar to ours in quality, no matter how much it surpasses it in degree) can hope to understand the production of even a tiny blade of grass from merely mechanical causes.

(§77, Ak 409 (353), G 279, P 294, M 66 [Pt II], B 258)

This example of the blade of grass invites us to consider how the perception of natural beauty fits into the perception of natural objects as natural purposes. As noted earlier, the two perceptions are akin, and we can see this once more in reference to Kant's definition of purposiveness in comparison to his account of the non-provability of the presence of a purpose that our power of judgment forces us to assume. The two are as follows:

> An object or state of mind or even an action is called purposive – even if its possibility does not necessarily presuppose the representation of a purpose – merely because its possibility for us can only be explained and conceived insofar as we assume as its ground a causality according to purposes, i.e., a will that has arranged them so in accordance with the representation of a certain rule.
>
> (§10, Ak 220 (33), G 105, P 65, M 61–62, B 55)

> We must therefore remain with the above fundamental principle of teleology, viz., that according to the constitution of human understanding, nothing other than the intentionally working causes can be presupposed for the possibility of organized beings in nature, and the mere mechanism of nature can by no means be adequate for an explanation of these products; [but this is said] however, without wanting to decide anything through this fundamental principle in regard to the possibility of such things themselves.
>
> (§78, Ak 413 (360), G 282, P 298, M 71–72 [Pt II], B 262)

In the experience of beauty, the apprehension of an object's systematic form is so impressive to our scientific (i.e., cognitive) sensibilities that we cannot but assume that the organically-unified object is the product of design, even though we realize the logical possibility that the object might have arisen by accident. No specific intention or purpose is associated with the object and the raw intelligibility of the object's form resonates with our cognitive faculties to produce a universal satisfaction.

In the experience of a natural purpose, the apprehension of an object's systematic form is so impressive to our scientific (i.e., cognitive) sensibilities that we cannot but assume that the organically-unified object is the product of design, even though we realize that our ascription of some unknown purpose to the object can never be proven. We associate a specific intention with the object as its ground or purpose, but we cannot define what this is. However, our conception of the object's essence stands as an approximation to whatever this purpose might actually be, assuming there is one. Kant's illustration of the beauty of a flower is illuminating in this respect, for the biologist would see the flower as having a reproductive purpose, whereas the appreciation of the flower's pure beauty would involve contemplating only its rational form independently of this purpose.

In the cases of both natural beauty and natural purposes, however, there is no knowledge of the object's purpose (except for the one case of human beauty, where the purpose is known *a priori* as being a moral purpose). In natural beauty we suppose that the object, as an aesthetic idea, is the expression of some indeterminate rule; in natural purposes, we suppose that the object, plant or animal, as it may be, is the expression of some determinate rule, but one that we cannot conclusively specify. One could say that the divine intelligence responsible for these items is postulated as being more genius-minded in the production of natural beauty and more literalistically or scientifically-minded in the production of natural purposes. In the case of the human being, the divine intelligence is more morally-minded. Reason, in sum, leads us to speculate that God underwrites truth, beauty and goodness.

An upshot for the theory of beauty is that owing to their organic unity, natural purposes will be perceived among the set of material objects as being more obviously paradigmatic of natural beauty. With respect to exemplars of natural beauty, this supports a preference to tulips, animal forms, and living forms of all sorts as opposed to crystalline or mechanically-derivable forms. In the apprehension of both natural beauty and natural purposes there is the appreciation of an organic unity in the objects' respective forms that appears to be explainable only in reference to an intelligently-derived intention, and in both cases Kant believes that we are led to contemplate the possible existence of God. We do not find Kant referring to natural purposes as symbols of morality, but their self-sufficiency and self-determination as living organisms suggests a similar analogy.

One might ask at this point, how can natural purposes be paradigms of natural beauty, if natural purposes defy mechanical, scientific analysis, and if the satisfaction in the harmony of the cognitive faculties that grounds judgments of beauty is itself caused by the apprehension of a purposive form that aesthetically confirms that our scientific quest is favored by nature? How can objects that defy scientific analysis confirm that nature favors our scientific endeavors? This seems to make no sense.

An answer resides in how the organic structure of living things represents an ideal for scientific inquiry, perhaps even because their living quality remains so mysterious. Their organic unity is so strong and their inner rationality so conspicuous, that they stand as formal representatives of the organic unity and integration we would hope to achieve within the structure of the best scientific theories. In this respect, living organisms exemplify how nature is understandable in both mechanistic and teleological terms, since their organic unity of structure is so complicated, concentrated, and suggestive of an underlying intelligence.

The priority of living organisms over natural mechanisms with respect to the apprehension of natural beauty suggests that the most beautiful natural objects would be ones that exhibit life, but that in addition to this, exhibit an organization that is governed by the activity of rational self-consciousness. These would be living human bodies insofar as they behave rationally. If we combine this reflection on the ideal of beauty (§17) with Kant's account of natural purposes as indicating the activity of a divine intelligence, we arrive at a situation where beauty in general can be defined as the sensible appearance of the divine, where the human body is the most intense example of this appearance, and where morality derived from the subjective side of the human being coincides with, on the objective side, the rationality of the underlying substrate of nature.[7]

Such connections are speculative and non-provable, but they indicate the nuclear role of *human beauty* in Kant's theory of beauty in general with respect to the project of integrating nature and morality, and by implication, the more substantial moral role of adherent beauty as opposed to free beauty. Free beauty may be the symbol of morality and even the symbol of science, but the beautiful living human body that acts morally integrates goodness, empirical truth and beauty all at once in a more direct, concrete fashion.

By arguing for the compatibility between mechanical causality and the teleological causality associated with natural purposes, it is now more obvious that Kant has a larger goal in mind. After having established to his satisfaction the compatibility between any given natural purpose and mechanistic explanation, he then extrapolates to the following global conclusion: the entire realm of empirical mechanical laws is compatible with the entire realm of teleological natural purposes, similar to his expansive style of thought in §66. It is consequently consistent to suppose that the mechanical ways of nature, the intentional ways of God, and the moral aims of humanity are, in principle, or could approach a condition of being, in one-to-one correspondence.

THE MORAL ARGUMENT FOR GOD'S EXISTENCE (§§79–91)

Teleology Provides a Method, but not a Proof

[§79: "**Whether teleology must be treated as belonging to natural science**"] The final section of the Critique of Teleological Judgment and of *Critique of the Power of Judgment* as a whole concerns the "methodology of the teleological power of judgment" and Kant begins by explaining his use of the term "method" in this context. He asks initially whether teleology belongs to the scientific account of nature or whether it belongs to theology, since teleology posits a behind-the-scenes intelligence as the divine author of nature, but also guides scientific inquiry. He rejects both options. Teleology does not itself provide any empirical knowledge, even though it is necessary for knowing nature scientifically. Neither does it prove God's existence with metaphysical certainty. Its main purpose is to guide scientific inquiry and the suggestion that God exists arises only in relation to the subjective need for a scientific guide.

Teleology emerges from the critique of the powers of judgment in the effort to identify *a priori* principles that govern our acquisition of empirical knowledge. Its principle, as we have seen, is the principle of the objective purposiveness of nature that prescribes to us how we must judge nature (viz., as the product of a divine intelligence), if we are to assume an economy of nature and a potential comprehensibility of empirical laws. Kant accordingly states that the principle of the objective purposiveness of nature provides us with a *method* for approaching nature, and this method is to judge it anthropomorphically, *as if* it were a divine work of art. Only in this way can we proceed to formulate empirical laws of nature in an economic manner, given the confusion of infinite possibilities. In sum, teleological considerations are mainly methodological ones, and are defined in relation to our quest for empirical knowledge.

[**§80: "Concerning the necessary subordination of the principle of mechanism to the teleological principle in the explanation of a thing as a natural purpose"**] There is nonetheless a double problem that accompanies the effort to understand nature in exclusively mechanistic terms. First, mechanistic causality cannot stand alone, since we need a general teleological principle of the objective purposiveness of nature to guarantee an economy of empirical natural laws. Second, when mechanistic causality encounters living things, it hits an impasse in the attempt to explain their living quality. The principle of the objective purposiveness of nature guides the formulation of mechanical laws that govern the organism, but insofar as it ascribes a purpose to the organism with respect to its condition as a living organism *per se*, this purpose is not comprehensible in mechanistic terms. Efforts to compose a mechanistic explanation of nature that can account for the presence of life are therefore in vain and Kant believes that no such biology-comprehensive mechanical system will ever be forthcoming from the human intellect.

In reference to method, however, Kant adds that the *authority to pursue* a merely mechanical explanation of all natural products is in itself completely unlimited and that we should aim for this ideal, since this is the only way to advance in empirical knowledge. In this effort, for instance, he states that with respect to the investigation of living things in general, we can develop mechanical models from the study of comparative anatomy. This is an objective study of bodily structures and it can partially help to illuminate the nature of life. One can expand even further than this and consider the entire array of genus and species, reaching down to the qualities of raw matter from which life appears to have arisen. We will never comprehend everything, but neither will the scientific progress ever end.

After taking such a broad view of nature, it is inevitable that some basic principles, entities, and processes will be set forth, such as those found in contemporary theoretical physics. Kant maintains that at this foundational level, we cannot but hypothesize some purpose as the ground of the entire array of nature. In more modern terms, we cannot but ask questions about the source of the assumedly contingent foundations of the physical world such as "Why are there this many as opposed to that many fundamental particles, and why do the elementary cosmic processes have the structures they do?"

To answer such questions rationally, Kant maintains that we must go beyond anything that science can offer and postulate some intelligence that stands behind nature. He believes that a self-sufficient natural system will not suffice, since not only will an account of the foundational contingency of things be lacking, but that, for us at least, an account of life cannot follow from mechanical explanations alone. To make ultimate sense of things, he believes that we need to postulate a single purpose to the physical universe that lies supersensibly beyond it.

At this point it is worth pausing to clarify two different scientific projects that are combining in Kant's discussion. The first refers to understanding the workings of inanimate nature in mechanical terms; the second refers to understanding living organisms in mechanical terms. When understanding inanimate nature in mechanical terms, we need to regard nature as having been produced by an intelligent cause for the sake of theoretical economy.

When understanding living things in mechanical terms, we also need to regard them as having been produced by an intelligent cause, not for the sake of theoretical economy, but because their living quality defies scientific understanding. Nonetheless, the demands of scientific inquiry and the acquisition of empirical knowledge motivate us to attempt to understand living things exclusively in terms of mechanical causality. In sum, we have a reciprocal relationship between the two different scientific projects mentioned above. We regard inanimate things as works of divine art, even to the point of their potentially being organically unified in the manner of a living organism; we regard living organisms as mechanically understandable in principle, even though this seems to be impossible.

The logic of this situation recalls Kant's earlier discussion of the relationship between nature and art (§45), where he claimed that we should regard nature as if it were the product of art, and the beauty in art as if it were a product of nature. Objects of natural beauty match the position of inorganic nature in their requirement to be regarded as the product of an intelligence; beautiful works of art match the position of natural purposes in their requirement to seen as merely natural products. The difference resides in their respective functions. Objects of natural beauty and beautiful works of art require a supersensible intelligence as a condition for appreciating their beauty; inorganic products of nature and natural purposes require a supersensible intelligence as a condition for comprehending them.

The Highest Good as the Ultimate Natural Purpose

[§81: "Concerning the association of mechanism with the teleological principle in the explanation of a natural purpose as a natural product"] When discussing the nature of life, it is inevitable to reach a point where an understanding of the nature of reproduction becomes necessary. One question is how the motivating purpose, or life-principle, of each new organism is embodied respectively in each new material body, if, as Kant is assuming, this purpose must be judged as having a non-natural, supersensible origination. Either the divine intelligence introduces this purpose into the new organism on the occasion of every new birth and creates life in every new instance, or the purpose is introduced long beforehand (from our standpoint) and is intrinsically present more generally in some overall motivating plan of nature that precedes the birth of any particular organism. For the sake of simplicity and rationality, Kant advocates the latter view.

The thought of a larger motivating and enlivening plan, in reference to which the purposes of new organisms can be explained, points back to the origins of life in lifeless matter and the hypothesis that independently infused in the lifeless matter is a divine plan that accounts for the emergence of life. Kant cannot conceive that lifeless matter could contain within *itself* the principle of life, and having thereby rejected hylozoism, he has no recourse but to postulate that the motivating plans that characterize natural purposes have their source in a supersensible being. His position is shared by his contemporary, Johann Friedrich Blumenbach (1752–1840), professor of anatomy, whose views Kant reports supportively:

> He starts off all physical explanation of these structures from matter that is organized [by God]. That raw matter could have formed itself on its own according to mechanical laws, that life could have arisen from what is lifeless, and that matter could have arisen in the form of a self-preserving purposiveness, he explains correctly as running counter to reason . . .
>
> (§81, Ak 424 (379), G 292, P 311, M 85–86 [Pt II], B 274)

In this picture, God imparts an original organization to lifeless matter and endows it with the potential for producing life through its mechanical activity. This hypothesis brings individual natural purposes into a closer correspondence with mechanical causality. There is also some paradox here, insofar as the aim is to conceive of a flower's purpose, for instance, as intrinsic to the flower. In one sense, at least, the purpose will be intrinsic to the flower on this model, since the flower emerged from a long series of mechanical causes without any added entrance of supersensible influence at the point of the flower's origination. The life and purpose of the flower is explained indirectly as the long-term effect of a single encompassing and complex, life-giving divine plan that included the flower's existence and purpose.

Such a theory, though, only obscures how the flower's purpose is in fact imparted from the outside, and how the flower's motivating plan is not intrinsic to the flower in the sense that we would look only to the flower's being to explain its life. The effort to put some distance between God's life-giving activity and the flower's emergence only accentuates how there is an implicit attempt and theoretical need to conceive of the purposes of natural products as intrinsic to them, as opposed to being placed there from the outside by a divine and supersensible hand. The philosophical theorizing takes this direction because a genuinely intrinsic account of natural purposes has been precluded with the rejection of hylozoism and the assumption of nature's contingency.

As is now evident, this tension between considering the motivating plans of natural purposes as expressions of divine activity and considering natural purposes as having their motivating plans intrinsic to themselves recurs periodically in Kant's discussion of natural purposes. The idea of natural purposes as instantiated in living things not only presents an impediment to understanding nature in terms of mechanical causality, their position as being for us neither fully within nature (since the structure of a natural purpose defies understanding in terms of mechanistic causality) nor fully without it (since natural purposes are instantiated in objects in space and time) tends to destabilize the sharp distinction between mechanical nature and supersensible teleology that Kant wishes to preserve.

[§82: "Concerning the teleological system in the external relationships of organized things"] Up until this point, Kant has been speaking freely about how we need to regard nature as having an intelligent designer, both in light of our need to suppose an economy of empirical natural laws and in light of our perception of living beings. He now looks more soberingly at how inanimate nature is constituted, observing that the oceans and larger natural processes neither appear to have the welfare of human beings in mind, nor appear to be governed according to a rationally-humane principle. For example, the ocean can overflow terribly at any time as a result of some natural accident, earthquakes can occur, and volcanoes can erupt to destroy an overwhelming amount of human life. The presence of natural evil, i.e., where nature appears to act despotically or demonically, seems to contradict the hypothesis of a rational, moral, and divine intelligence that is ultimately governing nature.

In an initial reaction to such reflections on natural evil, Kant states that the principle which leads us to postulate an intelligent ground for natural processes is only a subjective principle of our judgment, and, hence, does not give us knowledge of how things are in themselves. We have thus a tension between how we rationally need to think about nature and how inanimate nature often presents itself as being indifferent to our existence. Sometimes nature helps us to realize our plans; sometimes it hinders us.

The peculiarity of the situation is revealed by how our own principle of judgment leads us to ascribe to ourselves an outstandingly elevated status. Kant offers a description:

> For what reason are these plant-eating animals present? The answer could be: for the meat-eaters, who can feed only on what has life. Finally, though, the question is: For what good are these along with the above [mentioned] natural kingdoms? [It is] for the human being, whose understanding teaches diverse uses for all of those creatures. The human being is the ultimate purpose of the creation here on earth, because the human being is the only earthly being who can make a concept of purposes for itself, and who through his reason can make a system of ends from the aggregate of purposively constructed things.
>
> (§82, Ak 426–27 (382–83), G 294–95, P 314, M 88 [Pt II], B 276)

From the mechanistic perspective, human beings are not much more than one type of being among an uncountable variety of natural products. From the teleological perspective, human beings are the end-all of nature itself. It is difficult to imagine a more polarized self-conception, as the human being sees itself as both a mechanically-driven physical body and as a free, rational, self-consciousness.

The human condition is not completely broken in two by this immeasurable gulf between mechanical nature and human freedom, however, since the human being's living body as a natural purpose (as well as the experience of natural beauty along with the activities of artistic genius, as we have seen earlier in Kant's aesthetic theory) stands as the reconciliatory intermediary between these mechanical and supersensible extremes. This is another reason for conceiving of a natural purpose as having its motivating plan intrinsic to it. Otherwise, life itself would need to be explained with its rational principle outside of it, as an example of divine art, and the role of the living body as an intermediary between nature and freedom would be diminished, since the body's life would derive artifactually from outside of nature in God.

[§83: "Concerning the ultimate purpose (*von dem letzten Zwecke*) of nature as a teleological system"] Consistent with the Hebrew Scriptures in the Book of Genesis, Kant believes that human beings are set above the rest of nature owing to their capacity for reflection – a capacity which allows them to know the difference between right and wrong. In this respect, as described above, human beings can be regarded as the culminating point towards which the natural and animal kingdoms aim. But human beings are also driven by more rudimentary, animal qualities and they are not angelic beings who simply happen to inhabit a non-distracting and non-influential physical form. Our animality significantly constitutes who we are as living beings, often in competition and conflict with our reason and capacities for reflection.

Well aware of the inner tensions between reason and physiologically-driven inclination, Kant asks where within the human being we can locate the special feature that allows us to have a perspective that stands above the determination of natural processes. This, to him, is obviously identifiable as our capacity for rationality and self-consciousness, but Kant philosophically formulates this traditional idea with more complexity, using terms that fit closely with the present context of trying to understand the source of the motivating plans that natural purposes exhibit.

To reach this formulation, Kant begins with an initial and critical reflection on what many people believe to be the point of human existence, namely, happiness – an empirical condition where all of our most important natural inclinations are satisfied. Desires, however, vary from person to person, physical circumstances themselves vary from context to context, and people's desires, moreover, tend to be difficult to satisfy. There is no universality to be found in reference to the contents of happiness, for much depends on the good or bad fortune of accidental circumstances. Owing to its empirical, variable and contingent nature, and mirroring his reasons for rejecting hylozoism, Kant maintains that it is inconsistent to believe that human happiness could be the common, universal and unconditional purpose towards which the natural and animal kingdoms have been developing. For the same reason, neither can it stand as a foundation for morality.

Kant does not maintain simply that human happiness, as the satisfactory sum of all our inclinations, provides an inadequate measure for life's ultimate value. In a remarkable footnote to §83, Kant adds that a life based exclusively upon happiness, i.e., "what one enjoys" (*was man geneißt*) is not merely worthless. He asserts that its worth "sinks below zero" (*sinkt unter Null*). He sincerely believes that no one, if thinking clearly, would choose to exist, if it were known beforehand that the only point of living was to experience sensory enjoyment. The underlying thought here is that, virtually by definition, life's *ultimate* value must be *unconditional*, and sensory enjoyment does not fit this description.

Looking instead for a more universalistic and steadfast feature of human beings, Kant identifies generally our capacity to make plans and to put them into action, independently of any specific plans that we might formulate (e.g., independently of the plan to become happy, or the plan to act rationally as much as one can, and so on). Abstracting from the content of everyone's possible plans, he identifies the formal quality of being able to make plans *per se* as a universal human quality. Kant believes that this capacity is compatible with what nature itself can produce in the human being, since being able to make plans in relation to all kinds of practical skills and physiological needs (e.g., building houses, obtaining food) is expressive of the capacity for planning in general.

Kant refers to this generic capacity for planning as a quality of human culture, and maintains that human culture operates fundamentally to educate people to develop their planning skills. To the degree that people can become more cultured, the less crude and driven by instinct they will be, and the more power they will have to express their freedom and autonomy. In this respect, Kant notes that the development of civil society towards an integrated cosmopolitan state, the refinement of aesthetic sensibilities, and the development of scientific inquiry all help to educate and positively form the human character.

Ultimately, for Kant, the purpose of developing human culture is to foster people's more specific capacities to make *moral* plans.

The more we become adept at rational planning in general, the more power we will have to act rationally and consistently, i.e., morally. He harbors no illusions about the task that faces cultural education, however, and he believes that given the presence of animalistic desires, it is unlikely that people will develop the capacity to behave morally all of the time. Kant offers only an ideal against which we can measure our collective moral achievements.

We can optimally realize this ideal only, supposedly, if we direct our activity towards a supersensible reality, and settling into this intellectual focus is challenging in itself. Kant accordingly states that even though our role as the purpose of the natural and animal kingdoms *ought* to be realized, there is no guarantee that it *will* be realized, and that its realization depends heavily on how we choose to conduct ourselves:

> As the only being on earth who has reason, and hence a capacity to set and freely to choose purposes for himself, he is indeed the entitled master of nature and, if one regards nature as a teleological system, his calling is to be the ultimate natural purpose. This is, however, always only on the condition that he has the understanding and will to give to nature and to himself such a relationship to a purpose that can be independent from nature and sufficient to be an ultimate purpose, which must not at all be sought in nature.
>
> (§83, Ak 431 (390), G 298, P 318, M 93–94 [Pt II], B 280–81)

[§84: "Concerning the final purpose (*von dem Endzwecke*) of the existence of a world, i.e., of creation itself"] Kant wonders why things exist at all, and logically, any reason offered needs to be final in the sense of its being a self-sufficient and unconditional reason. The final purpose of existence cannot be arbitrary or dependent upon anything outside of itself, and it has to be a perfectly good reason. A God who is irrational and whimsical is thereby ruled out, since what is arbitrary amounts to no reason at all.

Kant takes some steps to locate within the human being a capacity that stands independently of mechanistic causality and that is compatible with the idea that the human being, with respect to some ideal characterization of it, is the purpose of the natural and animal kingdoms. This capacity is the above-mentioned one of making and carrying out plans, and Kant defines it in relation to the activities of human culture. Such a general capacity does not in itself prescribe any plans, rules, or concepts that have an unconditional content, however, so if we are to define an exact purpose that humans serve, as opposed to leaving the human condition completely open-ended and free in the most indeterminate sense, we need to consider the human being's inner constitution is a less generalized manner.

In his moral theory Kant identifies an unconditional rule of human behavior that is expressive of the human being's rationality. This is the rule to act consistently, such that the maxim of one's individual action can be generalized to define a course of behavior that would apply necessarily to anyone in similar circumstances. Kant develops his moral theory upon this categorical imperative, and in the present context we can see that this unconditional moral ground for action appropriately characterizes that feature of human beings that is consistent with the ultimate purpose of the world's existence. In other words, when postulating what the ultimate purpose of the world might be, and wondering what God might have had in mind, we encounter the unconditional idea of morality, and furthermore encounter the same idea in ourselves as the basis of our own supersensible being. For this reason Kant maintains that:

> . . . only in the human being, but only in the human being as the subject of morality, do we encounter unconditional legislation in relation to purposes, which makes him therefore exclusively capable of being a final purpose, to whom the entirely of nature is teleologically subordinated.
>
> (§84, Ak 435–36 (399), G 302–3, P 323, M 100 [Pt II], B 286)

One of the more interesting aspects of this characterization is Kant's remark that we are "capable" of being an ultimate purpose, which suggests that we might not live up to the moral agreement between our rational selves and nature. Although it is not preordained that we will in fact realize our moral potential, it unconditionally remains that we ought to give the world an ultimate meaning through our good-willed action.

The Teleological vs. the Moral Argument for God's Existence

[§85: "Concerning physico-theology"] After introducing the idea of how morality provides an unconditional content to action, Kant reflects upon his discussion of the teleological judgment of material things as natural purposes that has led to the postulation of God's existence. His question is how far this mode of reflection can take us with respect to understanding God's qualities more determinately, especially in connection with ascertaining God's ultimate purpose in creating nature.

If Kant's views on the limits of mechanically causal explanation are correct, then upon observing living things, every human being will wonder about the nature of life and will be led to speculate that some underlying intelligence or intelligences are responsible for the presence of life on earth. If we remain within the empirical realm and attempt to draw implications based on how nature looks in general, then the array of natural purposes and natural products will not obviously yield as a matter of implication the concept of a single, wise, all-good, all-knowing, and all-powerful being. Nature is too wild, destructive, and chaotic to support such a conclusion.

The more straightforward supposition, for Kant, is that nature is driven by an array of gods with finite capacities that are perhaps in conflict and competition with one another. Such speculations indeed occupy a great deal of ancient thought, and Kant believes that polytheistic outlooks arose owing to the teleological need to postulate an intelligence that governs nature, in conjunction with a predominantly empirical orientation towards the world. Whether or not this is historically accurate, it remains that from an exclusively empirical standpoint – and this is Kant's main point – unconditional principles and a single, benevolent, wise, and powerful God cannot be inferred.

If we initially assume an empirical standpoint and, upon reflecting about the nature of life, are led to suspect that some form of supersensible intelligence exists, some supplementation of this standpoint will be needed to arrive at a determinate conception of what the unconditional purpose of the world is. This is also to say that a teleological argument for the existence of

God – one that infers a divine intelligence from the intelligent structure of the physical universe, while being unable to say whether one or many gods are implied – can at best indicate in only a generalized fashion that there is some intelligence or intelligences governing nature. So if we use empirical methods alone, we can never prove unconditionally that there is a god or gods, let alone prove unconditionally that there is a single, infinitely intelligent God.

[**§86: "Concerning ethico-theology"**] Kant's identification of an unconditional content within the field of morality has some powerful implications for the question of what the human being's place is in the grand scheme of things. Indeed, Kant is so impressed with the moral substance of human beings that he maintains that without human beings in their moral presence the whole of creation would have no absolute value at all. If we were purely scientific intelligences, even this would fail to introduce an unconditional value to the world, since the notion of an ultimate purpose would be lacking. In itself, science collects only contingent facts.

Within the moral sphere, considered generally, Kant reiterates his claim from §83 that absolute value – the value in reference to which the value of the rest of creation is here being determined – cannot not reside in happiness, since happiness depends upon contingently-derived sensory gratification. This reveals that the aesthetic appreciation of pure beauty, since it abstracts from sensory gratification, is independent of happiness as well. Beauty, as we have seen, is more akin to morality in this universalistic aspect. In the end, Kant claims that it is "only through a good will that human existence can have an absolute worth, and in relationship to which the existence of the world can have a final purpose" (Ak 443 (412), G 309, P 332, M 109 [Pt II], B 293).

If the realization of morality – given this teleological outlook – is nature's unconditional purpose, then it follows that nature's realization of its own purpose coincides with the realization of our own purpose, since our own unconditional purpose is moral. Upon supposing this coincidence between mechanistic causality and teleological causality, we are presented with a question of what the conditions for the possibility of such a coincidence happen to be, given the assumption that nature is the product of a divine intelligence.

Kant argues that in order to render mechanical nature compatible with moral purposes, it is necessary to ascribe specific qualities to the divine intelligence that has already been introduced to explain the presence of life and the possibility for the economy of empirical natural laws. Neither the mere observation of life nor scientific knowledge provides these added qualities, but now that we have in hand a definition of nature's purpose in reference to the unconditional quality of morality, some further specification of God's qualities becomes possible. Kant writes:

> From this so-defined principle of the causality of the original being, we must think of it not merely as an intelligence and law-giver for nature, but also as the law-giver in general in a moral kingdom of purposes. In relation to the *highest good* that is alone possible under such a sovereignty, namely the existence of rational beings under moral laws, we can think of this original being as *all-knowing* . . . ; as *all-powerful* . . . ; as *all-good* and at the same time *just* . . . In this way *moral* teleology supplements the deficiency of *physical* teleology and first grounds a *theology* . . .
>
> (§86, Ak 444 (413–14), G 310, P 333, M 110–11 [Pt II], B 295)

The introduction of moral content supplements the principle of the objective purposiveness of nature that leads us to assume that a divine intelligence governs empirical natural laws in an economical way that supports scientific comprehension. God, in effect, plays the role of making science possible and of making a moral world possible by arranging the mechanisms of nature in a way that supports the realization of moral purposes, and, hence, the realization of nature's purpose itself. To account for how the realization of moral purposes is possible, we need to ascribe to God the traditional divine qualities of omniscience, omnibenevolence, and omnipotence and advance beyond ancient and empiricistic polytheistic conceptions.

[§87: "Concerning the moral proof of God's existence"] The requirements for making scientific theorizing possible lead us to assume a divine presence behind nature to preserve economy. The presence of life leads to the same assumption, given how living organisms defy comprehension in mechanical terms alone. Kant now adds independently to this double-indication of God a third and stronger one, by claiming that moral considerations alone lead us to suppose God's existence.

The moral argument for God's existence is that, first of all, morality within us obligates us to act rationally. If everyone were to act rationally, then this would satisfy the objective condition for a thoroughly moral world. This is not sufficient for such a world, however, since it is contradictory to suppose that in a thoroughly moral world everyone would be unhappy. Human happiness thus needs to be coordinated with the realization of moral purposes. Kant consequently claims that "the highest and best thing in the world (höchste Weltbesten) is a happiness of rational beings that harmoniously coincides with the conformity to the moral law," and this ideal condition is that towards which both nature and human morality ultimately aim.

Nature and morality, however, operate with different rules of causality, so some way to conceive of moral content as being compatible with natural processes is also necessary. The only way to do this is to conceive of moral content as being infused into, or coordinated with, the natural processes themselves. This becomes possible if we assume that the intelligence that we need to suppose underlies nature is not simply intelligent in both scientifically favorable and life-creating senses, but also has a moral nature. Hence, for the sake of fulfilling our moral obligations, we need to suppose that a morally-constituted God exists whose activity directs nature in a way that is compatible with our moral interests.

Kant adds to this argument an even more dramatic and thought-provoking implication. He recognizes that human beings are subject to physical accidents and that the human race could become physically extinct before its moral obligations are realized, where everyone, good and bad alike, would be thrown "back into the abyss of the purposeless chaos of matter from which they were taken." This implies, lest the unconditional nature of moral obligation be reduced to an illusion, that our existence cannot be merely physical and that a thoroughly moral society could exist outside of the spatio-temporal realm.

Objects of Faith and the Moral Argument for God's Existence

[§88: "Limitation of the moral proof's validity"] It is tempting to conclude that the moral argument for God's existence is as rock-solid as a scientific proof, but Kant disagrees with this. He is careful to keep the realms and logical styles of science and morality distinct, and he associates provable knowledge – the only genuine type of knowledge that we have concerning what exists – exclusively with scientific knowledge and theoretical understanding.

To articulate this distinction between science and morality, Kant argues that although moral principles in themselves do not provide knowledge of a provable sort, they do provide us with an unconditional ground for our behavior. There are many ways to conduct one's life, but according to Kant, the moral and rational way is the only universal and necessary way and, in a broad sense, is the only authentic way to live. Nonetheless, his moral theory is not a scientific theory, and we find nothing within it that serves to illuminate, for instance, the chemical constitution of things or the laws of physics. The moral sphere of discourse is entirely distinct.

This relativizes the status of the moral argument for God's existence to the very status of morality, which in human beings is an unavoidable and intrinsic mode of interpreting our experience. Kant illustrates the depth of the moral perspective by noting how it contradicts our inner voice of reason to imagine that a life morally-well lived could ever be equivalent in value to an evil life. This sort of question is biblically addressed in the Book of Ecclesiastes, when it is asked despairingly and nihilistically what the value of striving for wisdom could possibly be, given that both wise and foolish people face the same grave and ultimate extinction. Kant expresses the situation in more positive terms:

> As soon as people began to reflect upon right and wrong, during a time when they still looked upon nature's purposiveness with indifference, using it without considering it to be anything beyond the usual course of things, they [nonetheless] unavoidably must have made the following judgment: that in the end it must make a difference whether a person has acted honestly or falsely, fairly or violently, even if up until the end of his life, at least as far as can be seen, he has received

neither reward for his virtues, nor punishment for his crimes. It is as if they perceived a voice in themselves saying that it must come out differently . . .

(§88, Remark, Ak 458 (438), G 322–23, P 349–50, M 128–29 [Pt II], B 309)

For Kant, such feelings unveil an unshakable moral foundation in the human being, and it is in reference to the rational solidity of this foundation that he advances the moral argument for God's existence. Moral laws are given independently of experience and they are unconditional in Kant's view. They are at the same time, however, grounded in a rationality that, as far as we can tell, stems only from within the human perspective. This indicates a subjective aspect to morality in the sense of its being human-relative. The unconditional content of moral laws combined with the "ought" that they carry considerably offsets this human-relative quality, and inspires us to believe that the moral laws do not apply only to human beings, but apply to the world as it is in itself.

Kant describes the basic and ideal moral prescription as follows:

Through reason, we are determined *a priori* to further what is best in the world [*das Weltbeste*], and this is constituted by the union of the greatest welfare of rational beings with the highest condition of their good, i.e., of universal happiness with the most law-governed morality.

(§88, Ak 453 (429), G 318, P 343, M 122 [Pt II], B 304)

If such an ideal world is to be possible, as noted, we need to suppose that nature has in itself, quite independently of our presence and projections, a moral ground that allows mechanical causality and teleological causality to coincide. The moral argument for God's existence tries to establish this by drawing an implication from the necessity of postulating a moral ground for nature itself, to an intelligence beyond nature that is the source of that moral ground. After showing that God exists based on moral considerations, we can then suppose God's activity within nature.

Kant believes that the above inference from a moral teleology to a theology, however, is not logically valid for a subtle reason: it is possible that from the absolute standpoint of the intelligent being that gives a moral meaning to nature there might not be a finitude-generating distinction between mechanical and teleological causality. The divine intelligence that produces the economy of natural laws might be operating with a type of mentality and causality all of its own that does not have a specific moral content, but has this content amalgamated with the natural, mechanical content all at once. In short, it is logically possible to conceive of a supersensible intelligence that is so different from our own, that our projections of moral goodness would not make sense, despite the fact that such an intelligence produces a natural situation that allows for the coincidence of our moral aims with nature. What is unconditional in us (viz., morality) might not be unconditional in things in themselves, in other words.

Kant adds, though, that such a peculiarly-formed supersensible intelligence is impossible for us to conceive of as genuinely giving a moral meaning to nature. For this reason, given the constitution of our faculty of reason, we cannot conceive of nature's final purpose "without an author and ruler of the world who is a moral law-giver at the same time."

To underscore how the force of the moral argument for God's existence is limited, Kant offers a second avenue to the same qualified conclusion. We can see this by reflecting upon his overall philosophical project and style. In each of his *Critiques*, Kant identifies *a priori* principles and then discusses how they apply to the world of experience. This leads him to ask, first of all, how can such *a priori* principles apply to our experience at all. After overcoming this basic difficulty, he then explores the extent to which the *a priori* principles regulate and constitute our experience. In the *Critique of the Power of Judgment*, as we have seen, he introduces the principle of the objective purposiveness of nature in reference to the need to secure an economy of empirical laws. This concerns the compatibility of the empirical presentations of nature with our quest to formulate lawful and mechanical cause and effect relationships.

We can conceive of the limits concerning the moral argument for God's existence in similar terms. Once again we have a set of *a priori* principles – in this case they are moral principles and not science-grounding ones – whose compatibility with empirical nature is the subject of inquiry. And once again, we have an appeal to a supersensible intelligence as a way to establish the highest degree of compatibility, harmony, or optimal attunement between morality and nature. It is one and the same intelligence in both cases, except that in the scientific aspect, this intelligence supplies an economy of empirical natural laws, and in the moral aspect, this intelligence supplies a style of mechanical operation of the empirical natural laws that is consistent with the realization of moral laws. Both involve lawlike behavior, rationality, and the postulation of a supersensible intelligence. In sum, God coordinates the respective regulations of body and mind, or the starry skies above us with the moral law within us, as we can recall from Kant's famous formulation.

The crucial point is that these speculations about the presence of a supersensible intelligence that regulates nature for the sake of both scientific inquiry and moral behavior are set forth owing to an overriding rational demand for coherence and total comprehension. Without such conditions being met, we would have no way to conceive of nature as other than being potentially unreceptive to our attempts to behave in a moral way. The conditions for doing science and for acting morally are essentially the same, since both sets of conditions lead us to postulate God's existence. This postulation, however, is only relative to our general quest for comprehension.

At a more fundamental and immediate level, we aim to integrate the *a priori* way in which we constitute our experience in space, time, and mechanical causality, with the *a priori* necessity to act morally. This is to say that the effort to understand the compatibility of mechanical nature and teleology within our experience is simultaneously an effort to understand how two aspects of ourselves – the theoretical (i.e., scientifically-minded) and the practical (i.e., morally-minded) – are integrated. Reflections upon the nature of beauty and living things, as we have seen, serve this function. Kant thus concludes:

> The reality of a highest morally law-giving author is therefore sufficiently established merely *for the practical use* of our reason, without

theoretically [i.e., scientifically, in terms of logical proofs] determining anything in connection with this author's existence.

(§88, Ak 456 (434), G 320, P 346, M 125 [Pt II], B 307)

[§89: "Concerning the use of the moral argument"] It might initially seem disappointing that the moral argument for God's existence does not succeed in proving God's existence with mathematical certitude, but this limitation has a positive utility. Since the moral argument is limited in scope, it constrains expansive dispositions towards dogmatic assertions of God's existence. At the same time, its focus upon exclusively moral content constrains extravagances in the other direction towards ascribing too many anthropomorphic qualities to God. In the same respect, since it explicitly restricts the conception of God to a moral conception, it also discourages the worship of God for either selfish or fearful reasons, along with discouraging beliefs that the highest being can be satisfied by means other than through developing the expression of one's goodwill.

Also on the positive side, since Kant believes that metaphysical questions are altogether beyond the reach of scientific inquiry, the conception of God as a moral being based on the requirements of our moral dispositions and the nature of our judgment take a step in the direction of giving some speculative content to the scientifically unknowable origin of the universe. The moral argument for God's existence and the moral conception of the world stand as a way to temper uncontrolled speculation and arbitrary fancy in one's conception of God, while they nonetheless provide a conception of ultimate purposes that is unconditionally grounded in human reason.

[§90: "Concerning the kind of assertion involved in a teleological (i.e., moral) proof of God's existence"] Kant reiterates that the moral proof for the existence of God does not provide knowledge, and emphasizes that its strength cannot be enhanced by adding considerations that derive from teleological reflections on living things. As we have seen, aside from the moral argument, there are two independent avenues to the postulation of a supersensible intelligence that underlies nature, namely one that derives from the principle of the objective purposiveness of nature in reference to the economy of empirical laws, and one that derives from our reflections on the origins of life. The moral argument introduces a third *independent* avenue by postulating a supersensible intelligence in order to render possible the realization of our duty in the physical world. Fusing either of the first two avenues with the moral one, however, only confuses the moral argument.

Kant also underscores how there is some logical slippage between the concept of a moral purpose to nature and that of supersensible moral being who is inferred to have infused that purpose. He states that our postulation of God is based on an analogy, and adds that analogies do not involve an exact correspondence between their elements. A beaver can build a dam, or a bird can build a nest, but how this is done remains unknown; we can assert only that there is some analogy between their behavior and how we build houses according to rational plans.

Similarly, conceiving of an intelligence that underlies objects of natural beauty on the analogy of how we make works of art also guarantees no exact correspondence between our sort of teleological causality and what we ascribe to God. Insofar as no exact correspondence is implied, our inference from the need to conceive of nature as having a moral content that has been infused from an external source, to a moral and rational God who infused it there, is only as strong as is the analogy between our own intentional behavior and God's.

[§91: "Concerning the kind of assertion attained through a practical faith"] Kant concludes the *Critique of the Power of Judgment* with reflections on the status of the idea of God and the meaning of having faith that God exists. This continues his discussion of the status of morality in contrast to scientific understanding, and much that Kant says about God here continues to derive from his conception of morality.

To characterize what it means to have faith in God's existence, he identifies three legitimate, fact-related sorts of object, in the broad sense of the word "object." The first are opinions. Their truth can in principle be verified by some possible experience, although at present the experience has not been forthcoming. An example would be an opinion about whether life exists on other planets.

The second type of objects comprises actual facts, the reality of which is confirmed by the presentation of things that express the facts. These cover a wide range of subject matters and include mathematical facts along with facts associated with ordinary experience (i.e., empirical facts). But this is not all. Kant includes the concept of freedom among the set of facts:

> ... the concept of freedom [*Freiheitsbegriffe*] ... sufficiently establishes its reality through the causality of reason with regard to certain effects in the sensory world which are made possible through reason, and which are irrefutably postulated in the moral law.
>
> (General Remark, Ak 475 (468), G 339, P 369, M 150 [Pt II], B 328)

That people act freely upon occasion is a fact for Kant, and this recognition has the effect of locating facts in both the scientific and the moral realms, upon which cognitions of one sort or another can be based. Grounding beliefs on science, or on freedom in connection with morality, in other words, is not a matter of fancy, speculation or arbitrary construction.

This brings us to the third sort of object in addition to opinions and facts of a scientific or moral sort, namely, matters of faith (*Glaubenssachen*), which are closely tied to the fact of freedom. In the preface to the second edition of the *Critique of Pure Reason*, Kant stated profoundly that he found it necessary to deny knowledge in order to make room for faith (*Glaube*). It is easy to assume incorrectly that what Kant means by "faith," is the freedom in metaphysical, speculative matters, to believe whatever one wants. He has rather a specific, morally-focussed conception of faith that contrasts with fanciful metaphysical speculation:

> (3) Objects, which must be thought *a priori* in relation to a duty-conforming use of pure practical reason ... but which are transcendent [*überschwenglich*] for the theoretical use of reason, are mere *matters of faith*. Such an object would be the *highest good* in the world to be achieved through freedom, whose concept cannot be proved for us in any possible experience in terms of its objective reality ... but which consequently must be assumed to be possible nonetheless, since its use for that purpose to the best possible effect is commanded by pure practical reason.
>
> (§91, Ak 469 (457), G 333, P 362, M 142 [Pt II], B 321)

Matters of faith are what we need rationally to assume for morality to be realizable, where the possibility of the assumed objects or principles remains undecidable in principle. The highest good – the combination in everyone in the form of a social system, of happiness and behavior motivated purely by a respect for one's duty – could be an unrealizable ideal for the earthly situation. However, since it remains an ideal towards which we are morally determined to aim, we need to suppose as possible the significant realization of this ideal on earth, along with the conditions that would allow this realization to occur. Kant includes among the conditions for the realization of the highest good, the existence of God, and the immortality of the soul. We must assume their possibility, and although we cannot prove that these concepts are internally consistent, neither can it be proved that they are inconsistent.

What it means to have faith in God's existence therefore defines a special sort of rational attitude towards God. It does not amount to believing that God exists for any arbitrary reason at all; it amounts to believing specifically that God exists as a condition for fulfilling our rational vocation to realize moral obligations and to foster happiness that is consistent with those obligations. Morality is the paramount concern.

Kant carries this theme to the conclusion of the *Critique of the Power of Judgment*, and the third *Critique* ends with a conception of God that is tailored to include all and only those qualities such as omnibenevolence, omniscience, omnipotence, justice, wisdom, eternity, and omnipresence that express what we must assume in a being that serves to ground the significant realization of morality in the natural world. The list of qualities is substantial and it reflects a traditional monotheistic conception well.

At the same time, however, this divine conception issues only from the universal and unconditional morality that we find within ourselves. It amounts to saying that if we are to fulfill our obligations and respect ourselves as rational beings, then we need to explain how our own moral reflection can inhabit nature itself, lest nature otherwise remain an alien being. Once this is achieved through the postulation of God's existence, we are in the position to overcome not only the resistance that inanimate nature sets in our path but also, through faith in God's presence, the resistance that the animal drives within our own bodies pose to the realization of the highest good. Faith in God, as does the experience of beauty, thus serves also to unify the conflicted individual human personality for the sake of humanity's moral destiny.

CONCLUSION

THE MUSIC OF THE SPHERES AND THE IDEALIZATION OF REASON

If we return imaginatively to ancient Greece, we encounter the Pythagorean fascination with numbers, geometry, numerical ratios, and, in conjunction with this, a conception of the universe as having a thoroughgoing rational harmony. This is captured in the idea of the "music of the spheres" – a vision of the solar system inspired in part, by observing how a ball on a string, when spun rapidly in a circle through the air, produces a whirring, whistling tone. Each planet revolving around the sun is like a ball on a string, and can be thought analogously to produce a resonating tone appropriate to its speed and distance from the sun. In the larger picture, the set of planets in their simultaneous movements can be thought to produce the equivalent of a musical chord, like a kind of cosmic harp. This classical association of planetary movement and musical tone extends all the way into the writings of Johannes Kepler (1571–1630) – in his *Harmonices Mundi Libri V* (*Harmonics of the World, Five Books* [1619]) – who similarly hypothesized that each planet has its own sound, and that the movement of the planets can express a musical harmony upon the occasion of an ideal arrangement of the planets' positions.

Aristotle succinctly described the Pythagorean interest in music and harmonic resonance in his *Metaphysics*, and their ideas surrounding musical strings, harps, and spiritual attunement found their way into his own theory of human character, in the form of his famous doctrine of the mean. According to this Aristotelian doctrine, the virtues reflect temperate forms of behavior whereas the vices express the extremes. Every virtue stands as a mean, or intermediary, between two respective vices, as courage is the virtuous mean between the vices of rashness and cowardice, or as proper pride is the virtuous mean between the vices of vanity and humility. The development of virtue is consequently comparable to tuning a harp, where relative to each virtue, one could be initially either strung too tightly (e.g., rashness or vanity) and strung too loosely (e.g., cowardice or humility). Aristotle's doctrine of the mean, as here described, transports the image of musical attunement from its original location in the sphere of astronomy or, more generally, natural law, into the sphere of morality.

With respect to Kant, it has become a commonplace to note how Kant personally displayed only a limited taste in music, and how within his aesthetic theory, he ranked music as the lowest of the arts. His short account of music, along with his association between music and joke-telling in §54, also adds little to the prevailing impression that, for Kant, music is not to be counted among the most profound arts. There is one sense, though, in which this impression of Kant's lack of affinity for music has the effect of obscuring our appreciation of his entire philosophy.

If we consider, not Kant's explicit remarks about music, but his philosophical terminology, a different picture quickly emerges. At the forefront is the stated key to his theory of pure beauty, namely, the harmony between the cognitive faculties of understanding and imagination as they operate in reference to cognition in general (§9). To describe this harmony, Kant uses the words "*Übereinstimmung,*" "*Stimmung,*" "*Zusammenstimmung,*" and "*harmonische Spiel*" (harmonic play), all of which denote an accord, agreement or mutual attunement. He also refers to an optimal "proportion" (*Proportion*) between the understanding and imagination in relation to their mutual attunement. The set of terms suggests an accord, harmony or tuning that invokes an association with musical resonance or sympathetic vibration in tone.

The effect of Kant's verbal characterization of the harmony of the cognitive faculties is to suggest that when we perceive a beautiful object, something "rings true" in the object in an almost literal sense, since the object causes a harmony of the cognitive faculties and, hence, is related via cognition to truth and knowledge, while doing so in a non-conceptual, generalized way that escapes determinate conceptualization. So the "universal voice" (*allgemeine Stimme*) – one where the word, *Stimme* (voice) is closely related to "*Stimmung*" – with which we pronounce an object to be beautiful, can be regarded as more of a musical, or singing, voice, where we expect others to be able to join in with, or sympathetically resonate with, the "ring" that our own mind experiences in the apprehension of a beautiful object. In light of such reflections, we can consequently appreciate some strong musical associations at the basis of Kant's theory of pure beauty, despite the limited treatment that music officially receives in his analysis of the fine arts. The universal feeling of pure beauty provides the musical, aesthetic tone for the more conceptually-articulate universal voice of moral reason, one could say, just as music combines with words in a song.

What adds significance to this association of music and pure beauty is that the presence and application of this idea of mutual attunement is not limited to the foundation of Kant's theory of beauty, but is central to his philosophical vision as a whole. This sort of attunement is exactly what Kant aspires to define – in a whole host of ways – between the system of moral laws and the system of natural laws. Beauty as the symbol of morality defines an attunement between the universal qualities of judgments of pure beauty (e.g., freedom, disinterestedness) and moral judgments. Beauty as the symbol of scientific completeness defines an attunement between the systematicity of a beautiful object's structure and the systematicity of the ideal scientific theory. Human beauty in the abstract defines an attunement between morality and beauty, through the amalgamation of moral content with a generic human form. Human beauty in a concrete living person defines an attunement between morality, beauty, and nature, in the organic presence and activity of a person. Fine art, as the product of genius, defines a corresponding attunement between morality, beauty, and nature, in the creation in some material object whose form is beautiful and whose content is moral. In each case, there is some proportion, harmony, tuning, agreement, or mutual correspondence involved.

Kant's use of this idea of mutual attunement is reminiscent of the "music of the spheres" alluded to above or, more simply, reminiscent of a harp's strings. Kant is very careful about demarcating from one another, the respective spheres or realms of morality, of nature, of beauty, of the understanding, of imagination, of reason, of judgment, and so on, such that their boundaries do not melt and confuse into one another. Each is like a planet in the solar system that resonates with its own particular sound and which, ideally, resonates harmoniously with all of the other planets in celestial accord.

And it is here – in the term "ideally" – where we can appreciate what Kant offers in his various *Critiques* and here as well in his theory of beauty: he offers us an ideal to which we can aspire. His thought is governed by an absolute respect for reason and the maximal systematicity associated with it. A perfectly systematic scientific theory is only an ideal, as is a perfectly rational moral agent, as is a judgment of pure beauty, as is a happiness-filled world where everyone does the right thing. The amazing achievement of Kant's philosophizing is that, despite the existentially incredible quality of the perfect conditions he articulates, he shows that every dimension of these idealizations is grounded unconditionally within our very nature as rational beings. Such ideals thus stand as unshakable grounds upon which we can set our scientific and practical goals, and Kant's challenge to anyone otherwise minded is to show how any other alternative grounds could be as unshakable as the ones he has articulated.

In this sense, then, Kant's aesthetics can be regarded as one string in an ideally-tuned philosophical harp, constituted and played by our reason. The sounding of this philosophical harp historically preserves the religious idea of music as a divine art – an art expressed in the music of the spheres, in the *musica coelestis* of medieval angelic singing, along with many other representations of a musical accord between layers of the cosmos. In tune with such analogies, Kant can be regarded not as someone whose musical taste extended merely to local military marches in a limited and provincial fashion but, in a more celebratory fashion, as a philosophical descendent of Orpheus – the greatest musician and poet in Greek mythology, whose music was so beautiful that it could bring all of nature into harmony. By using philosophical terms at the core of his philosophy that express musical relationships, Kant achieved this same integrative effect with words, concepts, and reason, rather than with a harp but, to all those who appreciate his philosophy, he demarcates a set of crystalline spheres – of idealized morality, idealized nature, and idealized beauty – that resonates harmoniously and inspiringly as an ideal world that resonates within us all.

Notes

PREFACE AND ACKNOWLEDGMENTS

1   See, for example, the wide variety of writings by Paul Guyer and Henry
    E. Allison. All contemporary studies of Kant's philosophy, including the
    present one, owe an enormous debt to these two theorists. As a testa-
    ment to its intellectual strength, after more than 25 years since its pub-
    lication in 1979, Guyer's *Kant and the Claims of Taste* is still being
    actively discussed in the secondary literature on Kant's aesthetics.
    Henry Allison's *Kant's Theory of Taste – A Reading of the Critique of
    Aesthetic Judgment* (Cambridge, 2001) is now probably the most
    authoritative, relatively recent book on Kant's aesthetics available in
    English. It provides an accurate, detailed and intellectually probing
    treatment of Kant's aesthetic theory, engaging critically and thoroughly
    with the secondary literature, both in English and in German. It thus
    stands implicitly as an excellent, valuable guide to the interpretations
    of other writers.

2   A useful exception is Werner Pluhar's 1987 thoughtful introduction to
    his translation of the third *Critique*. This introduction sets the work in
    context by summarizing the associated purposes of each of Kant's
    three *Critiques*, viz., the *Critique of Pure Reason*, the *Critique of
    Practical Reason*, and the *Critique of the Power of Judgment*. John

Zammito's *The Genesis of Kant's Critique of Judgment* (Chicago & London: University of Chicago Press, 1992), also offers a more historically-focussed effort to provide an integrated account of the third *Critique*. A more recent (2005) holistic condensation of Kant's aesthetics and teleology that sketches the contents of the third *Critique* is Hannah Ginsborg's entry in the *Stanford Encyclopedia of Philosophy* (online). There is also Angelica Nuzzo's *Kant and the Unity of Reason* (2005) that attends primarily to Kant's published Introduction, but which focusses in principle on the entire third *Critique*. Although all of these have technical dimensions as works of philosophical argumentation in their own right, they have significantly helped to provide a wider vision of the third *Critique* that extends beyond the first half of the book.

3　The quotations from Kant's aesthetics will be noted with page numbers from the standard German edition (*Kants Werke, Akademie-Textausgabe* [1902], Band V [Walter de Gruyter & Co., Berlin 1968]), with Kant's pagination in parentheses, the Guyer–Matthews translation [G], the Pluhar translation [P], the Meredith translation [M], and the Bernard translation [B], so that whatever English translation happens to be available, the textual reference can be easily traced.

INTRODUCTION

1　An exemplary place to see this is in Kant's first paragraph in his discussion of the Antinomy of Pure Reason in the *Critique of Pure Reason* (A406 / B432), where he refers to the four functions of all judgment and the three formal species of syllogisms as structuring his exposition.

2　This is suggested by Henry E. Allison (*Kant's Theory of Taste*, p. 305).

3　The main works involved in the German aesthetics influence are Baumgarten's *Metaphysica* (1739) and *Aesthetica* (1750 and 1758), Meier's *Gedanken von Scherzen* (*Thoughts on Jesting* (1744 and 1754)), and *Anfangsgründe aller schönen Wissenschaften* (*Foundations of All Liberal Arts* (1748–50)), Mendelssohn's *Briefe über die Empfindungen* (*Letters on Sensations* (1755)), *Über die Hauptgrundsätze der schönen Künste und Wissenschaften* (*On the Main Principles of the Fine Arts and Liberal Arts* (1757)), and *Über das Erhabene und Naïve in den schönen Wissenschaften* (*On the Sublime and Naïve in the Liberal Arts* (1758)).

The English texts that Kant had read included Hutcheson's *Inquiry Into the Origins of Our Ideas of Beauty and Virtue* (1725; German translation, 1762), Kames's *Elements of Criticism* (1762, German translation, 1763), Gerard's *Essay on Taste* (1759; German translation, 1766), and *Essay on Genius* (1774; German translation, 1776), Burke's *A Philosophical Enquiry into the Origin of Our Ideas of the Sublime and Beautiful* (1757, German translation, 1773). Kant certainly read segments of Hume's philosophy, but whether he read "Of the Standard of Taste" (1757; German translation, 1759) although likely, is still a matter of debate. Similar themes are addressed by Kames, in any case.

4   The main source is Leibniz's *Discourse on Metaphysics* (1686), Section XXIV. In addition to the taxonomy of obscure vs. clear knowledge, etc., this section contains Leibniz's often-cited remark that when we judge that a poem is good (or bad), we apprehend the poem clearly, but in a confused manner, noting only that it has a "*je ne sais quoi*" (I know not what) quality that makes it good.

More substantially influential, given its contents, could have been Leibniz's short essay "On Wisdom" (c. 1690), where he repeats the "*je ne sais quoi*" phase in a similar context, but combines this with reflections on wisdom whose contents are programmatically reflected throughout Kant's third *Critique*. See "On Wisdom," trans. Anita Gallagher, *Fidelio*, Vol. III, No. 2, Summer 1994.

1   THE PLEASURE IN PURE BEAUTY (§§1–22; §§30–40)

1   Examples would be "This is red" (positive), "This is not-red" (negative), and "This is non-red" (unlimited).

2   In the *Critique of Pure Reason*, the ordering of the first two moments is reversed, viz., first moment is that of quantity, and the second, that of quality. Kant reverses the order here to establish, first of all, that the judgment of taste is aesthetic, since this fact grounds the rest of his analyses.

3   Necessity is the key feature of the *a priori* judgments for which Kant is well known. He writes in the *Critique of Pure Reason* that "if we have a proposition which, in being thought, is thought as *necessary*, it is an *a priori* judgment" (B3). In contrast, judgments that have the logical form of universality (e.g., "everything is made of water" or "every event has a cause") can either admit of exceptions or not; if they do not, then they are necessary judgments and are hence *a priori*. The second and

the fourth moments of Kant's present discussion are thereby closely connected. His discussion in the second moment (§9), although officially concerned with the judgment of pure beauty's universality, also does much to associate necessity with such judgments as well.

Judgments of pure beauty are not universal judgments in the sense of the above two examples, however, since their logical "quantity" is singular, e.g., "This flower is beautiful." Their universality resides in what can be called their "assent-value" viz., that *everyone* ought to agree. The possibilities for such values are: (1) "everyone necessarily agrees," (2) "everyone ought to agree," and (3) "no one need agree." Judgments of pure beauty fit (2).

4 The word here translated as "feeling of approval" is "*Wohlgefallen*," which could be translated more literally and directly as "liking." The English term "satisfaction" can also be used, since it has an advantage in how it dually captures the pleasurably psychological dimension of "liking," but also additionally and importantly, the epistemological dimension of how a given object can "satisfy" a definition or conceptual condition. As we will see in §9, in the case of pure beauty, we have the presentation of an object that energetically satisfies the conditions for cognition in general. The phrase "feeling of approval" is also appropriate since Kant's discussion is framed within the context of making evaluative judgments of one sort of another. As a rule, either "feeling of approval" or "satisfaction" will be used to translate "*Wohlgefallen*," to capture the epistemological and evaluative relationship to cognition in general when the positive feeling involved refers to beauty.

5 *Critique of Practical Reason*, Ak 30 (Vol. 5). This first version of the categorical imperative is also expressed in the *Groundwork of the Metaphysics of Morals*, Ak 421 (Vol. 4).

6 If a person plays a game of tennis for its own sake (i.e., just for fun, and not to win), one could say that the person's enjoyment is disinterested. Since the person is not playing and enjoying the game "as a human being," however, one could not expect the other player to have the same disinterested enjoyment. The universality of the judgment of pure beauty arises from the disinterestedness (as in the tennis game) coupled with the universal persona one adopts – a persona which is essentially the same as one's universal persona as a moral agent, minus the interests that morality carries with it. Kant tries to define "disinterested" in a way that directly implies this universal persona,

and this is why he believes that disinterestedness implies universality within the context of judgments of pure beauty.

7   This account refers to cognitive structures that can be known *a priori*, viz., ways of knowing that carry with them a strict universality and necessity (*Critique of Pure Reason*, B4). Kant's arguments for the *a priority* of space and time along with the transcendental deduction of the categories characterize how human beings similarly structure their experience. Kant's analyses in the Second Analogy and in his Refutation of Idealism provide some supplementary argumentation to the same effect. When a set of beings with the same cognitive structures is given content from (i.e., become aware of) the same mind-independent reality, they consequently experience a public world whose publicity derives in part from their shared cognitive structures, and in part from the fact that it is single mind-independent reality of which they are aware.

8   Kant distinguishes two types of free play that are easily confused. One is a free play between the imagination and the understanding; the other is a free play within the imagination alone. As a rule, Kant refers to the former (e.g., as here crucially in §9, in the key to the critique of taste) as an aesthetically positive free play between the imagination and the understanding that characterizes the pleasure in beauty. The other is an aesthetically neutral free play located within the imagination itself, which, when it happens to conflict with the lawfulness of the understanding, results in the judgment that something is not beautiful.

Kant refers to the free play of the imagination alone in §26 (quoted below) in his discussion of the sublime (which in its counter-purposiveness is non-beautiful), and to the combination of the two sorts of free play in §49. In §26 (explicitly) and §49 (implicitly) Kant maintains furthermore that the free play within the imagination alone can be alternatively related to the understanding (in the case of beauty) or to reason (in the case of the sublime). A further reference to the free play within the imagination alone is in Mary J. Gregor (trans.), *Anthropology from a Practical Point of View* (The Hague: Nijhoff, 1974), p. 109.

9   Paul Guyer emphasizes this important distinction between "form of purposiveness" (or "form of finality") and "purposiveness of form" (or "finality of form") in his *Kant and the Claims of Taste* (Cambridge and London: Harvard University Press, 1979), p. 219.

10 Kant's use of the term "adherent" is sometimes, if not typically, neutral. In the Introduction (VII), for example, he states that the satisfaction in pure beauty adheres {in one sense} to a given empirical representation ("Die Lust ist also im Geschmacksurtheile zwar von einer empirischen Vorstellung abhängig ... " (Ak191 (V)); in the unpublished Introduction, he states that the satisfaction in pure beauty adheres [in another sense] only to reflection and its form (" ... das Gefühl der Lust ... [ist] nur als der Reflexion und deren Form ... anhängend ... ") (Ak 249 (XX)). In this decisive context, it is clear that the term "adherent" can only be neutral.

11 The importance of this quote can be seen in how it foreshadows the concluding remark in the Critique of Aesthetic Judgment (§60) that taste is at bottom (im Grunde) a capacity for judging the sensible presentation of moral ideas.

12 A troubling intellectual descendent of this method can be seen in the attempts (e.g., those of Francis Galton [1822–1911], the cousin of Charles Darwin) to discern the face of the typical criminal through the use of composite portraiture. In this process, various photographs are superimposed over one another to form a generic image.

13 In the characterization of the common sense referred to in this section on the deduction, there is no mention of an "optimal attunement" between the understanding and imagination – the notion that provided a fairly refined and idealized characterization of the common sense in §§21–22. In the present context (§40), the common sense is instead characterized in a more generic way (similar to how it was described in §20) as referring simply to a feeling associated with the harmony of the faculties in general (this is also similar to §9), rather than to a feeling associated with an ideal attunement of them. This is to say that the more refined (and theoretically informative) idea of optimal attunement from §§21–22 – although Kant might be presupposing it – plays no explicit role in Kant's deduction and that the deduction is formulated at a more generic level of discussion.

2 THE SUBLIME AND THE INFINITE (§§23–29)

1 An alternative taxonomy would be the following, but it leaves no clear room for aesthetic judgments of sensation under either of the two main categories:

I. Determining Judgments
  A. Determining Cognitive Judgment
II. Reflecting Judgments
  A. Reflecting Cognitive Judgment
  B. Reflecting Aesthetic Judgment
    1. Judgments of Pure Beauty
    2. Judgments of Sublimity
[Aesthetic Judgments of Sensation]

2 One can imagine an alternative analysis of the sublime that, although it would run contrary to the spirit of reflecting judgment that proceeds from object to concept, could paint the imagination in a less negative light. This analysis would work in the other direction, like determining judgment, starting with the concept of an infinite totality, and then proceeding to the exemplifying realm of sensation. In this case, space and time (as infinite in their own right) would "schematize," or exhibit for sensation, the rational idea of an infinite totality, and in particular instances overwhelmingly large or powerful objects would do the same. Such objects could consequently be regarded as the finite appearances within sensation of an infinite totality (i.e., they would be representations of the divine towards which we would project our respect). Consistent with the process of determining judgment, this would be theoretically analogous to the procedure of starting with abstract moral imperatives and then showing how they can be instantiated in actual experience. In a related vein, Kant refers to poetry as a "schema for the supersensible" in §53.

3 As seen in the last chapter, Kant's account of the experience of pure beauty is interpretable as expressing the phenomenological side of his theoretical view that knowledge arises from the application of concepts to intuitions, for the harmony of the cognitive faculties of understanding and imagination expresses this application of concepts to intuitions in general. That is, one could say that Kant's theory of pure beauty describes *the phenomenology of his epistemology* as it is described in the theoretical terms of the first *Critique* that detaches its components from specific sensory content. In light of this, that we encounter phenomenological correlates to arguments for God's existence in Kant's theory of sublimity is in keeping with his style of philosophizing in the present Critique of Aesthetic Judgment as a whole, which can be described generally as phenomenological and aesthetic.

3 THE FINE ARTS AND CREATIVE GENIUS (§§41–54)

1 This abstraction from origin explains why Kant can indiscriminately use natural objects (e.g., flowers) along with art objects (e.g., abstract wallpaper design) as examples of free beauty in §4. What is relevant is not their origin, but how such objects present mere linear configurations for us to contemplate. The inclusion of art objects as examples of free beauty in §4 does not entail that there must be some form of artistic beauty *per se* that is "pure" or "free."

2 This refers to a free play within the imagination itself.

3 This refers to a free play between the imagination and the understanding.

4 BEAUTY'S CONFIRMATION OF SCIENCE AND MORALITY (§§55–60)

1 In his *Elements of Criticism* (1762) – a book which Kant read – Lord Kames begins his concluding Chapter 25, "Standard of Taste," with the proverb, "there is no disputing about taste." After some discussion of how judgments of beauty vary from person to person, Kames ultimately asserts that our common human nature nonetheless provides a standard of taste that is applicable to everyone. This discussion helps set the tone of the historical scene for Kant's present discussion of the antinomy of taste. David Hume also addressed the issue in his essay "Of the Standard of Taste" (1757), but it is uncertain whether or not Kant had read this particular essay by Hume. That Kant did, though, becomes probable in light of how some of Hume's verbal formulations come very close to Kant's (e.g., as Hume's reference to a "standard of taste" that can adjudicate between competing judgments of taste according to a definite rule).

2 An alternative translation of "*streiten*" is "quarrel."

3 There is some small doubt here with respect to the text's archeology, since §55 uses the phrases "critique of taste" and "transcendental critique of taste" which date originally from 1787. This was when Kant first conceived of entitling the projected manuscript that became the *Critique of the Power of Judgment*, the *Foundations of the Critique of Taste*.

4 Paul Guyer makes this important observation and develops this alternative in *Kant and the Claims of Taste* (1979). Another option might be to introduce the concept of "purposiveness without purpose," but this is less plausible because we are looking specifically for an indeterminate

concept that would directly explain how we, as Kant states in the antithesis, "demand the necessary agreement of others to this judgment." The concept of the harmony of the cognitive faculties or the concept of "cognition in general" justifies our demand for such agreement from others, but the concept of "purposiveness without purpose" does not itself harbor enough systematic implications to fulfill this function.

5   The essential publicity of knowledge can be understood to imply that our disposition towards society and communicability is not merely an empirical and variable contingency, as Kant suggests in §41, but is an *a priori* feature of our cognition in general. Without a presupposed conception of society or community, the concept of a judgment's universal validity that involves demanding the agreement of others is a contradiction in terms. For this reason, Kant's remark in a note to §2 which asserts that moral judgments are disinterested but carry an interest with them, whereas judgments of pure beauty are disinterested and do not carry any interest with them, needs to be regarded in a careful light. What he states is accurate: judgments of pure beauty are disinterested, and do not force us to refer the judgments to actually existing objects (as do moral judgments). Nonetheless, they do require us to regard the objects judged "as if" they were actual. Judgments of pure beauty carry with them an interest that is satisfiable in imagination, or fictionally, one could say, whereas moral judgments carry with them an interest that is only satisfiable in actual spatio-temporal behavior.

6   This formulation also has a subjective as well as an objective aspect. The former is parenthetical.

7   This is ambiguous between saying that the concept is in us, insofar as it refers to some underlying personal reality in us, or that the concept is our projection (and hence, in us) of a nonetheless mind-independent, objective being.

8   This is different from Kant's standard account whereby the artist takes some definite purpose or definitive subject matter and then expands it in the direction of reason by means of an aesthetic idea relative to that finite subject. Here, we instead have a rational idea that is not fully expressible in sensory experience, and an especially resonant representation (an aesthetic idea) associated with it that brings us closer to the rational idea via sensation.

9   A third way is to compare the formal systematicity of the beautiful object with the formal systematicity of the ideal society where everyone

acts morally. Kant does not mention this further symbolic correspondence in his account of beauty as the symbol of morality.

10 There is a revealing parallelism between Kant's conception of the unity of human consciousness in its actual organizing activity, and the unity of the divine supersensible being in its projected, or postulated, organizing activity. According to Kant, the "I," or abstract activity of the self, gives unity to sensations, to space and time, and to the pure concepts, and allows them to be coordinated thereby in an act of empirical knowledge. The supersensible, divine consciousness, as rationally postulated, gives an analogous unity to the empirical laws of nature, to living things, and to moral activity, and allows them to be coordinated thereby in a system of nature. The human unity of self-consciousness functions to give comprehensiveness to human experience, and the unity of divine consciousness is postulated to function analogously to give comprehensiveness to the universe as a whole.

5 LIVING ORGANISMS, GOD, AND INTELLIGENT DESIGN (§§61–91)

1 For an exposition of the concept of *logos spermatikos* as it appears in Stoicism (e.g., Diogenes Laertius), see Maryanne Cline Horowitz, "The Stoic Synthesis of the Idea of Natural Law in Man: Four Themes," *Journal of the History of Ideas*, 35, (1), 1974, pp. 3–16.

2 A candidate for a perfect instantiation would be a thoroughly conceptual system whose components are mutually dependent, self-sustaining, developmentally interconnected, and, in general, organically unified. The dialectical systems of German Idealism (e.g., Hegel's) aimed to instantiate this living quality in their theories.

3 For instance, William Paley's (1743–1805) well-known argument in *Natural Theology* (1800) – published ten years after Kant's third *Critique* – explicitly compares watches to living organisms in connection with the teleological argument and, given the complexity of living organisms, extrapolates to assert the existence of a divine intelligence.

4 i.e., recognizing a "descending" and "ascending" series of causes referred to in §65. Both the mechanical kind (descending series) and teleological (descending and ascending) kind of causality are consistent with Kant's elementary analysis of causality in the *Critique of Pure Reason*. In this analysis, the concept of causality derives from and

expresses the logical form of judgment "*if A, then B*" (e.g., see A91 / B124 and A90 / B122). Mechanical causality straightforwardly extends this "*if A, then B*" format in a linear fashion, and is consistent with the structure of deductive reasoning; teleological causality doubles, or loops, the "*if A, then B*" format back onto itself, biconditionally, and does not support deductive reasoning, owing to the structure's inherent circularity. Kant's unshakable position is that we cannot avoid thinking generally in an "*if A, then B*" fashion, but there are different ways to elaborate this elementary structure, either linearly or circularly.

This is to say merely that there is no direct conflict between the elementary characterization of causality that Kant provides in the first *Critique* (e.g., "every event has a cause") with his claim here that we need not interpret everything in terms of linear, mechanical causality. The very causal phraseology of §64, where Kant states that a natural purpose must be "cause and effect of itself" implies that we are here dealing with an elaboration of the elementary structure of the hypothetical form of logical judgment (viz., "*if A, then B*") that underlies the basic concept of causality.

5   One way to conceive of this higher, presumably infinite, perspective is through a geometrical analogy. We have characterized mechanical causality as a linear formation of the elemental "*if A, then B*" logical format, and teleological causality as a circular formation of that format. If we conceive of this difference as analogous to the qualitative one between a line and circle, then a compatibility between the two forms of causality can be visualized analogically by considering how a circle can transform into a line, if one demarcates some finite segment of the circle and then observes how it flattens out as the circle's diameter is constantly increased. As the circle's size increases, the curvature of the finitely-demarcated segment proportionally decreases; when the diameter is extended to infinity, the curvature becomes zero and would paradoxically turn into a straight line. This reflection is from Nicholas of Cusa (1401–64), who maintained that the circle and the line coincide in the infinite, and who associated God with the infinite and with the coincidence of opposites.

6   Kant added "(a God)" in the second edition of late 1792. This could very well mean "some deity or other," i.e., "a god."

7   These are the key ideas in Hegel's aesthetics as well, and the present discussion hints at how close Hegel's aesthetics actually is to Kant's.

BIBLIOGRAPHY

WORKS BY KANT (IN ORIGINAL AND IN ENGLISH TRANSLATION)

Kant, Immanuel. *Anthropology from a Practical Point of View*, trans. Mary J. Gregor. The Hague: Nijhoff, 1974.

———. *Critik der Urtheilskraft von Immanuel Kant*. Berlin and Libau: Lagarde und Friederich, 1790.

———. *Critique of Judgment*, trans. J. H. Bernard (1892). New York: Hafner Press, 1951.

———. *The Critique of Judgment*, trans. James Creed Meredith (1911 / 1928). Oxford: Clarendon Press, 1952.

———. *Critique of Judgment*, trans. Werner S. Pluhar. Indianapolis: Hackett Publishing Company, 1987.

———. *Critique of the Power of Judgment*, The Cambridge Edition of the Works of Immanuel Kant, trans. Paul Guyer and Eric Matthews. Cambridge: Cambridge University Press, 2000.

———. *Critique of Pure Reason*, trans. Norman Kemp Smith. New York: St. Martin's Press, 1929.

———. *Critique of Pure Reason*, The Cambridge Edition of the Works of

Immanuel Kant, trans. Paul Guyer and Allen Wood. Cambridge: Cambridge University Press, 1998.

——. *Kants gesammelte Schriften*, 29 Vols. Berlin: Walter de Gruyter, 1902. (*The Critique of the Power of Judgment* is in Volume 5.)

——. *Observations on the Feeling of the Beautiful and Sublime*, trans. John T. Goldthwait. Berkeley and Los Angeles: University of California Press, 1960.

——. *Opus postumum*, The Cambridge Edition of the Works of Immanuel Kant, trans. Eckart Förster. Cambridge: Cambridge University Press, 1993.

——. *Practical Philosophy*, The Cambridge Edition of the Works of Immanuel Kant, trans. Mary J. Gregor. Cambridge: Cambridge University Press, 1996.

BOOKS ABOUT THE *CRITIQUE OF THE POWER OF JUDGMENT*

Allison, Henry. *Kant's Theory of Taste – A Reading of the Critique of Aesthetic Judgment*. Cambridge: Cambridge University Press, 2001.

Burnham, Douglas. *An Introduction to Kant's Critique of Judgment*. Edinburgh: Edinburgh University Press, 2001.

Cassirer, Heinrich Walter. *A Commentary on Kant's Critique of Judgment*. London: Methuen & Co., 1938.

Cohen, Ted and Guyer, Paul, eds. *Essays in Kant's Aesthetics*. Chicago and London: University of Chicago Press, 1982.

Coleman, Francis X. J. *The Harmony of Reason: A Study in Kant's Aesthetics*. Pittsburgh: University of Pittsburgh Press, 1974.

Crawford, Donald W. *Kant's Aesthetic Theory*. Madison: University of Wisconsin Press, 1974.

Crowther, Paul. *The Kantian Sublime, From Morality to Art*. Oxford: Clarendon Press, 1989.

Fricke, Christel. *Kants Theorie des reinen Geschmacksurteils*. Berlin and New York: Walter de Gruyter, 1990.

Ginsborg, Hannah. *The Role of Taste in Kant's Theory of Cognition*. New York and London: Garland Publishing Company, 1990.

Guyer, Paul. *Kant and the Claims of Taste*. Cambridge and London: Harvard University Press, 1979.

——. *Kant and the Experience of Freedom, Essays on Aesthetics and Morality*. New York and Cambridge: Cambridge University Press, 1993.

—— (ed.). *Kant's Critique of the Power of Judgment: Critical Essays*. Lanham, MD: Rowman and Littlefield, 2003.

Kemal, Salim. *Kant and Fine Art, An Essay on Kant and the Philosophy of Fine Art and Culture*. Oxford: Clarendon Press, 1986.

Knox, Israel. *The Aesthetic Theories of Kant, Hegel and Schopenhauer*. New Jersey: Humanities Press, 1936.

——. *Kant's Aesthetic Theory: An Introduction*. New York: St. Martin's Press, 1992.

Kulenkampff, Jens. *Kants Logik des ästhetischen Urteils*. Frankfurt am Main: Vittorio Klostermann, 1978.

Makkreel, Rudolf A. *Imagination and Interpretation in Kant, The Hermeneutical Import of the Critique of Judgment*. Chicago and London: University of Chicago Press, 1990.

McCloskey, Mary A. *Kant's Aesthetic*. London: Macmillan, 1987.

McFarland, J. D. *Kant's Concept of Teleology*. Edinburgh: Edinburgh University Press, 1970.

McLaughlin, Peter. *Kant's Critique of Teleology in Biological Explanation: Antinomy and Teleology*. Lewiston, NY: Edwin Mellon Press, 1990.

Nuzzo, Angelica. *Kant and the Unity of Reason*. West Lafayette: Purdue University Press, 2005.

Pillow, Kirk. *Sublime Understanding: Aesthetic Reflection in Kant and Hegel*. Cambridge, MA and London, England: MIT Press, 2000.

Rogerson, Kenneth R. *Kant's Aesthetics: The Roles of Form and Expression*. Lanham, MD, New York, and London: University Press of America, 1986.

Savile, Anthony. *Aesthetic Reconstructions: The Seminal Writings of Lessing, Kant and Schiller*. Oxford: Basil Blackwell, 1987.

Schaper, Eva. *Studies in Kant's Aesthetics*. Edinburgh: Edinburgh University Press, 1979.

Schlapp, Otto. *Kants Lehre vom Genie und die Entstehumg der 'Kritik der Urteilskraft.'* Göttingen: Vandendoedt & Ruprecht, 1901.

Souriau, Michel. *Le jugement réfléchissant dans la philosophie critique de Kant*. Paris: Librairie Félix Alcan, 1926.

Wenzel, Christian. *An Introduction to Kant's Aesthetics: Core Concepts and Problems*. Oxford: Basil Blackwell, 2006.

Zammito, John H. *The Genesis of Kant's Critique of Judgment*. Chicago and London: University of Chicago Press, 1992.

ARTICLES ABOUT THE *CRITIQUE OF THE POWER OF JUDGMENT*

Allison, Henry E. "Kant's Antinomy of Teleological Judgment." *Southern Journal of Philosophy*, 30 (1992), supplemental volume, pp. 25–42.

Ameriks, Karl. "New Views on Kant's Judgments of Taste." *Kants Ästhetic, Kant's Aesthetics, L'esthétique de Kant*, ed. Hermann Parret. Berlin and New York: Walter de Gruyter, 1998, pp. 431–47.

Baxley, Anne Margaret. "The Practical Significance of Taste in Kant's Critique of Judgment: Love of Natural Beauty as a Mark of Moral Character." *The Journal of Aesthetics and Art Criticism*, 63 (1) (2005), pp. 33–45.

Caranti, Luigi. "Logical Purposiveness and the Principle of Taste." *Kant-Studien*, 96 (3) (2005), pp. 364–74.

Crawford, Donald W. "The Place of the Sublime in Kant's Aesthetic Theory." In *The Philosophy of Immanuel Kant*, ed. Richard Kennington. Washington: Catholic University of America Press, 1985, pp. 161–83.

Crowther, Paul. "Fundamental Ontology and Transcendental Beauty: An Approach to Kant's Aesthetics." *Kant-Studien*, 76 (1985), pp. 55–71.

Ginsborg, Hannah. "On the Key to Kant's Critique of Taste." *Pacific Philosophical Quarterly*, 72 (4) (1991), pp. 290–313.

——. "Lawfulness Without a Law: Kant on the Free Play of Imagination and Understanding." *Philosophical Topics*, 25 (1997), pp. 37–81.

——. "Review of *Critique of the Power of Judgment*." *Philosophical Review*, 111 (3) (2002), pp. 429–35.

——. "Aesthetic Judging and the Intentionality of Pleasure." *Inquiry*, 46 (2) (2003), pp. 164–81.

——. "Two Kinds of Mechanical Inexplicability in Kant and Aristotle." *Journal of the History of Philosophy*, 42 (1) (2004), pp. 33–65.

Gracyk, Theodore A. "Sublimity, Ugliness, and Formlessness in Kant's Aesthetic Theory." *The Journal of Aesthetics and Art Criticism*, 45 (1) (1986), pp. 49–56.

Guyer, Paul. "Formalism and the Theory of Expression in Kant's Aesthetics." *Kant-Studien*, 68 (1977), pp. 46–70.

———. "Disinterestedness and Desire in Kant's Aesthetics." *The Journal of Aesthetics and Art Criticism*, 36 (1978), pp. 449–60.

———. "Kant's Distinction Between the Beautiful and the Sublime." *Review of Metaphysics*, 35 (1982), pp. 769–73.

———. "Autonomy and Integrity in Kant's Aesthetics." *The Monist*, 66 (1983), pp. 67–88.

———. "Feeling and Freedom: Kant on Aesthetics and Morality." *The Journal of Aesthetics and Art Criticism*, 48 (1990), pp. 137–46.

———. "Kant's Conception of Fine Art," *The Journal of Aesthetics and Art Criticism*, 52 (1994), pp. 175–85.

———. "Free and Adherent Beauty: A Modest Proposal." *British Journal of Aesthetics*, 42 (2002), pp. 357–66.

Hudson, Hud. "On the Significance of an Analytic of the Ugly in Kant's Deduction of Pure Judgments of Taste." In *Kant's Aesthetics*, ed. Ralf Meerbote. Altascadero, CA: Ridgeview, 1991.

Kemal, Salim. "Aesthetic Necessity." *Kant-Studien*, 74 (1983), pp. 176–205.

Kreines, James. "The Inexplicability of Kant's *Naturzweck*: Kant on Teleology, Explanation and Biology." *Archiv für Geschichte der Philosophie*, 87 (3) (2005), pp. 270–311.

Kulenkampff, Jens. "The Objectivity of Taste: Hume and Kant." *Noûs*, 24 (1990), pp. 93–110.

Longuenesse, Béatrice. "Kant's Theory of Judgment, and Judgments of Taste." *Inquiry*, 46 (2) (2003), pp. 146–63.

Lüthe, Rudolf. "Kants Lehre von den ästhetischen Ideen." *Kant-Studien*, 75 (1984), pp. 65–73.

MacMillan, Claude. "Kant's Deduction of Pure Aesthetic Judgments." *Kant-Studien*, 76 (1985), pp. 43–54.

Maitland, Jeffrey. "Two Senses of Necessity in Kant's Aesthetic Theory." *British Journal of Aesthetics*, 16 (4) (1976), pp. 347–53.

Meerbote, Ralf. "Reflection on Beauty." In Ted Cohen and Paul Guyer (eds.) *Essays on Kant's Aesthetics*, Chicago and London: University of Chicago Press, 1982, pp. 55–86.

Matthews, Patricia. "Kant's Sublime: A Form of Pure Aesthetic Reflective

Judgment." *The Journal of Aesthetics and Art Criticism*, 54 (1996), pp.165–79.

Pippin, Robert B. "The Significance of Taste: Kant, Aesthetic and Reflective Judgment." *Journal of the History of Philosophy*, 34 (1996), pp. 549–69.

Pluhar, Werner S. "How to Render *Zweckmäßigkeit* in Kant's Third Critique." In Moltke S. Gram (ed.) *Interpreting Kant*, Iowa City: University of Iowa Press, 1982, pp. 85–98.

Rind, Miles. "What is Claimed in a Kantian Judgment of Taste?" *Journal of the History of Philosophy*, 38 (1) (2000), pp. 63–85.

——. "Critique of the Power of Judgment" (review). *Journal of the History of Philosophy*, 39 (4) (2001), pp. 594–96.

——. "Can Kant's Deduction of Judgments of Taste be Saved?" *Archiv für Geschichte der Philosophie*, 84 (2002), pp. 20–45.

Rogerson, Kenneth F. "The Meaning of Universal Validity in Kant's Aesthetics." *The Journal of Aesthetics and Art Criticism*, 40 (1981), pp. 301–08.

——. "Kant on Beauty and Morality." *Kant-Studien*, 95 (3) (2004), pp. 338–54.

Shier, David. "Why Kant Finds Nothing Ugly." *British Journal of Aesthetics*, 38 (1988), pp. 12–18.

Tonelli, Giorgio. "La formazione del testo della Kritik der Urteilskraft." *Revue Internationale de Philosophie*, 30 (1954), pp. 423–48.

——. "Von den verschiedenen Bedeutungen des Wortes 'Zweckmäßigkeit' in der *Kritik der Urteilskraft*." *Kant-Studien*, 49 (1957–58), pp. 154–66.

——. "Kant's Early Theory of Genius." *Journal of the History of Philosophy*, 4 (1966), Part I, pp. 109–31, Part II, pp. 209–24.

Wenzel, Christian. "Kant Finds Nothing Ugly?" *British Journal of Aesthetics*, 39 (4) (1999), pp. 416–22.

Wicks, Robert. "Dependent Beauty as the Appreciation of Teleological Style." *The Journal of Aesthetics and Art Criticism*, 55 (4) (1997), pp. 387–400.

——. "Kant on Beautifying the Human Body." *British Journal of Aesthetics*, 39 (2) (1999), pp. 163–78.

White, David A. "On Bridging the Gulf between Nature and Morality in the *Critique of Judgment*." *The Journal of Aesthetics and Art Criticism*, 38 (1979), pp. 179–88.

Zeldin, Mary-Barbara. "Formal Purposiveness and the Continuity of Kant's

Argument in the Critique of Judgment." *Kant-Studien*, 74 (1983), pp. 45–55.

Zuckert, Rachel. "Boring Beauty and Universal Morality: Kant on the Ideal of Beauty." *Inquiry*, 48 (2) (2005), pp. 107–30.

INDEX

Material in endnotes is signified by the page number followed by 'n.' and the note number.

RELATED TITLES FROM ROUTLEDGE

ROUTLEDGE PHILOSOPHY GUIDEBOOK TO
NIETZSCHE ON MORALITY
BRIAN LEITER

'This work is simply the best, most sustained, book length exposition of Nietzsche's *Genealogy of Morals*. As such it will be the reference point for all further scholarly work on the subject.' – *Ken Gemes, Birkbeck College, University of London*

'Offers one of the most comprehensive and compelling interpretations of Nietzsche's critique of morality to date. With its distinctive emphasis on naturalistic themes, it forms a very significant contribution to the study of Nietzsche, and is poised to become a work of reference in the field.' – *Notre Dame Philosophical Reviews*

Nietzsche is one of the most important and controversial thinkers in the history of philosophy. His writings on moral philosophy are amongst the most widely read works in philosophy – many of his ideas are both startling and disturbing.
  Nietzsche on Morality introduces and assesses:

- Nietzsche's life and the background to his writings on morality
- The ideas and text of *The Genealogy of Morals*
- Nietzsche's continuing importance in philosophy

ISBN10: 0-415-15284-4 (hbk)
ISBN10: 0-415-15285-2 (pbk)

ISBN13: 978-0-415-15284-6 (hbk)
ISBN13: 978-0-415-15285-3 (pbk)

Available at all good bookshops
For ordering and further information please visit:
www.routledge.com

RELATED TITLES FROM ROUTLEDGE

ROUTLEDGE PHILOSOPHY GUIDEBOOK TO HUME ON MORALITY
JAMES BAILIE

'Clearly written and well structured discussion of Hume's contribution to moral philosophy ... not only an excellent introduction
to Hume on morality, but also an excellent introduction to moral
philosophy.' – *The Philosopher's Magazine*

' ... A superb example of sober thinking and meticulous attention to
detail ... generate interest that it deserves.' – *Journal of Consciousness
Studies*

David Hume is widely recognised as the greatest philosopher to
have written in the English language. His *Treatise on Human Nature*
is one of the most important works of moral philosophy ever written.
  Hume on Morality introduces and assesses:

- Hume's life and the background of the *Treatise*
- The ideas and text in the *Treatise*
- Hume's continuing importance to philosophy

ISBN10: 0-415-18048-1 (hbk)
ISBN10: 0-415-18049-X (pbk)

ISBN13: 978-0-415-18048-1 (hbk)
ISBN13: 978-0-415-18049-8 (pbk)

Available at all good bookshops
For ordering and further information please visit:
www.routledge.com

RELATED TITLES FROM ROUTLEDGE

ROUTLEDGE PHILOSOPHY GUIDEBOOK TO
KANT AND THE *CRITIQUE OF PURE REASON*
SEBASTIAN GARDNER

'This is a quite outstanding introduction to the *Critique* ... It will help students not only to study the *Critique*, but also to see why it is so worth studying ... deserves to find itself, and pretty certainly will find itself, at the very top of the reading list for any course on the *Critique*.' – *The Philosophy Quarterly*

'In his clear and well-organized book, Gardner succeeds in providing a charitable and compelling reading of the most important sections of Kant's text, while also offering fresh and lucid interpretations of Kant's most provocative arguments. The result is an invaluable companion to the *Critique* that helpfully illuminates a notoriously opaque work ... Gardner's book is an invaluable resource for any student of Kant and, thus, for any student or teacher of philosophy.' – *Mind*

'The major virtues of Gardner's book are clarity, accuracy, and its focus on the key concepts and arguments of Kant's notoriously complex work. Both serious students and Kant scholars will benefit greatly from Gardner's contribution.' – *Philosophical Books*

RELATED TITLES FROM ROUTLEDGE

KANT, DUTY AND MORAL WORTH
PHILIP STRATTON-LAKE

'A sure-footed and elegant argument . . . that he is able to cover so much ground, exegetical and philosophical, in this relatively short work is one mark of the elegance of the sustained argument he makes.' – *Philosophical Quarterly*

'This book will surely be mandatory reading for anyone interested in the foundations of Kant's moral theory.' – *Kant-Studien*

Kant, Duty and Moral Worth is a fascinating and original examination of Kant's account of moral worth. The complex debate at the heart of Kant's philosophy is over whether Kant said moral actions have worth only if they are carried out from duty, or whether actions carried out from mixed motives can be good. Philip Stratton-Lake offers a unique account of acting from duty, which utilizes the distinction between primary and secondary motives. He maintains that the moral law should not be understood as a normative moral reason but as playing a transcendental role. Thus a Kantian account of moral worth is one where the virtuous agent may be responsive to concrete particular considerations, whilst preserving an essential role for universal moral principles.

    Kant, Duty and Moral Worth is a lucid examination of Kant's moral thought that will appeal to Kant scholars and anyone interested in moral theory.

ISBN10: 0-415-20524-7 (hbk)
ISBN10: 0-415-33557-4 (pbk)

ISBN13: 978-0-415-20524-5 (hbk)
ISBN13: 978-0-415-33557-7 (pbk)

RELATED TITLES FROM ROUTLEDGE

PHILOSOPHY OF THE ARTS 3RD EDITION
GORDON GRAHAM

Praise for the first edition

'A textbook for students needs to satisfy many criteria . . . These criteria are amply met by Gordon Graham's excellent book . . . Graham's introduction to aesthetics informs, illuminates, and should elicit lively discussions in any courses that utilize it.' – *British Journal of Aesthetics*

'Graham's account is subtle and seductive . . . attractive and readable.' – *European Journal of Philosophy*

'Graham's book rivals Dickie's [*Introduction to Aesthetics*, OUP, 1997] for its clarity and excellent organization, but Graham's more expansive style is more accessible to those who are new to philosophy.' – *Journal of Aesthetics and Art Criticism*

'Graham's discussion is thorough, authoritative, and accessible; one always feels in sure hands.' – *Philosophy in Review*

ISBN10: 0-415-34978-8 (hbk)
ISBN10: 0-415-34979-6 (pbk)

ISBN13: 978-0-415-34978-9 (hbk)
ISBN13: 978-0-415-34979-6 (pbk)

Available at all good bookshops
For ordering and further information please visit:
www.routledge.com